BEST SERVED COLD

BEST SERVED COLD

The Rise, Fall and Rise Again of Malcolm Walker

MALCOLM WALKER

ICON

'I have known Malcolm Walker for many years. His drive, tenacity and knowledge of his business remained with him throughout his turbulent period away from Iceland, and I was not remotely surprised by his great comeback. His story demonstrates that, regardless of any setback, if you know your business, care about your business and wake up every morning loving what you do, you have a great chance of making it a success. Well done, Malcolm.'

Sir Philip Green
(CEO, Arcadia Group)

'Having competed with Iceland, and therefore Malcolm, throughout my retail career, the insight this book provides into what makes him tick would have been invaluable to me, had it been published twenty years ago! A great comeback story written by one of the true characters of recent retail history.'

Justin King
(CEO, Sainsbury's)

'An inspiring story and a cautionary tale. Malcolm Walker built Iceland into a household name but a botched merger and management succession threatened to undo a life's work. They say "never go back" but Malcolm felt he had to in order to save the company and restore his reputation. Amazingly he succeeded and revealed a genius for retail we can all learn from.'

Sir Terry Leahy
(Former CEO, Tesco)

Malcolm Walker CBE
Founder, Chairman & Chief Executive, Iceland Foods Ltd

Malcolm Walker co-founded Iceland in 1970 and was its Chairman and Chief Executive through 30 years of continuous sales growth.

He left Iceland under a cloud early in 2001, but returned four years later to lead a transformation in its performance. Iceland today has sales of £2.6 billion, 800 stores and 25,000 employees, and is recognised as one of the Best Companies to Work For in the UK.

Malcolm has been married to Rhianydd for more than 40 years, and they have three grown-up children and eight grandchildren. Outside work, Malcolm's greatest enthusiasms are for his home, garden and family, good food and wine, skiing, sailing and shooting.

Published in the UK in 2013 by
Icon Books Ltd, Omnibus Business Centre,
39–41 North Road, London N7 9DP
email: info@iconbooks.net
www.iconbooks.net

Sold in the UK, Europe and Asia
by Faber & Faber Ltd, Bloomsbury House,
74–77 Great Russell Street,
London WC1B 3DA or their agents

Distributed in the UK, Europe and Asia
by TBS Ltd, TBS Distribution Centre, Colchester Road,
Frating Green, Colchester CO7 7DW

Distributed in India by Penguin Books India,
11 Community Centre, Panchsheel Park,
New Delhi 110017

Distributed in South Africa by
Book Promotions, Office B4, The District,
41 Sir Lowry Road, Woodstock 7925

Distributed in Australia and New Zealand
by Allen & Unwin Pty Ltd,
PO Box 8500, 83 Alexander Street,
Crows Nest, NSW 2065

Distributed in Canada by Penguin Books Canada,
90 Eglinton Avenue East, Suite 700,
Toronto, Ontario M4P 2Y3

ISBN: 978-1-84831-700-0 (hardback)
ISBN: 978-184831-703-1 (paperback)

Typeset in Adobe Text Pro by Marie Doherty

Printed and bound in the UK by
CPI Group (UK) Ltd, Croydon CR0 4YY

Contents

Acknowledgements   xi

Chapter 1: Prologue   1
Chapter 2: 'You're Fired!'   7
Chapter 3: The Strawberry Sellers   22
Chapter 4: A Multiple Retailer   29
Chapter 5: The Takeaway   37
Chapter 6: Moving up a Gear   45
Chapter 7: 'Get it Bought'   55
Chapter 8: Another Day, Another Deal!   66
Chapter 9: Riding a Rocket   81
Chapter 10: 'Let's Go Hostile'   93
Chapter 11: Conquering the World   112
Chapter 12: Killing the Sacred Cows   126
Chapter 13: Losing Sleep   142
Chapter 14: Flying Again   160
Chapter 15: The New Millennium   175
Chapter 16: The Deal   189
Chapter 17: A Bad Start   198
Chapter 18: The Booker Prize for Fiction   209
Chapter 19: I've Got My Job Back   221
Chapter 20: The Share Sale   228

Chapter 21: Breaking and Entering   239
Chapter 22: Everything Hits the Fan!   254
Chapter 23: Animal Farm   266
Chapter 24: Starting Again   280
Chapter 25: The Vikings   291
Chapter 26: Full Circle   300
Chapter 27: Long-Term Greedy   312
Chapter 28: On Top of The World   316
Chapter 29: The Auction   326

Index   333

To my wife Rhianydd, who has been my unstinting supporter since I was fifteen years old. She has given me the most amazing family and always allowed me the freedom to build the business, never complaining about the late nights or the many knocks we have had along the way.

It's one of life's ironies that enjoyment of our present success has been tempered by her illness, which has prompted our support for the work of Alzheimer's Research UK.

Acknowledgements

A company is never built by one person. Iceland is the result of the combined effort, enthusiasm and in many cases the dedication of our staff. I would like to thank them all.

Particular thanks go to:

My wife and family for their support, encouragement and understanding; Peter Hinchcliffe for 25 years of partnership in the business; Bill and Norman Woodward for being our early mentors; Nigel Woodward for 43 years of support and friendship; John McLachlan for his shrewd investment; Geoff Mason and Barry Owen for taking me under their wings; Peter Bullivant for his friendship and advice; Tarsem Dhaliwal for his loyalty, support and constant encouragement; Nigel Broadhurst and Nick Canning for running the company and letting me feel I'm still in charge; Andy Pritchard for sharing the Dark Ages and Cooltrader; Kathy Wight for running my life so loyally and efficiently; Jon Asgeir Johannesson and Gunnar Sigurdsson for believing in me; Larus Welding for lending us the money in 2005, and for his guidance through Icelandic politics; Steven Walker for his friendship and for pushing me to do the deal; Russell Edey for protecting us from ourselves; Majid Ishaq for masterminding the management buyback in 2012; Dan Yealland for his advice and friendship in the brief time I knew him. I miss him; Keith Hann for all his help and advice; Peter Pugh for publishing this book; Bill Grimsey for giving me the opportunity to have a second career. And everyone else who has helped and encouraged me in my adventures, in business and elsewhere.

1

Prologue

'Happy birthday, Ranny.' Rhianydd looked at Debbie, and the two of them started crying again. It was 30 January 2001 and we were in the bar at the Four Seasons Hotel in London. Andy Pritchard and I raised our glasses and glanced at each other without embarrassment.

My mobile phone rang. The Four Seasons is a business hotel so there were no hostile looks from the staff. John Berry, our Company Secretary, was calling from his room upstairs. He said he was going to have room service and wouldn't be joining us for dinner and please would I understand how difficult it was for him. 'Christ almighty, what's his problem?' I thought aloud. I'd taken the guy on eighteen years ago and had seen him every day since.

'Aren't you even going to have a drink with us? It's Ranny's birthday.'

'No, I can't,' he said. 'But I think it will be OK to bump into you at breakfast.'

'Bloody wimp,' I mumbled.

Apparently the two Bills, Grimsey and Hoskins, were making a point of staying in some cheap hotel and had already told John that this would be the last time he would be staying at the Four Seasons. I suppose he had conflicting emotions. I'm sure he felt a great loyalty or maybe just sympathy for me, but he had the rest of his career to think of. Already Andy and I were bad news in the new Iceland regime. We finished the champagne and moved into the dining room.

I couldn't decide how I felt. On the one hand there was great relief at being out of the company, which I'd been trying to achieve for the past two years but, on the other, bewilderment and even anger at how it had happened. Ranny was in emotional turmoil. I kept reminding her of our son Richard's words the night before: 'Don't worry about it,' he said, 'happy endings only happen in fairy tales!'

Debbie was worried for different reasons: how were they going to make a living? What were Andy's chances of ever getting another top job after this?

Although I stayed in the Four Seasons whenever I was in London, I never ate there. The food was too fussy for my liking and the meal always took too long. Tonight was different. It was certainly going to be a memorable occasion. It was also the last meal on expenses and Andy, ever the wine connoisseur, decided to sting the Bills for a couple of bottles of Palmer '86.

Throughout the evening we kept churning it all over. 'I've only had two jobs and I've been fired from them both!' I thought this was a great line but the girls kept asking how it could happen and why we hadn't stopped it.

'Because I couldn't,' said Andy.

'Because I didn't want to,' I said, more than once.

'But it's your company, you started it, you *are* Iceland,' the girls reminded me.

'Ranny, Grimsey is welcome to it,' I said.

The press had been horrific over the past week and I knew over the next couple of days it would get a lot worse. That made it impossible for any of us to draw a line under things. Not unnaturally, the girls thought about their friends and their Mums and what people would think. For myself, I had got used to the idea over the past week and persuaded myself I didn't care.

The board meeting had lasted until lunchtime; nineteen people around a long table at our lawyer Herbert Smith's offices. Iceland directors, advisers and professionals – friends, too, I thought, but impotent while the charade was played out. Some of the advisers were already negotiating with their own consciences about where their loyalties lay and where their continuing fees would come from. I just wanted to get it over with. It would have been ludicrous for me to try to take the meeting as Chairman, so I handed over to David Price, our senior non-executive director.

David did a good job in trying to give Andy a fair hearing, even though Bill Grimsey didn't want Andy to present papers to defend himself. I made a short speech first and then said that, much as I wanted to, I didn't propose to resign unless the board asked me to. Edward Walker-Arnott, the much respected and now retired senior partner of Herbert Smith, had advised me not to resign when I consulted him privately, as a friend, three days earlier. 'It will look as if you have done something wrong. Under no circumstances should you resign for at least a couple of months,' he had told me. At the lunchtime break the non-executives did ask me to resign, so I was delighted to oblige. Andy and I both resigned as directors of the company but not as employees. We all agreed we should stay on the payroll until March to give us time to decide on our respective positions. I asked David Price if he would take over as Chairman and he said he would, but only until a permanent replacement could be found.

My recent share sale had now become a potential issue. Before my resignation, Tim Steadman of Herbert Smith agreed that I had followed the correct procedure, but had said that in view of all the bad press an investigation by the United Kingdom Listing Authority (UKLA) was almost inevitable. He also said there wouldn't be any conflict in his firm advising me personally despite their connection with Iceland. I couldn't get used to that idea as I had first used them in 1984 and felt that they worked for me. After lunch, Tim suggested I should spend some time with Stephen Gate, their compliance expert, and review all the events around my share sale. Gate worried me. I explained to him how I had telephoned each non-executive director in turn and asked their permission to sell shares.

I'd also asked several of our advisers and no one had had a problem.

'What did you say when you spoke to the non-execs?' he asked.

'Well, I said I wanted to sell some shares and was that OK?'

'Yes, but what were your exact words, what exactly did you say?'

'I can't remember but I asked their permission to sell and asked if they had any problems with that, and they didn't. David Price even remarked that shares weren't family heirlooms to be kept for ever.' I was certain I had followed the correct procedure. I couldn't understand what he was getting at.

The red wine was relaxing me as I repeated the conversation. 'That guy is not on this planet. You won't believe what he said next. He said, "When you asked the non-execs for permission to sell, did you say, 'I am ringing pursuant to paragraph 5 (a) of the model code for share dealing to formally request permission to sell shares in the company'?"'

'Are you serious?' I said. 'Nobody speaks like that. I know these guys well and would never use language that formal.'

'Well, you should have,' he insisted.

'People like him probably do talk like that,' said Andy.

The conversation with Gate had gone on for hours and, although he was supposed to be advising me, I felt his line of questioning was increasingly hostile. I was totally exhausted.

I saw Grimsey briefly at about 6.30pm and told him I would clear my office by the weekend. He expressed no regret at what had happened. I told him he had got everything he wanted now and asked him to play fair by Andy with his pay-off. 'Don't ask me to do anything that would jeopardise the interests of the shareholders' was his only response. I had heard this line so many times over the past few weeks that it held no credibility for me. He reminded me of some kind of religious zealot preaching high-minded religion and burning people at the stake at the same time.

The four of us met for breakfast next morning and John Berry came over to talk to us but sat at a separate table. For the first time in 30 years there seemed to be no urgency to get on with the day. A great weight had been lifted off my shoulders only to be replaced by uncertainty. I signed the hotel bill but decided to pay for the wine and champagne personally. I didn't want to give Grimsey an excuse to make an issue out of it.

Harnish met us in the hotel lobby. As our London chauffeur he always heard enough of what was said in the back of the car to work out what was going on. He looked bleak and visibly upset. He drove us to Northolt airport and gave everyone a tearful hug as we boarded the plane. That upset Ranny. He'd worked for us for years and been privy to many of our adventures.

It takes only 35 minutes for the Citation jet to get to Chester airport and this was of course the last time we'd be using it. We'd had a company plane for sixteen years and this had been our first brand new one, bought in 1995. It was still immaculate. We'd always made a profit on selling them and while company planes are often considered an emotive issue, I'd long since given up caring what people thought about it. As a national retailer we'd always found it an invaluable business tool and I'd defend it to anybody. I couldn't imagine Grimsey keeping anything as extravagant, though. My lifestyle was going to change dramatically now but I couldn't have been happier about it.

Kathy Wight, my PA, had packed 30 years of personal files into boxes and wrapped up all the accumulated clutter in my office. She'd organised a Transit van to be there the following Saturday morning to take the stuff home. The office was deserted but Janet Marsden, our Personnel Director, was there. I'd employed her twenty years ago as the youngest member of our team. She was obviously embarrassed and upset to be there. Grimsey had asked her to watch me take my possessions out of my office and ensure I didn't nick any company papers. She said if I took any company documents she was required to make a list of them, but then she offered to go to her office and wait until I'd gone.

Andy was packing up at the same time but he had a lot less junk than me. I'd tended to keep a lot of my personal files at the office. So many adventures over 30 years had generated a lot of memories. We had a librarian who worked four hours each week keeping the archives and all the memorabilia and old photographs carefully filed. A few years earlier I'd realised that most of that kind of stuff had vanished over time and we'd decided to conserve what was left and also keep current items of interest for the future. I left it all behind without much thought.

We'd built a company from nothing to annual sales of over £5 billion. We employed over 30,000 people and probably as many again among our suppliers and support companies. We'd paid hundreds of millions to shareholders and at least £10 million to charity and made many people very wealthy, including some of our staff.

Then the letters and emails started to arrive from friends and colleagues in the business and I had plenty of time to reflect over the next few weeks about how it all began ...

2
'You're Fired!'

A.V. Green was God. At least to Woolworth's trainee managers he was. I'd been in his office only once before when I was promoted to deputy manager of Woolworth's Wrexham branch. It was the biggest office I'd ever seen, dark and wood-panelled with his massive desk in one corner. It was certainly impressive. Last time it had been a handshake and a word of congratulations: the motivation factor of ten minutes with God was deemed to be worth a day out of the store with petrol expenses for the drive to the regional office in Dudley, Birmingham. Head office in London was something too important and remote for me even to contemplate. This time my visit was to get fired. It apparently didn't occur to anyone to wonder why Johnnie Walton, the Wrexham store manager, couldn't do it. Deputy store managers were important in the hierarchy and firing one was an event that required some drama.

Peter Hinchcliffe and I drove down to Birmingham together. Peter was called into Green's office first and I had to wait in the corridor outside. It was only five minutes before it was my turn and I was given a speech about wasting an opportunity. I told Green that the company owed me about 10,000 hours in unpaid overtime but he didn't seem impressed. His parting words to me were: 'So, go and run your fish and chip shop or whatever it is.'

It was 27 January 1971, almost 30 years to the day before I was fired for the second time.

We drove back to Oswestry. Peter was deputy manager of Woolies there and that was where we had opened our first Iceland store three months earlier. We were both earning £26 per week at Woolies but our dismissal package had included our holiday pay and pension money so we figured we could last the next few months without drawing anything from the new business. I'd worked at Woolworth's for seven years, the only job I'd had since leaving school, but I was glad to be out of it. I was bored and I wasn't doing very well in the company. I was a little scared about the future but also excited: I was 24 and ready to make my fortune.

I joined Woolworth's after a conversation with the careers teacher at school.

'What are you good at?' she asked me, obviously knowing it wasn't academic studies.

'I like organising things,' I replied.

'In that case you should go into retailing,' she said. So I did.

I was born in 1946 and brought up in a mining village called Grange Moor in the West Riding of Yorkshire. My Dad was a colliery electrician but he was also something of an entrepreneur. He ran a smallholding of eight-and-a-half acres in his spare time. He grew vegetables and also kept poultry. He was one of the first to install the new battery cages, which were rapidly improving egg production at the time. I used to help him on the farm and like to think I developed my work ethic from him in those early days. In 1955 Dad had an accident at the pit when a coal-cutter crushed his foot, and he then went full-time on the poultry farm. Eventually he set up a small grocery shop near Huddersfield with my Mam and sold a lot of home-grown products and the sponge cakes Mam baked at home. He died young at 52, from cancer, when I was fourteen.

Although I failed the eleven-plus and went to a secondary modern school, I eventually got into grammar school as a late entrant in the second year. I still didn't do very well: I managed four O-levels in four attempts. I was remembered at school for all the wrong reasons. I was always in trouble for some prank or other, and had also started going out with a very pretty girl in the fourth form called Rhianydd Jones. Rhianydd is a Welsh name, which Yorkshire kids could never hope to pronounce, so everybody called her Ranny. She was academic and something of a swot. The headmaster, Mr Faires, was anxious she shouldn't be corrupted by my bad influence. Corporal punishment was a daily fact of life and I got the cane or the slipper more often than most. On one occasion Mr Faires had me in his study and counselled me to 'keep away from Rhianydd'. 'I'll cool your ardour,' he said, selecting a cane from his collection. At that moment we both noticed, through his window, the vicar walking down the school drive. He hesitated and said: 'I think you should go now. I'll deal with you later.' I don't think I've ever been so pleased to see a vicar.

I remember my last day at school. We had just finished our final assembly and sung 'Lord dismiss us with thy blessing'. As we were filing out of the school hall I had a water pistol and squirted the maths teacher. His name was Evans and he had a minor speech impediment which caused him to end every sentence with 'err'. We called him 'Ker-man'. He dragged me out of the hall by my ear and gave me three strokes of the slipper. I must be a conformist at heart because I bent over when he told me to, even though I'd technically left school 60 seconds earlier.

Grange Moor was a pretty godforsaken place, and at night there was nothing to do except hang around the local village fish and chip shop. There were no youth clubs or anything like that. So I decided to liven things up by organising a dance in the local church hall. This was pretty ambitious stuff and involved three local bands. It was a really successful evening and all the proceeds went to Cancer Research. Flushed with success and my enhanced reputation in the village, I decided to organise another event where this time the proceeds would go to me. This was while I was still at school and I was soon running a small business organising dances at different venues in Huddersfield, booking some of the most popular live bands in the country at the time. All the commercial dance halls were already in use on Saturday nights, which only left church halls for me to book, but they were usually too small. Then I found St Patrick's Hall in Huddersfield, which took 300 people. I ran a series of dances there, and one day I took a phone call from another small-time impresario called Peter Stringfellow (later of the famous London lap dancing club) who wanted to take over my venue. How different my life might have been if I'd gone into partnership with him.

I didn't question my career teacher's advice about going into retailing and applied to all the major chains: Littlewoods, Marks & Spencer and Lewis's of Leeds. Littlewoods and Lewis's turned me down because I failed their arithmetic test but the local M&S manager called me into his store to explain they only took graduates at 21 years of age. He offered me tea and spent a couple of hours telling me how to go about getting a job. He was really helpful and I realised then, in 1964, that M&S was a very special organisation.

I applied to Woolworth's because I'd been told it wasn't very difficult to get in – they took more or less anybody – but also because their store managers were by far the best paid in the business (they were paid a percentage of their store profits). In the 1960s Woolworth's were at the tail end of 50 years of fantastic success and were the eighth largest company in the UK. Stories were legion about former managers and head office staff who had Rolls-Royces and chauffeurs. Those glory days were gone, but senior managers still did pretty well for themselves and the legend was enough to attract people like me. The catch, but also the incentive, was that absolutely everybody from the Chairman down had started at the bottom, sweeping the floors in the stockroom, and promotion was 100 per cent from within the company. Their selection process really took place during the job itself, which meant that the dropout rate was enormous.

I started working in the stockroom of the Huddersfield store at £6 for a six-day week. The stockroom manageress, Loui Maltis, was really butch and was always trying to prove she was ten times tougher than any man. She terrified me. The training programme was quite simple: there wasn't one. You worked hard, tried to impress your boss, put in more hours than anybody else to prove how keen you were and, gradually, you worked your way up the ladder. You could go from the stockroom to the sales floor, through various positions of responsibility to store manager, area manager (or 'superintendent', as Woolies quaintly called the job, a real hangover from the past) and on until you made Chairman. At least that was the theory.

I worked in the stockroom at Huddersfield for two years. I swept the sales floor, stoked the old coke boilers twice a day and took my turn baling cardboard. If a child dropped an ice cream or a dog made a mess on the floor a shout would go down to the stockroom for someone, usually me, to come and clean it up. This tended to happen when my mates from school were in during their lunch hour from their 'suit jobs'. 'I'm a trainee manager, honest I am,' I would tell them as I stood in my brown overall with a shovel and a brush in my hand. This was the real cutting edge of retail training.

I was still running my dances while at Woolies and I had also developed a new side-line in selling potatoes. Every spring, tons of seed potatoes would be delivered for the gardening counter. There were no garden centres to speak of then and the Woolies garden counter was big business. The potatoes came in hundredweight sacks, and I had to spend about three weeks in the store basement repacking and weighing them into seven-pound bags on an old kitchen scale. As the season came to an end we had about ten sacks (half a ton) left, which had to be dumped as the potatoes were already sprouting and it was getting too late to sell them. I asked the store manager if I could have them and he said I could. I organised a mate with a van to take them home, then paid a local farmer to plough our field so I could plant them. That October I employed kids in the village to harvest about ten tons of potatoes, which I sold back to Woolies for their canteen. Every morning I had to walk a mile to get the bus to Huddersfield and for weeks I did this carrying a sack of potatoes. I seem to remember I was paid about ten shillings (50 pence) for each half-hundredweight sack.

After two years in the stockroom I became worried about my lack of progress. The store's deputy manager, Dan Gillette, who gave me the job, had moved on and a new deputy was in place. Dan had employed me as a 'trainee manager' but had forgotten to tell anybody. The store manager was Arnold Ravenhill, an alcoholic of the old school, always immaculately groomed and held in high regard by the company. He would spend most of each afternoon locked in the Horse and Jockey across from the loading bay door. He was a decent man but not easily approachable. I think he was also scared of Loui Maltis. One day I plucked up the courage to ask him about my career. He didn't know I was a trainee. I felt my world had ended and I'd wasted any chance of a future.

Within a week or two I'd been offered a chance to prove my worth. I was asked to go to Heckmondwyke, a small town near Huddersfield, to a store where they were short-staffed in the stockroom. I remember arguing politics in the staff canteen with the girls in the store. Harold Wilson was the man of the moment but the real novelty was being in a mixed-sex canteen. Woolworth's had a canteen in every store and provided a cooked breakfast and lunch. In most stores they had a separate canteen for stockroom males, who weren't allowed to eat with management or female staff. But given that the store manager and I were the only men in the store it made sense even to Woolies to have just one dining room!

I must have done a good job in Heckmondwyke because soon after I was promoted to 'junior' trainee manager on the sales floor and moved to Leeds 5. This was one of the biggest stores in the country and the fifth store that Frank Winfield Woolworth had opened when he came to the UK from America. Charlie Beck, who was famous throughout the company, managed Leeds 5. Even though he was 'only' a store manager his status was considered to be higher than that of area managers and even 'merchandise managers', who were distant figures from head office in London second in importance only to buyers, the true aristocrats of the company. Charlie had an office like the bridge on a ship overlooking the ground sales floor (there were three sales floors in Leeds) and he was reputed to earn £12,000 per year. In 1965 that was a fortune – the equivalent of £300,000 in today's money. Merchandise managers and buyers occasionally visited the store and arrived in their Jaguars and Humber Super Snipes; the young trainees, including me, got to drive them to the car park. Charlie, though, drove a van. He was near retirement and considered an eccentric, but devoted to the company. He worked six days a week, often came in on Sunday, and never took holidays. You could always tell when he was supposed to be on holiday or having a day off because he wore suede shoes to work. His van was for customer deliveries, which trainees did after the store had closed. This was Charlie's idea, unheard of anywhere else in the company, but he would try anything to help sales.

I often drove Charlie's van on deliveries but I also had my own Mini van, which was sometimes commandeered for deliveries too. Every Friday evening, on my way home, I had to deliver six cases of cat food to an old lady who lived on the outskirts of Leeds with a houseful of cats. One night she met me in tears. She had to move out of the house so the cats had to be put down: please would I take them to the vet next Friday when I called? A week later I arrived and she loaded a couple of cardboard boxes full of cats into the back of my Mini van. Goodness knows how many there were but apparently they weren't all boxed up and she kept finding the odd cat and shoving it into my van. The cats weren't at all impressed with this and there was a great deal of hissing and scratching going on. It was a nightmare straight out of an Alfred Hitchcock film. As I drove through Leeds to the vet, more and more cats escaped from the boxes and rocketed around the van. The cats were wild and I was shaken and bleeding when I reached my destination. As I got out of the van two or three cats streaked out of the door, never to be seen again. The vet came out carrying a long pole with a noose on the end, opened the van door a crack and fished inside until he caught one. I reckon he caught about half and the others escaped to become town cats.

Charlie took quite a shine to me and I had eighteen wonderful months working in that store. He had a sense of mischief, and one morning I caught him filling the lock of the shop next door with glue. The owner had upset him by complaining about one of his products. There were about twelve trainee managers in the Leeds store, an assistant manager and a deputy manager called Sherwood who had the most amazing halitosis. Trainees were graded as junior man, advanced man, ready man and then deputy manager. It was odd even then to have the job title 'ready man'. Everyone dressed smartly in dark suits and most trainees wore detachable collars on their white shirts. Even in 1965 collarless shirts were becoming hard to find, but Marks & Spencer still sold them and Woolworth's had a line in disposable stiff paper collars, which we thought looked really good. They could be reversed when they got dirty.

I soon learned the culture of the business. Trainees were almost encouraged to be arrogant because 'Woolworth', as we all called it without the 's', was considered the only professional retail business in the country. Any other company was regarded as 'Mickey Mouse'. I remember one store manager observing in all seriousness that he could run Marks & Spencer in his lunch hour. Every store had four coloured lights at a high level on the sales floor and each trainee was called to the telephone by a different combination. We were addressed by our surnames, and I was told to answer the phone as 'Walker'. It was considered presumptuous to put 'Mr' before your name and first names were never used.

My first departments were crockery and glassware. I was responsible for displays, the ordering of stock and managing the staff. Technically I was in charge of the crockery supervisor who had been there for 40 years but you can imagine how she took to a nineteen-year-old trying to tell her what to do. Any store manager would rather lose a trainee than an old hand who knew the business inside out. That was obvious to me and obvious to the crockery supervisor. In that situation you learned pretty quickly how to get the best out of people.

I had had to leave home when I started work in Leeds. In Grange

Moor if you didn't go to university, and nobody did, you lived with your parents until you got married. Woolworth's was my university. I lived in a flat with two other trainees and learned to cope with the launderette, a little cooking, late nights and a lot of drinking. Work started at 8am, or 7am if it was your turn to let in the bread man, and you never finished before 9pm – sometimes 10pm. If you took a day off you were considered not to be 'keen'.

One of my first surprises in Leeds was that every product had two prices. The correct 'list price' ticket was put into the ticket holder and then an inflated price was displayed on another ticket placed over the top. Customers were charged the higher price, which was what you thought you could get for the product, but if a head office visitor came into the store the top price tickets would be quickly whipped off so that he saw only the official price. As soon as he'd gone the other tickets would be put back. The idea was that the extra money would cover 'shrinkage': stock loss caused by breakage or pilfering or by having to cut prices to clear old stock. It's not possible to run any retail business without shrinkage, but a good manager will minimise it, while a bad manager might let it get out of control. Controlling shrinkage seemed to be the only thing that mattered at Woolworth's and managers got up to all kinds of tricks, not just to control it, but to cover it by generating extra money which wasn't accounted for in the book-keeping system.

I don't know how it happened but perhaps one careless manager once generated more money than he lost through shrinkage so that, after the year-end stock-take his store showed a stock 'overage'. That is not possible in a properly run store but the extra profit must have been appreciated because instead of being fired the manager was promoted. However it started, the bizarre situation existed through-out the company that managers were promoted for overages and fired for showing any shrinkage. The bigger the overage the better. This encouraged all kinds of 'fiddles' as managers inflated prices and became ever more inventive in finding ways to generate cash outside the system to hide shrinkage.

Charlie even had a spare cash register on the sales floor. The money taken through that till was not recorded in the books but collected separately, then used for buying stock for cash, which was sold in store. Since there was no record of the transaction in the books the profit on the product covered shrinkage. You could only sell official Woolworth's merchandise but several suppliers cooperated with Charlie in selling to him for cash instead of through the official ordering system. His van was useful for supplier collections as well as customer deliveries. This crazy situation existed throughout my seven years with Woolworth's. You had to fiddle the system to create an overage and gain promotion but you would be fired if you were caught doing it! If you showed even a small shrinkage – which, if you played it straight, you couldn't avoid – you also got fired.

Trainee managers were moved periodically to another store in the region, usually at a week's notice. I was promoted to 'advanced man' at a salary of £15 per week and moved to Scarborough on 8 May 1967. The prospect of doing a summer season at Scarborough was exciting and I enjoyed my time there. Typically you left your old store on a Saturday night and the company would generously pay only your first night's accommodation at a hotel in your new town. That tended to be on a Sunday night so that you could arrive at your new store at 8am on Monday morning, shoes polished and ready to go. At about 6pm on that first day you might ask your manager if it would be OK to slip off early and find somewhere to live. In practice trainees already in the store knew about flats or digs and you were usually invited to share so it was never really a problem, but the system certainly taught you to be self-reliant and resourceful.

After Scarborough I was moved to Lincoln, then on to Rhyl in North Wales where I was promoted to 'ready man' at a salary of £18 per week. Since the store wasn't big enough to warrant a deputy manager, I was also the assistant manager.

It was usual to have a session in the pub when you left a store, and the party at Lincoln sticks in my memory. I was standing in the pub toilet a little the worse for wear and smoking a cigar, when a voice from next to me said: 'That cigar stinks.' I looked at the man who'd spoken. 'You don't recognise me, do you?' he said. Then it dawned on me who he was and I went cold. I had to pretend I didn't know him, which gave my friend a little time to slip away for help. Shoplifters were always a problem in Woolworth's and I'd caught this guy some months earlier. I'd been a witness in court when he was sent to prison for six months. He was a big bloke and out for revenge, but luckily he'd only half strangled me before the cavalry arrived to rescue me.

I drove home to Yorkshire the following evening before going on to Rhyl the next day. I managed to crash my Mini van five miles from home so I arrived in Rhyl by train on a cold, foggy, miserable night on 13 October 1968. I thought it was the most godforsaken place on earth.

Tony Coyle was the Rhyl store manager: a tall, energetic, ambitious man with jet-black curly hair. He was desperate for promotion. On my first morning he took me into his tiny office to explain how he saw things. He was going to go far in the company, of that he had no doubt, and nobody would stand in his way. I could go with him, which meant doing things his way and specifically delivering the biggest overage the company had ever seen, or ... well, the alternative wasn't even to be contemplated. I hastily assured him of my commitment and enthusiasm and promised my support. I liked Tony but he wasn't generally well liked by other managers. Even in a company where ambition and enthusiasm were everything he was considered really over the top. Tony's speciality was cost control. Woolworth's managers generally felt they couldn't influence the sales line: poor sales were considered the fault of buyers not delivering the right products. You had to do what you could, of course, but managers could more directly influence the profits of the store and their own pay packet by controlling costs.

Tony believed he wouldn't spend more than two years in Rhyl before being promoted so the problems he was going to leave behind would be left for someone else to sort out. He had a simplistic attitude to cost control. You could cut the store electricity bill by switching off lights, so he kept the sales floor on half lighting throughout the quiet winter months. The problem was, he cut his electricity bill for the first year but it couldn't be allowed to rise again in the second, so the store had to go on quarter lighting. The third year was going to be someone else's problem. This philosophy extended across all areas of overhead. In most retail companies it would be a crime to run out of paper bags but Tony encouraged staff to persuade customers that they didn't need bags. Nothing in the store was ever repaired, nothing was painted and if a customer brought a faulty product back, under no circumstances could you give them a refund. 'Tell them you'll send it back to the manufacturers,' he'd say, 'and the next time they come in, tell them you've not heard anything. They'll soon get fed up.' Attitudes like this contributed to the decline of the company, but the system encouraged it and, to a lesser extent, similar practices were widespread. Tony's obsession with cost control even extended to his private life. Every day he drove to work in the green Zephyr Six that was his pride and joy, and he always told us on arrival how far he'd got without switching on his lights during the dark winter mornings. One day, on the drive in to work, a golf ball landed on his bonnet and dented it. He was distraught.

In many ways Tony was a good manager. He spent time with his trainees every evening when we all had to tell him how much 'shrinkage cover' we had made that day. He made us all feel part of a team. He was misguided but he could motivate. He trusted no one. I learned a lot about shrinkage control from him. Everyone, he said, was trying to rip us off. 'Back door shrinkage' is a term in retailing that refers to the stock you lose or is short delivered by suppliers at the loading bay. Tony lost not one penny. However, he did have one big fault as far as I was concerned: he insisted that when the store was open all I did was 'watch service', that is make sure that staff were moved from one counter to another as it got busy. All other work had to be done after the store was closed so the hours I worked were phenomenal, but during the day I just walked round and round the store and was bored rigid.

I was still going out with Rhianydd and we were getting quite serious. She came to stay in Rhyl for a few weeks during her college holidays and although it was strictly against company rules for managers to go out with staff, Tony gave her a temporary job in the cash office. One day John Richards, the Superintendent (area manager) gave me a major bollocking for something I'd done wrong, which Ranny overheard. I really liked Richards, partly because you knew where you stood with him. He didn't harbour grudges but could give you a serious telling off and then wink at you, just to let you know it was immediately forgotten. Ranny was incredulous at how one human being could speak to another in that way. You had to be thick-skinned to be a retailer.

At the start of the summer season a bloke who obviously knew Tony turned up at the store. He set up a 'seaside' backdrop at the front of the store and took your picture with a primitive Polaroid camera, then mounted it inside a plastic key ring. He charged five shillings (25 pence) for this and made a fortune. He paid rent for his pitch to Tony, which was one more way of covering shrinkage. This gave me an idea. I'd become friendly with Louis Parker, the son of one of the local amusement arcade tycoons. (Louis later opened a nightclub in Rhyl, which was a huge success, largely because he invented something called the 'Miss Wet T Shirt Competition'.) I persuaded him to sell me a second hand candyfloss machine for £25.

A candyfloss machine is nothing more than a spinning drum with an electric heating element at the centre. A teaspoon full of ordinary sugar dropped on the hot element is whizzed out into candyfloss threads in seconds. A touch of cochineal dye on the sugar makes it red. All you do then is pick up a ball of it on a stick and you have converted a few grains of sugar into one shilling (five pence). I asked Tony if I could rent a space at the front of the store to sell candyfloss, to which he agreed. I employed a student for the summer holidays and had made enough money by the end of the season to buy Ranny a decent engagement ring.

We got married in October 1969 and for the grand sum of £25

each we took one of the first ever package tours and honeymooned in Ibiza. At the same time I was moved to Wrexham as deputy store manager and I agreed to rent a farm cottage nearby. I told Ranny about the outside toilet while we were on honeymoon but she thought I was joking – until we got back.

All I knew about Wrexham was that Arnold Ravenhill, my old boss from Huddersfield, had retired there. The Wrexham store was an old building with a wooden floor and was overrun with mice. They were eating everything and had defeated Rentokil. The trainees seemed to spend half their life catching mice. The only thing that worked was to smear glue into a circle on a piece of cardboard and put chocolate in the middle. We had to put several of these on the floor every night, and next morning dozens of mice would be stuck fast on each one, still alive.

Soon after I arrived, the store manager retired and a new manager, Johnnie Walton, was appointed. He was considered to be of the right calibre to oversee the move from the old Wrexham premises to a brand new flagship store up the street. It was probably the last megastore that Woolworth's ever built. Johnnie Walton was one of the most objectionable men I have ever worked for. His favourite trick was reserved for when sales reps and other visitors came up to him on the sales floor. They would usually thrust out their hand to shake his in greeting. Walton was a big man with a large gut and he would draw himself up to his full height and look down at them as if they had crawled from under a stone, keeping his hands firmly behind his back. It was the ultimate put-down and I never understood why he did it.

I disliked Walton and he disliked me. His hobby was keeping parrots and he had me labouring for several weeks at his house building an aviary. Gradually I started to hate my job. I decided I would never make a successful career at Woolworth's. I was working long hours at Wrexham, usually six days a week, and I also had to 'check the store' on Sundays. Since I still hadn't replaced my crashed Mini van that meant I had to go in to work on the bus. On Sunday, when buses were less frequent, it meant if I jumped off the bus when it arrived at Wrexham bus station and ran like hell, I could check round the store and usually get back home on the same bus. If I missed it, the afternoon was gone. I began to wonder what on earth I was going to do with my life. I'd spent seven years at Woolworth's, I couldn't see a future and felt I'd wasted an important start to my career.

One day another trainee manager from the Oswestry store, Peter Hinchcliffe, came over to help in Wrexham and we had a drink together after work. We got on well and saw quite a bit of each other, usually in the pub where we would moan about our jobs and put the company to rights. Of course, next day in the store we were both too frightened to say anything. I told Peter about my dances and how I wanted my own business, and Peter told me about the 'stamp club' he used to run through various children's comics. One Saturday night Ranny and I, with Peter and his girlfriend Jean, were going out for a drink in my newly acquired second hand Singer Vogue car. We drove past a strawberry seller at the side of the road. He was packing up, but on impulse we stopped and negotiated a discount price to buy all his remaining stock of about half a dozen boxes. The next morning we drove to the Horseshoe Pass, a local beauty spot, to resell them. Our business partnership had been born.

3

The Strawberry Sellers

Sex sells! That was our first lesson in marketing. We'd parked the car and arranged the boxes of strawberries in a nice display on the grass verge. We'd made a large sign displaying the price, which gave us a modest profit over what we'd paid, and propped it in front of the car. Then Peter, Ranny, Jean and I sat down to wait for customers. An hour later we hadn't sold a single punnet. It was at that moment I had an idea: Peter and I hid behind the wall and within minutes cars were stopping. The girls did a roaring trade and soon sold out. We packed up and went to the pub to spend our profits and decide what to do next.

Over the next few weeks the four of us kept meeting for a drink or a meal, usually at our rented cottage, to discuss various hare-brained business ideas and moan about Woolworth's. One day Peter turned up quite excited and showed me a chain letter he had just bought from a friend for £1. He was convinced he was going to make a lot of money out of it and did I want to buy one? He had three to sell. The idea was that you bought a letter, then sent £1 to the organiser of the chain and also returned a list, which came with the letter, with the names of eight people who had bought letters previously, having added your own name and address to the bottom of the list. You sent £1 to the person at the top of the list and the organiser sent you back three new letters and lists with your own name moved up a notch. You had to sell these three new letters for £1 each, so you got your money back. Then you waited for the chain to spread and your own name to move up the list. Eventually thousands of people would be sending you £1 postal orders.

That was the theory anyway but I couldn't see this working and thought the chain was bound to fizzle out. I said to Peter, 'The only person making money out of this is the organiser. Why don't we start one ourselves?' We soon convinced ourselves this was the quickest way to make our fortune and set about organising everything. We decided on a name that we thought would lend gravitas to our new business: 'Investors Services'. We rented an accommodation address in Liverpool to have our mail delivered, and printed thousands of the letters we'd need, which explained everything. We also acquired an old typewriter, as everyone sending in their £1 postal orders would need the list of addresses retyping, leaving off the one at the top and adding theirs to the bottom.

The problem was starting the chain, so we typed a list of friends' names and addresses and added ourselves to the bottom so we could then sell the list claiming we'd bought it ourselves. Of course, we should only have sold three but we sold dozens to get the chain going and I really believed we were about to become rich. Soon postal orders started to arrive and we retyped the lists and sent them back. The people we'd put at the top of the list would wonder what on earth had happened when they started to receive postal orders out of the blue! I soon lost all interest in Woolworth's as I was convinced this was going to work. At first we thought it was quite funny when someone to whom we had sold a letter sent in their £1, and when we asked them if they had sold on their three letters they said they had, but we soon knew they hadn't because the letters didn't come back to Investors Services. That was the flaw in the system: many people found it difficult to sell letters on and the chain fizzled out quite quickly.

It didn't worry us though because Peter had found a new product that would make us even more money, and not in such a dodgy area as 'financial services'. He was an avid reader of *Exchange and Mart* and had seen an advert for 'Superflon'. This was an aerosol spray can that contained some magic fluid that gave aluminium pans a non-stick coating. Non-stick pans were still quite new and expensive and we thought the opportunity for people to make their existing pans non-stick would be in great demand. We decided the best way to sell these aerosols, which were quite expensive, was to demonstrate them at 'non-stick parties'. Tupperware was going great guns and we saw this as a similar opportunity for people to earn money by becoming 'non-stick agents'. We ordered twenty cases of Superflon and Peter's girlfriend Jean organised the first party in Oswestry, but by then we'd already moved on again. We had decided that if we were ever going to leave Woolworth's we should set up a proper business and stop messing about.

We decided to open a shop. The problem was, what should we sell? We had no money so we couldn't afford any type of business that required even a modest stockholding. A shoe shop, for example, would need shoes of every size, colour and style sitting on the shelves before you could open the doors. The same was true of most retail sectors. Woolworth's had departments that sold glassware and gardening, crockery and confectionery, hardware and hosiery; in fact most things you could think of. We knew a little about most departments but not a lot about any of them. The only product we could think of where you didn't need to carry much stockholding was fruit and vegetables. You had it delivered every day and sold it every day. We knew the suppliers from Woolworth's and figured we could set up a shop without any money. Provided we could get a week's credit from our suppliers we would always have a week's sales in the bank before we had to pay anybody.

Peter said he knew where there was an empty shop to rent in Oswestry, next door to the Queen's Hotel. We found out the landlord was Border Breweries in Wrexham so I went to see if we could do a deal. The shop was available to rent at £15 per week on a three-year lease, and we thought we should offer to take it, provided they allowed us a 'get out' clause after three months. This would provide us with some degree of safety if our project didn't succeed. We didn't plan to let Woolworth's know what we were doing and thought if we could keep it a secret for a few weeks, until we were sure it would work, then we had the option of carrying on with our careers if it didn't work out. We found a young solicitor, John Evans, and asked him to draw up a partnership agreement and finalise the lease terms with Border Breweries.

When I worked at Leeds 5, the Superintendent would occasionally ask all the trainees to go out in their lunch hour and come back with twelve ideas for new products to sell. He had to attend a regional meeting with the buyers and needed us to feed him with ideas. New products aren't that easy to find and usually ideas were for range extension with increased pack sizes or variations on what we already sold. On one such foray, I was looking round Lewis's department store and saw that they were selling 'loose' frozen foods. They had an open top freezer, crusted with ice and with plastic washing up bowls in the bottom full of frozen vegetables. These were scooped into plastic bags and sold by weight. I put the idea on my list of suggestions but I never heard anything back. In Wrexham more recently I had noticed a shop that specialised in loose frozen food called 'The Ice Box'. There were always queues outside its door. Few people owned a freezer at that time and supermarkets only had small frozen food cabinets with a limited range of Birds Eye and Findus products, which were nearly all sold in eight-ounce packets. Loose frozen foods were considerably cheaper as there was no packaging involved and you could buy just the quantities you wanted. I suggested we should sell loose frozen foods in our shop.

We had to fix up a bank account for our new business and my personal account was at Martins in Rhyl, which had just been taken over by Barclays. Fortunately I'd had more than my salary going through the account because of my candyfloss business. One afternoon I managed to slip out of work and drove like a lunatic to Rhyl to see the bank manager, then back again to Wrexham to find Woolworth's in uproar: my coloured lights were on and the manager was looking for me everywhere. Border Breweries agreed to our request for a three-month break clause in the shop lease and it almost seemed things were going too smoothly. I was half hoping something would go wrong to stop us in this foolhardy adventure. We had to put up a deposit of £30 each to cover the first month's rent of £60. This was the only money we ever put into our venture, and the shop was ours. We bought two open top freezers and two large chest freezers for storage, plus a scale and a cash register, all on hire purchase. The cash register was a massive and ornate contraption that would probably be worth a fortune now. We called it 'Big Bertha'. It had just been converted to decimal currency.

The next thing we had to do was to fix up supplies and choose a product range. Woolworth's bought their frozen chickens from a wholesaler in Rhyl called Woodward's and I dealt with them often. The company was owned by two brothers: Norman ran a depot in Rhyl, and Bill a branch in Oswestry. Bill insisted we should deal with his son Nigel, who was a similar age to Peter and me, and we met one night in the bar of the Queen's Hotel to agree products and prices. Nigel showed us the price list and we went through it item by item. I was surprised Nigel was offering big discounts to the list price, which made us feel special, but we soon realised that nobody ever paid list price for anything. Woodward's product range was primarily for the catering market and we chose a range of frozen vegetables, fish, meat and pastry products. We worked out we could sell competitively and make an average profit margin of 40 per cent.

One night we were in Peter's flat and trying to choose a name for the business. The Ice Box in Wrexham had set the tone and we considered Iceberg's, Penguin's, Eskimo's and Igloo's until Ranny suggested 'Iceland' and we all agreed that should be the name. 'Walker and Hinchcliffe' was excluded not for reasons of modesty but so that Woolworth's wouldn't find out.

We gave the shop a coat of paint and laid some plastic floor tiles, paying for everything with the loose change out of our pockets. Peter's girlfriend Jean was going to work in the shop full-time and brought in two of her sisters to help. I didn't really like the idea of friends and relations working for us as I thought it might lead to trouble. Ranny was a teacher and it wasn't sensible or necessary for her to give up her job.

We opened for business at 9am on Thursday, 18 November 1970. Peter took three days' holiday from Woolworth's but Johnnie Walton would never let me take any time off so I went sick. Those first three days were busy and we just knew the shop was going to be a success. We'd placed a full-page advert in the *Oswestry Advertizer* with our slogan: 'Why pay for fancy packaging when you can save up to 50 per cent by buying loose frozen foods?' Woodward's were only down the road and we had several deliveries every day. I helped in the shop, but Peter had to work in the back in case anyone from Woolworth's came in and recognised him. It was very exciting. I thought the shop looked very professional. There was some shelving on the walls when we took it over, which was not much use for frozen foods, so I bought some eggs from the farm where I lived and the rest we filled up with Superflon.

On Saturday night, after the first three days' trading, we worked out how much profit we had made. We thought it a fairly obvious thing to do. We had taken £360 in sales. We counted how much stock we had left and worked out the gross profit. Then we deducted the rent and wages, made a guess at the rates and telephone bill, and eventually came up with a net profit figure. We continued to do that every week. Apparently it wasn't such an obvious thing to do because accountants and other professionals we met for years afterwards were amazed that we produced weekly profit figures. The following Monday Peter and I were both back at Woolworth's and we ran the shop by visiting it every night and on Sundays.

Looking back it all seemed very easy. Woodward's had given us a week's credit on their supplies but we stretched it to four weeks before we paid them. In the first four weeks the only money we paid out was in wages so our bank balance just went up every week.

Things settled into a routine but my days at Woolworth's seemed unbearable. By early January we knew that they knew about the shop and by late January they knew that we knew that they knew. The girls in our shop used to tell us about Woolworth's supervisors hiding across the road to spy on us. It wasn't long before we were told that God wanted to see us in Dudley. We couldn't imagine that it was for promotion.

4
A Multiple Retailer

Sink or swim were the words that came to mind. I felt as if I'd been freed from jail and I couldn't believe how much I enjoyed going to work again. We'd actually got nowhere to go each morning except the shop in Oswestry and Jean and her sisters quickly got fed up with me spoiling their cosy working arrangements. I was soon labelled the bossy one as I tried to organise everybody. However, Peter and I got on well and before long it was felt best that the sisters left and got other jobs.

We constantly discussed the future and decided we were really serious about this venture. It just had to work and we agreed all our decisions would be taken for the long term. We were great admirers of Marks & Spencer and soon we were using their name not to describe their company but a certain attitude to business, which we thought they typified. This was a long-term, quality approach to every decision we made, and the opposite of everything we thought Woolworth's stood for. The Oswestry shop was doing OK but it wouldn't keep the two of us so we knew we had to expand fast. We also knew we should conserve cash so we agreed not to take any money out of the business until our Woolies pay-off ran out, and then we agreed we would only take £10 per week. It was ironic that, shortly after this, Peter found several hundred pounds' worth of out-of-date postal orders in his raincoat pocket from our Investors Services escapade! We recruited a manageress for the Oswestry shop, Mrs Arrowsmith, and paid her £11 per week, which was about the going rate. For many years we paid other people more than we paid ourselves.

Rhyl seemed like a good place to open our second shop. I knew the town and Woodward's also had a depot there. We set off in my car to do a search and called in to see the local estate agent, Jones and Beardmore. A young surveyor called Gareth Williams told us that a Mrs Twigdon had a dress shop just off the main street and she wanted to sell it. The Twigdons were big hitters in Rhyl. Mum had the dress shop and her son had a pet shop across the road. Dad owned a garage. We went to see Mrs Twigdon who explained that she couldn't sell us the lease on her shop until she had sold all her stock and that might take some weeks. Hot pants were just coming into fashion and were a large part of her stock. She refused to put a date on when the shop would be available or agree a sale until everything had been sold. We couldn't wait as we were desperate for a second store and wanted to open before Easter. We kept going back to try to persuade her but to no avail. One day we were just leaving her shop, downhearted at getting nowhere, when we stopped in her doorway. A popular television programme at the time was *Man at the Top*. It was about a hard and ruthless businessman and we discussed what he would do! It was obvious. We turned round and went straight back into the shop and said we would buy the shop and all her dresses and hot pants with it. It worked. We did a deal there and then for £750 plus stock at valuation and arranged to take over in about two weeks' time. In actual fact once she put a closing down notice in the window all her stock went pretty quickly and we didn't have to buy anything.

The shop in Rhyl was just one large room and Mrs Twigdon had divided it with a curtain. We realised there was a lot more work to do than when we had fitted out the Oswestry shop and we were short of time if we were to open by Easter. We decided to go to Rhyl with our sleeping bags and stay in the shop until we'd finished the entire fitting out work. The first thing we had to do was to build a dividing wall. We went down to the local builders' merchants who explained how to build a 'stud' partition. We spent several days at the sharp end of DIY, building the partition, putting up wall panelling, gluing down floor tiles and painting. We did all the work in the shop ourselves except for the electrical work. We did cause some local amusement when we were seen sticking mosaic tiles on the front of the shop one tiny little tile at a time. Mr Twigdon junior, the pet shop owner across the road, came over and explained that you stuck on whole sheets at once and then peeled off the brown paper backing when it had set! Our suppliers from Oswestry had delivered the till, scales and refrigeration and we were ready for opening the week before Easter. Iceland Rhyl opened with good sales and we were then able to claim we were 'multiple retailers'.

Peter and Jean were engaged by this time and planned to get married at Easter. They were married on Easter Monday and had their wedding reception at the Queen's Hotel next door to Iceland in Oswestry. Mrs Ward, the manageress of the hotel, came over to Peter in the middle of the wedding reception and whispered something in his ear. Peter turned to me and said Mrs Ward needed some more chickens for that night and would I go with him to the shop to help him get them! Peter and Jean had two days off for their honeymoon and were then back at work.

Our bank balance went up again with the opening of the second shop. We'd spent very little on fitting out and had no outgoings apart from staff wages, so we had four weeks' sales in the bank before we had to pay Woodward's for our supplies. We still felt we needed something else to help our cash flow along, however, and remembering our strawberry escapade we decided to try our hand on a market stall. We pitched up at Wrexham open air market one Wednesday morning at 8am and hung back with other 'casuals' while the regulars set up their stalls. Eventually the market superintendent allocated pitches to the casuals. The best and most prominent of the remaining spaces went to the 'regular' casuals and finally, if there were any odd spaces left, to the traders at the bottom of the pecking order like us. We later learned a little cash in the right direction helped get a better pitch!

In addition to frozen food and Superflon, we had a small range of grocery items on sale in our two shops and we always tried to choose slightly more unusual items that weren't commonly available in supermarkets. One such line was Knorr dried soup, in one gallon catering packs, which we bought from the local Booker cash and carry. For some reason it sold quite well. We decided to sell this on the market stall. Our first morning was encouraging enough for us to go back again the following week and we broadened our range with a very unusual product, which cost us nothing. Near the cottage where I lived was a pond in a field with bulrushes growing wild. Bulrushes are often used as dried flowers. I waded in and cut a load and we sold these on the market stall alongside the Knorr soup. The most bizarre product range you could imagine! We kept up the weekly market stall for several weeks but then decided our efforts would best be rewarded by concentrating on opening more shops.

We opened one more shop that first year in Flint, a small town in North Wales. This was a gamble as the town was very small, more of a village really. The landlord of the shop was an Italian, John Guanerri, who also owned and ran the snack bar next door called The Clwyd Diner. Everybody called him Johnnio. A few days before we opened he called in to chat as we were still fitting out and asked how much we needed in sales to break even. I told him about £300 per week. He thought for a moment and then decided we were doomed to failure as he judged (correctly) that there wasn't £300 worth of frozen food sold in a week in the whole of Flint. I'd never really thought of that but I suppose technically he was right, the market didn't exist. I often remembered Johnnio's reasoning years later when I saw management consultants overanalysing a situation. Analysis doesn't allow for either instinct or the possibility of creating a new market.

As it turned out Flint wasn't a roaring success and we hovered around break-even sales levels for more than a year until we slowly built up the business to about £1,000 per week. Our customers in Flint were a pretty conservative lot and we employed a manageress who was much younger than the other two. I was therefore quite shocked when, one day while discussing the poor sales figures, she told me that this new exotic product 'pizza' was a complete waste of time, none of her customers wanted it and she personally wouldn't eat it if we paid her!

The Flint shop had a first floor attic room, although there wasn't access to it by a staircase, only a ladder. As this was the only spare room we had in the business, we decided to make it our head office. We built a desk out of plywood, bought filing cabinets and set up the 'nerve centre' for our empire. Soon we became bogged down with the paperwork that faces anyone running a business. We checked the daily cash sheets and reconciled them with the money the shops paid into the bank. We matched delivery notes to invoices and checked that the prices we were charged were what we had agreed with suppliers. We set up a system to pay our suppliers and every week, and worst of all, we had to work out the wages and PAYE. We didn't employ any office staff and had to do everything ourselves. It was a real bind!

Gradually, more and more frozen food companies got to hear about us and while Woodward's were by far our biggest supplier we started to increase our range of products and deal with many other suppliers. Often sales reps would come to see us in 'the office' and it was always amusing watching them climb the ladder and then having to sit in a deck chair, which was the only spare chair we had.

We had put a sales graph on the wall, which we filled in every week, but we became increasingly concerned as the sales line started to go down for all three shops. We didn't realise it at the time but frozen food sales are seasonal and, after the summer peak, sales would decline until the end of October when the build-up to Christmas would begin. We really started to get quite worried in October and thought the frozen food boom was already over.

We had already started to think we were becoming

over-dependent on frozen food anyway. Three shops did seem quite a lot and we felt it was wrong to keep all our eggs in one basket. My Uncle Harry worked in Leeds and told me about a new shop that had opened there which was doing fantastic business, although it seemed such a simple concept. It was a small shop not much bigger than a kiosk and all it sold was sandwiches. It was situated away from the main shopping area in a part of town where all the banks and offices were. Peter and I went to look at it and thought it was a brilliant concept and we should open one. We found a tiny shop in Oswestry only 50 yards from Iceland and thought it would be ideal. We weren't sure if the idea would transplant from the Leeds city office district to a Shropshire market town but we thought with a few product additions we could probably make it work. We had also seen a shop in Wrexham called 'Bake and Take' which sold cooked pastry products to take away. Both shops were quite innovative at the time and certainly we'd seen nothing like them. We thought a mix of the two might work well.

We planned the shop to be very upmarket. We still had cash in the Iceland bank account and used some of it to set up the new business. We thought we should offer a wider product range than just sandwiches and pies so we added a rotissamat to cook chickens, a griddle and a chip fryer. As usual we fitted out the shop ourselves and spent a lot of money on equipment and decorating the shop to a really high standard. We called it simply 'The Takeaway'. About three weeks before we opened we found to our horror that someone else had had the same idea and were also in the middle of fitting out a takeaway type shop at the other end of town. It was too late for us to change our minds, we were already committed, but we reckoned if we could open first we might have the advantage.

It was now the middle of November and nearly one year since we had opened the first Iceland shop. We were very keen to work out how we were doing and had arranged to count all the stock in the three shops on the anniversary of the opening, 18 November, and then work out the profit result back in the office that same night. The

Takeaway was nearly ready to open but we had to break off to organise the stock-take and thought we would open the following week.

We worked until about 10pm on 18 November and I remember pulling the handle on the adding machine to come up with the final profit figure for the year: £5,000. We were delighted.

It was a cold night with the first frost of the year. We left the office and started the drive home, me in my old Singer Vogue and Peter in front of me in a maroon coloured old Rover. About three miles from Flint I suddenly felt the car sliding to one side, I saw bright lights and then all went black. I remember wandering in the road and actually turning my car radio off. I was then in a house waiting for the ambulance but I couldn't remember who I was or if I had a passenger in the car. In the ambulance someone covered in blood kept asking me what the hell I thought I was doing. It was the driver of the other car who turned out not to have been hurt other than a few cuts.

I was laid on a trolley in the hospital and I could feel my chest slowly filling up and tightening. I thought I was going to die. A young surgeon explained that I had ruptured my spleen and he was going to take it out. I had also broken some ribs and while he was in there he would look at my liver which also might have been damaged but not to worry, if he had to cut a piece off it would regrow! The anaesthetist was also there and asked me with some sarcasm if it 'had been a good party'? I told him I had been working but I'm not sure he believed me.

I spent a month in hospital in the men's surgical ward where everyone else seemed to be middle-aged and having their prostate removed. I could see that was a really messy operation and hoped I never had that problem. I lost my spleen but my liver was OK. I learned to play chess and soon became institutionalised. One of the older patients we all called 'The Major' christened me 'The Entrepreneur'. It was the first time I'd ever heard the word.

Peter came to see me after a few days. He'd been working round the clock and got The Takeaway open on time but I could tell he wasn't happy. Apparently sales were awful during the daytime, when we took hardly any money at all, but we were very busy at night and had great difficulty in getting staff so he and Jean had to work every night. He looked exhausted. I was happy to be alive and just felt we'd had a great first year in business.

5

The Takeaway

As soon as I was out of hospital I went back to work without much in the way of convalescence. During my first week back we bought a whole lorry load of 'frozzy pops'. These were polythene tubes of coloured water, packed in boxes of a hundred, which we would freeze and sell as iced lollies. I had to unload the whole lorry by myself and carry them into the back room of the Flint shop. I felt a little aggrieved that Peter wasn't there to help.

I couldn't wait to see The Takeaway but soon found that the original concept had evaporated in favour of an altogether more downmarket offering. Nobody was interested in our daytime business and we'd even stopped doing sandwiches. Most evenings were also quiet but Friday, Saturday and Sunday nights were something to behold.

The queues started to form at about 9pm and continued until well after midnight. No matter how fast we served the customers, no matter how quickly we prepared the food, people walking or driving past would join the queue but only if it was a certain length. Too long and people would pass by but just short enough and they would join the line. The queue never got any shorter. We soon realised we had an amazing business that could take an unlimited amount of cash, depending only on how fast we could serve the customers – but only on three nights per week.

A major problem was staff. We had no problem during the daytime and employed a very capable daytime manageress, who didn't have a lot to do, but, on the three nights per week when the cash was taken, we just had to be there ourselves to keep control.

Iceland was by now becoming a serious business and Peter and I would both work there all day and then take it in turns to run The Takeaway at night. Sundays were our only day off from Iceland and when it was my turn on duty at The Takeaway, a dark cloud would descend at about 4pm, as Ranny and I would leave home and drive to Oswestry.

We would start our shift preparing food and threading defrosted Iceland chickens on metal skewers for the rotissamat. Late at night our customers were often very drunk and rowdy and their culinary requests would typically extend to something like scampi and chips with gravy and a portion of curry on top, and then they would drop it in the doorway as they left the shop. Fights were not unusual and things would only quieten down at about 1am as we started the big clean up. Usually we would be driving home at daybreak, our clothes and hair infused with the smell of cooking fat.

However, The Takeaway was very profitable and, since we had decided it wasn't a business we wanted to expand, we were content to 'milk it' and supplement our £10 per week drawings from Iceland. Ranny and I had applied for a mortgage on the strength of our joint earnings, Ranny as a teacher and me as a half shareholder in a business making £5,000 per year in profits. We left our farm cottage and moved into a brand new house in St Peter's Park, a new housing estate, for which we had to pay £5,000. I remember thinking what a shame it was that we had missed the property boom. We could have bought the same house six months earlier for £4,500.

The Takeaway paid for all the furniture for our new house but after about twelve months of working day and night we could stand the pace no longer, whatever the reward. Fate intervened and during a routine visit by the local fire officer, he told us we would have to close down. The shop had a first floor, which served as the staff room and food preparation area. Everything had to be carried into the shop down a narrow wooden staircase which went right past the chip fryer. There was no other way of arranging things and the fire officer reluctantly gave us a month to close the shop. It was a relief really and we didn't argue. Then I had a brainwave.

I rang the owner of our competitor in Oswestry and suggested the town wasn't big enough for the two of us and one of us should close down and let the other take all the business. Since Iceland was our main business, we would be prepared to close our Takeaway shop provided he paid us £1,000 in cash. He agreed. We met one morning in Littlewoods' café for a cup of tea, 'him' carrying a very obvious briefcase! We went down the street to The Takeaway, which hadn't yet opened for business that morning, to count the money and do the handover. There was £1,000 in £1 notes, which I noticed as we counted them were still covered in salt and vinegar. Peter and I split the money between us and I finished furnishing the house!

Soon after we first opened The Takeaway we continued to plan Iceland's growth and recognised we could do better than buying from local wholesalers with deliveries every day to every shop. We really needed our own cold store and warehouse in order to take larger deliveries direct from the manufacturers, which we could then redeliver to our own shops. This would save us money, as we would be able to buy at better prices, and also operationally be more efficient. We reckoned we could build a small cold store (although we had nowhere to build one) for about £25,000. We set about visiting local banks to try to borrow the money. I'd never heard of a 'business plan' and we were armed only with a good story and our first set of accounts. Nobody would take us seriously as we didn't have a 'track record', just twelve months' trading history. We tried every bank in Rhyl and finally thought we were getting somewhere when we gained an appointment with the manager of Lloyds. We were shown into his office and left alone for quite a long time before the manager finally appeared. He was completely oblivious to our whole presentation and he kept ferreting around his office mumbling over and over again, 'Sorry about the gin'. It took a while for us to realise that someone as important as the bank manager could actually be drunk out of his skull!

It became clear we were not going to be able to borrow any money but out of desperation I did ring up my old landlord, the farmer from the cottage we used to rent. He had seen our early success and when we moved out of the cottage his last words to me were, 'Remember, if you ever need an investor in your business, come to me first.' Of course, he didn't mean it as I realised from his embarrassment when I contacted him. Though I bet he's regretted that a thousand times since!

Woodward's, our main wholesale supplier, was run by Bill and Norman Woodward, two brothers who couldn't be more different. Bill was an extrovert, a great wit and raconteur. Norman was quiet and dour. They had been impressed with the growth of Iceland, which by now was their largest customer, and suggested they should take a stake in our business. Norman was building a new giant cold store and his old one in Ernest Street, Rhyl, would soon be vacant. In return for a 50 per cent share of Iceland they would agree to rent us their old cold store at a market rent.

This was in one way very attractive to Peter and me and a great opportunity to expand our business, but it was hardly a fair deal. We also worried about losing our independence but convinced ourselves it was better to have half of a large cake than all of a small one. Bill was very persuasive and dazzled us with his wealth and influence. 'Look upon Norman and myself as your merchant bankers,' he told us, not realising I hadn't a clue what a merchant banker was. (Or perhaps he did know!) 'We have the experience and resources to help Iceland grow.'

We tried to do a better deal and in the end it was also agreed that the Woodwards would put £5,000 into Iceland, but since Iceland was by now reckoned to be worth around £10,000 it meant Peter and I would have to take out £5,000 to equalise things. The idea was to put money in, not take it out, and since Bill and Norman couldn't or wouldn't put in any more cash, the solution was for Peter and me to leave in our £5,000 and convert it into a loan or debenture. The deal was agreed in August 1972 but not signed until December, by which time we had opened our fourth store in Mold, North Wales. We also became a proper limited company as opposed to a partnership, with me as the Chairman and Peter and me as Joint Managing Directors. We moved from Barclays to Woodward's bank, the NatWest, where Bill and Norman had more influence. Even so, we still had to give personal guarantees and sign our houses over to the bank as security! We were gearing up.

Norman's old cold store was such an exciting opportunity and we couldn't wait to get hold of it. Expansion, however, meant we soon had an overdraft at the bank as we spent money refurbishing Norman's old offices and setting up our new headquarters in Ernest Street. We also opened a frozen food 'cash and carry' in part of the building to service Rhyl's catering customers. At last the great day came when we could move into the offices and the cold store. In my first eight years at Iceland I never took a holiday. Looking back now I realise I was stupid but at the time Iceland came first. Work was a holiday. Peter's wife Jean insisted from the beginning that they took holidays every year and their fortnight in Bournemouth coincided with the move into our new cold store. I didn't mind, I wouldn't have missed it for the world and I couldn't understand how Peter could miss such an important event.

Our new 'Central Services' generated a lot of additional over-heads for our business but it gave us the base from which to open a lot more shops. We employed our first office staff member as a sec-retary/telephonist/accounts clerk. We also recruited a driver, John Keegan, for our newly acquired second hand Transit van which was specially insulated to carry frozen food, and Gary Davies, a school-leaver, to run the cold store. Gary is still with us today. Peter and I shared not only an office but also the same desk. The first one to get in each morning sat behind it and the other, usually me, perched on the end. Peter and I had different working patterns. He would be in early but had to be home by 6pm. I could never manage to get in before 9am but would always stay late.

Our relationship with Bill and Norman was fantastic. We worried about them taking over but they left us to it. We met occasionally for a 'board meeting', which was usually a meal, and enjoyed their company and Bill's many stories, usually about his time as a pilot during the war. Bill insisted on weekly financial information being sent to him and in order to provide this in the form he wanted I invented something we called our 'Directors' Report'. This contained a mass of information on just one sheet of paper and I now know it would be called a 'spreadsheet' today. We listed all our shops with the weekly sales and the increase or decrease over the previous year. Goods were sent to our shops only from our own warehouse which made us the first food retailer in Britain to be 100 per cent central delivered. Because of this we knew the cost and selling price of goods delivered to each store every week and could therefore calculate the gross profit. We listed all store overheads and then apportioned central overheads to each store. This gave us a pretty accurate net profit figure for each shop and the company as a whole every week.

This degree of financial information was highly unusual for a company of any size let alone a fledgling business like ours. It was a laborious and time-consuming document to produce, especially when you think the calculator had only just been invented. We had just bought one for £80. It did, however, give us a fantastic control system, which became one of the cornerstones of our business success. We sometimes got behind with producing the Directors' Report but since we prepared full accounts every quarter we often didn't bother catching up and waited until the next quarter to start again. Whenever we did that it seemed like there had always been a problem in the business, a surprise in the profit figures or our overheads, which we would have been aware of and able to rectify if only we'd had our weekly report. It became our bible and we ran essentially the same system for the next 28 years, although eventually it became a complicated computerised document I could never understand.

Neither Peter nor I had a clue about book-keeping or accounts. We just invented our own common-sense 'Noddy systems' which seemed to work and serve us well. Retailing is a very simple business and only five things (key ratios) matter:

1. Sales obviously, but the percentage increase on the previous year tells you if the business is growing and is almost more important than the actual sales level.
2. Gross margin is the biggest factor in determining profitability and tells you the percentage profit on goods sold.
3. Cost to sell is the staff wages as a percentage of sales and needs to be carefully managed every week.
4. Shrinkage is the amount of stock losses and Woolworth's taught us the importance of managing that.
5. Overheads and, in particular, the cost of central distribution can become uneconomic and kill a business.

After 40 years in business I still can't read a balance sheet or a set of accounts but I don't consider it necessary. I know enough about generating profits and controlling overheads and am happy to let the accountants do the rest.

Once Ernest Street was up and running smoothly we set about the business of opening more shops with a vengeance. However, we also had the empty shop premises from The Takeaway that we had shut down, as agreed, but which was still costing us money in rent every week. One day Peter and I were talking about our favourite company, Marks & Spencer, and he told me about all their textile suppliers being based in Leicester where he used to live. Corah was a well-known manufacturer of knitwear among other things and they had a factory shop where they sold Marks & Spencer seconds, with the labels cut out, at really knock-down prices. We went to visit them and were most impressed with the range of products you could buy, and the fact that there were lots of market traders buying stock. So we came up with the idea of opening an M&S seconds outlet in the old Takeaway premises. This seemed as if it would be a lot easier than frying chips every night and might also make some money.

We converted the shop and bought a load of gear from Corah and we were soon in business. We had no difficulty recruiting a manageress and, best of all, we didn't have to be there ourselves. We could almost forget about the shop and let it run itself. Sales were good, we were in profit and we thought we'd stumbled on another good idea until after a couple of weeks we started to run low on stock and had to think about making another trip to Leicester.

Peter had a big Ford Granada, but Leicester was a long way away and we'd drive back from a buying trip almost unable to move or see out of the window with the car crammed to the roof with stock. It used to take us a whole day to make the journey. This soon became a regular pattern. Two or three weeks of good sales, then a few poor weeks until we could put off the trip no longer and then another journey to Leicester. We had much more important things to do in Iceland and the trip became a real nuisance. We learned a lot about colours and sizes, though. In knitted cardigans, or any other ladies' clothing, size 16 in blue was by far the bestseller. Size 10 pink or other funny colours wouldn't sell at all but Corah were wise to that and wouldn't let you buy just what you wanted. Cardigans came packed in twelve assorted colours and sizes and you would get stuck with all the slow sellers.

We soon became fed up with this latest venture and finally closed the business down, and eventually we got rid of the shop premises. We could now concentrate all our attention on Iceland.

6

Moving up a Gear

One of the first things Peter and I had to do was organise ourselves better. As partners, we both felt we should be involved in everything and every decision, and that led to a great deal of confusion. We both placed orders, we both visited stores, usually together, and we made all decisions jointly. This wasn't very productive so we had a long conversation about splitting responsibilities. We decided Peter's prime responsibility would be for all the product buying and I would be responsible for expanding the company. To begin with, this meant finding and fitting out new stores. The next thing we did to improve productivity was buy a second desk so we had one each!

We soon fell into a routine with Peter starting early and going home early while I did the later shift. Peter would spend most of the day buying products and fixing prices. Inflation at that time was rampant and prices seemed to increase every week, which wasn't bad news for a retailer. I would be out visiting stores and looking for new sites. Our new site appraisal system didn't really change much over the next 25 years and amounted to nothing more than 'intuition' or 'gut feel'. I would look at lots of properties and when I found one at the right rent that I thought we could trade out of, I had to persuade the landlord to let it to our new company, which he'd never heard of. I would draw up the plans myself and then organise the shopfitters.

I used a local firm based in Prestatyn, North Wales, called Arthur Hapgoods.

We opened shops in Wrexham, Chester, Shotton, Moreton, Neston, Prestatyn and Heswall and then we ran out of money. Bill Woodward had insisted we change from Barclays to his bank, the NatWest. It seemed to make more sense as Woodward's were a big company and would have more 'clout' with their bank than we did with ours. In truth we never built up any kind of relationship with the NatWest manager and I think he always viewed us as two young lads who needed keeping under tight control. He never visited any of our shops and had no interest in our business. We were always having to push for a bigger and bigger overdraft so we could expand the business but the manager had great difficulty understanding why we were so ambitious and often lectured us about 'overtrading'. I never knew what he meant.

In my search for new shop sites I met a Liverpool fruit and vegetable merchant called William Ross who had half a dozen greengrocery shops. We seemed to get on well but I thought his shops were the dirtiest, scruffiest places I had ever seen. However, they were all in good high street locations. It was an old family business, he seemed very well off and not too interested in his shops. He was just content to let them jog along. I convinced him that if he let us put a frozen food section in all his shops, he would make money both from our rent and from extra greengrocery sales because we'd bring in more customers. We would also clean the places up for him. This was going to be a very cheap and easy way for us to expand without upsetting the bank manager. We subsequently opened in Holywell, Caernarvon, Bangor and Bootle. We also expanded our product range to include 'serve-over deli' (cooked meats, loose bacon and cheese etc). It was very hard work and I soon learned the lesson that it's difficult to make money out of any serve-over operation except for loose frozen food. We always appeared very busy with lots of customers. I used to spend hours on the bacon slicer but would always be amazed at the end of each day by how little money we'd taken for so much work. We also had the political problem of keeping the William Ross staff happy. They saw us as interfering intruders who were trying to take over their shops. However, the shops were very profitable and they kept the momentum of expansion going when cash was tight. I did the buying for all the deli products and in order to be able to buy in decent quantities and fit in with our central delivery philosophy we bought an old garage behind our cold store in Ernest Street and converted it to a chiller room.

About this time we also took on our first area manager, a young guy called Alan Jones. We bought him a Mini van and paid him £45 per week. His job was to visit all the shops and keep them up to standard. Alan was a raging socialist and seemed to have a permanent chip on his shoulder about most things in life, but particularly about people who did well. Britain seemed to be in permanent crisis at that time and many people had a destructive attitude towards endeavour and success. A culture of envy was wrecking the country. By the end of 1973 the mineworkers had brought the pits to a standstill, the Prime Minister Edward Heath had declared a three-day working week and the electricity workers were on strike. Rubbish was uncollected in the streets and people in top jobs were leaving the country in something that became known as 'the brain drain'. A Labour government followed the 'Who governs Britain?' election of February 1974, inflation soared to 25 per cent and the Chancellor of the Exchequer Denis Healey did his best to split the nation into 'them and us' and tax enterprise out of existence. Better opportunities and lower taxes were available in other countries. Funnily enough, while Peter and I were obviously aware of all this, we were largely unaffected by it. We were in the food business and in the mass market and people always have to eat! We were too engrossed with the development of our own business to worry about the politics of the country.

Peter and I drew very modest salaries from the company but one advantage of being in business with Bill and Norman was that they were mad about cars and considered it entirely natural that Peter and I would be as well. After my car crash I'd bought a brand new

Ford Capri on the company but after the deal with the Woodwards I developed a good arrangement with Norman. He always had an exotic car which he changed every year and I would buy his old one. This ensured no hassle or criticism from Bill or Norman and meant I had an E-Type, a Lotus and a Ferrari in quick succession. I then decided I really should buy new and bought a red Porsche 911. The only real effect of the political climate at the time to trouble me was that I had to have the side resprayed on a regular basis because no matter where I parked it some envious soul would run a key down it.

Frozen food was proving a very popular market to be in. Lots of people were setting up new businesses as 'freezer centres' but just as quickly most of them would go bankrupt. People were seduced by the apparent high gross margins to be had, but didn't fully appreciate the high running costs of such a business or the controls that were necessary. Our product range had expanded so that in addition to the original 'loose' frozen food we sold a wider and wider range of packaged items. Loose frozen food was still very important to us and was featured prominently in every shop. It was a unique point of difference and the margins were very high at around 45 per cent.

We heard on the grapevine about a company based in Liverpool called 'Alpine Frozen Foods' that had just gone into receivership. They had a meat processing business based in Kirkby near Liverpool which traded as 'Coleman's'. They also had four freezer centres, which we decided we should buy. Alpine was run by John Murphy and Alan Birchall who we considered to be a couple of rogues. A company in receivership is just one step away from bankruptcy but can continue to trade under the control of a 'Receiver', who attempts to sell the business as a going concern on the basis that the creditors will get more money than if the business is simply closed down. I didn't understand the intricacies of this at the time and just saw that Birchall and Murphy appeared to be still running the show so I tried to buy the business from them.

Birchall was the chief negotiator and came across as an easy-going bloke full of bonhomie but we rapidly found out he was never very much up to speed on detail. His partner John Murphy seemed to have cast himself in the role of a mafia type gangster and always tried to look hard and intimidating. (This wasn't difficult given the size of him!) They made a great double act. We got nowhere very fast. Birchall was asking £200,000 for the freezer centres, a figure that seemed to be based on nothing in particular! We decided to cut them out and deal direct with the Receiver, Frank Taylor, who was a partner of the accountancy firm Huntingdon's in Liverpool. Frank was theoretically in charge but he did seem influenced by Birchall and Murphy and it became apparent that it was impossible to do a deal by excluding them. Negotiations went on for weeks but eventually we bought three of the Alpine shops, Old Swan and Maghull in Liverpool and Middleton in Manchester, for £25,000 plus stock. We were frightened of getting ripped off on the stock count, so on the morning of the takeover we had an army of our own staff in each store very early and it was all finished before Birchall and Murphy arrived. They were not happy!

We took over Alpine in 1977 and this proved to be a turning point for Iceland, because the acquisition opened our eyes to the benefits of bigger shops in bigger towns. Our existing shops were all very small units and sales were much lower than in the Alpine stores, which were really catering to the new and rapidly growing home freezer market. More and more people were buying large chest freezers, which they would typically keep in their garage and stock with large packs of frozen food. Buy in bulk and save money was the philosophy. We were keen to develop this new market but at the same time we didn't want to lose our existing 'loose' customers. We refitted the Alpine stores, which were pretty worn out and grotty, to a much better standard and we installed loose frozen foods in the Middleton and Old Swan branches. Then the real turning point came when we opened our new Stretford store.

The store was in the Arndale shopping centre in Stretford, Manchester. Woolworth's had just closed down and the empty shop unit was on the market. The rent seemed astronomical but we had to have the store. With the trading knowledge we had gained from Alpine, we were confident we would do well in this location, plus it was an old Woolworth's. We saw it as some kind of victory taking it over! I drew up the plans and at first included a loose frozen food section at the back of the store, but at the last minute we decided to take a gamble and see if the store would be viable without it. The store was over 4,000 square feet and would be our first 'proper' freezer centre. We opened in February 1978 and it was a great success. It was also our 'flagship' store and served as the template for future openings. Gradually we changed our trading style in the rest of the business, refitted most of our shops and pulled out the loose frozen food sections. We closed down some of the very small shops and converted the others into 'mini' freezer centres.

Iceland was on the verge of a big growth phase so, with hindsight, perhaps it wasn't the most sensible time for us to set up another new venture but it seemed like a good idea at the time! We went into the printing business. The rationale behind this decision was based on our difficulty in getting good quality printing done quickly. Our posters and price tickets were produced by a local silk-screen printer, who would literally turn them round for us overnight. We were his best customer. Our need for more standard print requirements such as forms, booklets, price lists and letterheads, was growing all the time. The process was always the same: Peter or I would inevitably leave it until the very last minute and then dash round to one of half a dozen local printers with a rush job. They all seemed to be based in old dirty premises without any kind of reception area. You would have to wait in a corridor until some old bloke emerged in a dirty brown overall to suck through his teeth and tell you how busy he was and no, he couldn't do the job for tomorrow but maybe a week on Friday. Knowing nothing about the printing industry but knowing a lot about our own requirements we decided we could do better. This would be a subsidiary of Iceland and we felt it would both make money and be of great benefit to the company.

We advertised for an experienced young printer who wanted the chance to run his own business. We met Roy Sheldon, who was not much older than us but seemed to have all the right experience. He must have thought it was Christmas when we told him he could set up a new printing workshop, we'd buy all the best equipment and give him a 40 per cent share in the company. We found the perfect premises, on a prominent street corner in Rhyl, and refurbished everything to our usual high standard. We built a reception area, a print workshop and a design studio. We bought two second hand printing machines of which one was a Heidelberg, reputedly the Rolls-Royce of printing machines. These were modern lithographic machines. At that time many of our local competitors were still using lead type. Our main marketing tool for the business was in the name, which we felt said everything about our point of difference. We called the company 'Hi-Speed Printers (Rhyl) Ltd'.

To begin with, everything worked really well. We had a drinks party to launch the business and invited everybody who was anybody in Rhyl! Business was reasonably good, Iceland alone provided enough work to take the business to 'break even' and Roy did a good job. A big surprise for us, and a constant source of frustration, were the print unions. Peter and I were fundamentally opposed to any kind of unionisation but in this business we had no choice. If our own art studio designed a newspaper advert, the paper wouldn't print it unless the actual artwork had the union stamp on it. They had a complete stranglehold on the industry.

We kept the business for the next few years but two things started to go wrong: Iceland soon outgrew the company's printing capabilities and our printing jobs couldn't always therefore be provided at the best price. We ended up giving work to the company just to support it. We also got worse service than the other customers as Roy always thought he could push us to the back of the queue if one of his 'real' customers had a rush job! This is a classic and common business situation and a good reason for not having subsidiaries provide a service to a company. Roy also turned out to be a bad choice. He ended up cheating on us and doing work for himself on the side. We took his shareholding from him and booted him out. We then sold the business to another printer called Charles Gill and continued to do business with him for many years. One part of the business we kept was the design studio. We moved this into the Iceland head office and it has been an invaluable asset to the business to this day.

When we moved our head office from Flint to Rhyl, we also moved to new firms of lawyers and accountants. It was more convenient but we also thought we should move to bigger firms. Our first company auditor was based in Wrexham and he was a really nice bloke who sadly died after a couple of years. In Rhyl we moved to Harold Smith and Son, who were one of the biggest firms of accountants on the North Wales coast. Our audit partner was a guy our age called Bernard Leigh and we were enormously impressed as he was newly qualified and had just been made a partner.

We also said goodbye to John Evans of James, James and Hatch in Wrexham and moved to Gamlin, Kelly and Beattie, a prominent firm of solicitors in Rhyl. The senior partner there had recently shot himself after some scandal or other and again a young guy our age called Bob Salisbury struck lucky and became senior partner. He was determined to make a name for himself and was very ambitious. One of the first jobs he ever did for us was the Alpine deal. Bob was larger than life and enormously likeable. We had a lot of fun with him.

Our small head office had expanded slightly but we were still weighed down with all the paperwork and the chore of completing the Directors' Report every week with our single calculator. We decided we should push the boat out and employ a book-keeper, but a cheap one. Mr Boardman answered the advert. He seemed ideal, as he was old (to us), semi-retired and happy to work part-time. We didn't know how to interview an accountant or what to ask him, so we gave him a column of figures to add up in his head. It was astonishing. He should have been on TV. He could run his finger down a column of twenty numbers in about two seconds and then give us the answer, faster than a calculator. We thought he had all the qualifications that would be needed so we took him on. We soon became aware of his shortcomings, however. He would always doze off at his desk after lunch, much to the amusement and giggles of the two young girls who shared his office. We had to get rid of him but who should we replace him with?

Peter and I talked it over and then went to put our idea to Bill and Norman. Iceland was going to grow quickly so we should be ambitious and not mess around any more with second best. Why didn't we poach Bernard Leigh from Harold Smith and Son? He was clearly a high-flyer and surely he would transform our business and deal with all the increasingly complicated paperwork that was coming our way. That would free up Peter and me to grow the company even faster.

Poaching Bernie took a long time. To be fair he had a lot to lose, he was already a partner in a respected professional firm and a comfortable future was assured. To join two 'market traders' like Peter and me with a very young business needed an act of faith and a lot of persuasion. He had worked with us as auditor for a few years and even helped with the Alpine deal so he knew how we operated. He also knew our company accounts inside out. He told us that of all his firm's clients, we were the only ones who did full quarterly accounts and a stock-take, tried to work out the result ourselves and then hassled him for verification. His usual clients never really wanted to know their results provided they were earning enough cash out of their businesses. Nevertheless it took several months, a lot of negotiation and many nights out to try to persuade him. Half-way through, he got involved with a serious girlfriend, Carol, so we had to start again and persuade her! We paid him a salary of £10,000 and gave him a car, plus a 10 per cent share of the business. That meant Peter and I and the Woodwards were diluted down to 22½ per cent each but we made Bernie's shares 'non-voting' so he couldn't upset the balance of power and his shares would never be as valuable.

We were quite excited at the prospect of Bernie joining us. We altered our headquarters at Ernest Street so we could provide him with his own private office. It was all decorated and ready for him when he arrived, and on his first morning he went in there, closed the door, and that was almost the last we saw of him! We waited and waited for him to emerge one day and announce he was changing everything. I imagined he would install all new systems and procedures but he never did. Perhaps it was a compliment that the Noddy systems we invented, our 'Mickey Mouse' Directors' Report and office systems, were actually very good and worked well. Bernie produced our quarterly accounts and was always there to give financial advice if we asked for it but he was never very proactive in coming forward with suggestions. He was dependable and reliable but never really 'joined in' or got involved in the day-to-day admin. We thought maybe it wasn't his role to deal with the detail and so, to get the best out of him, he should perhaps have an assistant who could organise the basics. We talked this through with Bernie and he suggested recruiting another young guy from Harold Smith called Peter Williams. Peter had failed his accountancy exams but seemed ideal as a lower cost 'office manager' and took the day-to-day organisation away from Bernie.

Now all we needed was more shops.

7

'Get it Bought'

Robin Greenway worked for Mason Owen and Partners, the Liverpool-based property agency, and had become our main contact there. We acquired one or two shops through him and I was fascinated by the stories he told me about Geoff Mason and Barry Owen, the founding partners of the firm. I didn't understand the property business at all but Geoff and Barry seemed to be legendary in the property world. Their clients included MFI and Kwik Save, both fast expanding retailers at the time. Albert Gubay had founded Kwik Save in the late 1960s as a direct copy of the German discount retailer Aldi. Albert had visited Germany with Geoff Mason when the idea was born and the two worked very closely together. Albert had gone public in 1972 and then soon after sold all his £22 million worth of shares in the company virtually overnight and disappeared off to New Zealand to start all over again. Kwik Save was based in Prestatyn and the company was now run by the two young guys who were left behind: Ian Howe, the accountant, and Michael Weeks, who looked after property and site finding. Michael Weeks was a very flamboyant character and quite the opposite of the penny-pinching Albert. Michael spent the majority of his time travelling the country in a chauffeur-driven Rolls-Royce looking for new shops.

Geoff and Barry were not much older than I was but seemed to live a glamorous lifestyle. Their offices in Union Court, Liverpool, were very stylish and modern, they seemed to own every exotic car imaginable and mix with all the big hitters in business. I was very impressed and it all served to strengthen my own ambitions. The first time I met Geoff was at Whelan's supermarket in Failsworth, Manchester. I actually pulled up alongside him in the car on the motorway driving there. He was sitting in a chauffeur-driven Aston Martin reading the newspaper. We met at the store with Dave Whelan, the owner, who was an ex-footballer. After he sold out his supermarket business and 'retired' he went on to make a bigger fortune by developing JJB Sports! At that time he had a chain of supermarkets and the one in Failsworth was in a massive old cotton mill with acres of spare space. Geoff had offered us the chance to rent some space in the store to put in a frozen food concession. He was there with Dave Whelan to do the deal. I was with Peter and we were both left dazed at the speed with which we were shown round the store – everything was settled in less than half an hour. Geoff obviously had to move on to more important things.

It was a while before I met Geoff again and this time he was driving a Ford Fiesta! A lot had happened to his firm that I was only vaguely aware of. The state of the British economy was far worse than I realised. There had been a property crash in the mid-1970s which led to many property companies, and the second division banks who had lent to them, going bankrupt for spectacular amounts of money. Geoff and Barry were involved in more businesses than just their property agency, which was still doing very well. One of the companies they owned was Telegraph Properties, a development company they had started and which had grown like a balloon and then gone bust. Afterwards, Geoff had concentrated on running the agency while Barry had spent all his time negotiating with the banks to which they owed money. He was trying to get out of the personal guarantees they had given and avoid personal bankruptcy. A deal was eventually done; they worked hard to pay the banks back something and 'downscaled' their lifestyles in the meantime.

Geoff came to see us in Rhyl and spent most of the afternoon with us. He told us the whole story about their business and what had gone wrong and the lessons he'd learned. He saw the potential of Iceland and was keen to work with us and help us acquire more shops. His energy was infectious. A deal he said he could do for us straight away was with 'Cee-n-Cee' Supermarkets, which was based in Staffordshire. This company was owned by another ex-footballer, Alex Humphries, but he had run into problems and Geoff was trying to broker a deal to sell the business to Michael Weeks at Kwik Save. There were several smaller stores Kwik Save didn't want and he could sell them to us. I asked why Cee-n-Cee was in trouble and Geoff explained they had made a profit of 2½ per cent two years ago, 1½ per cent last year and were on track for half a per cent this year. The business was only going one way and the reason, Geoff explained, was Alex. He was always frightened to employ anyone better than he was! That one piece of insight was a pure gem. Whether it was true or not in Alex's case, it always stuck with me and I tried to adopt it as a business philosophy: never be frightened to employ people better at the job than you are.

We wanted to take four of the Cee-n-Cee stores but this was now stretching our empire both geographically and with regard to management. We still had Alan Jones as an area manager and also a guy called Robert Robertson but they were not going to cope with more responsibility. We needed someone else. Someone of a much higher calibre than was necessary for the business as it was at that time, someone who would be capable of helping us run the company as it grew. Peter suggested we ring Dick Kirk. Dick had worked at Woolworth's at the same time as Peter and me. I had met him a couple of times, most recently at the side of the road in Rhyl. Dick was now the youngest ever area manager in Woolworth's and by coincidence Rhyl was on his patch. He was doing really well in the company and was well paid too, so I think he was a bit surprised when I overtook him one day in my E-Type. He was driving a cheaper Lotus! We pulled over and had a chat. Peter had worked with Dick for a while and rated him highly. I rang him and asked if he would like to join us if we matched his salary (without knowing what it was!). To my surprise he said he'd think about it. It didn't take long and we met soon afterwards in a hotel room and he agreed to join us. I explained we would pay him well as the company grew but there could be no equity share for him. He said he didn't care about that, he was just ready for a change. In truth, I don't think he knew what 'equity' was. (I'd only just learned the word myself!)

Dick resigned from Woolworth's a couple of days later and was asked to leave immediately. He joined us the next day. We gave him the title of 'Stores Controller' and his job was to run the shops. Dick was enthusiastic and aggressive and he soon made his presence felt. Alan Jones and 'Robbo' took an immediate dislike to him and the whole company felt the effects of his shake-up. He couldn't see what Peter Williams or Bernie did for a living and wanted to get rid of them both. Gradually he settled down.

I was now able to spend more time looking for new shops (site finding) and also spent more time at the offices of Mason Owen and Partners (MO&P). At that time I had little to do with Barry, who spent most of his time on investment property, but I spent time with Geoff and a young surveyor called John Prestt who was put in charge of our account. John had started out his career at MO&P but when the property crash came a lot of people were made redundant from the firm, so he bought a sailing boat with a few mates (none of them could sail) and disappeared around the world for a couple of years. He had just got back and resumed his career at MO&P. I was to spend two or three days every week for the next few years with John, in the car, site finding.

Geoff inspired me with his enthusiasm. One day, I was talking to him and Barry (you couldn't really have a conversation with only one of them as they shared an office) and Geoff was telling me how I should get better organised. He told me if I wanted to take more shops I should get a specialist property lawyer who could act quickly. He said I should move to Bullivant's. That name rang a bell.

A couple of years earlier I had moved house from St Peter's Park to an impressive mock Tudor house called Pinewood Lodge. The asking price was very expensive at £32,500. I bartered the seller down to £30,000 but a house sale always seems to take ages to go through and Bob Salisbury, my solicitor, was doing his 'searches' and messing about with the contract. One night the seller rang me to say he had some bad news. He'd sold the house to somebody else. I was stunned and heartbroken, as I really wanted this house. He explained that someone else had offered the full asking price and he had sold it to him. I put the phone down and after talking it over with Ranny for five minutes I rang him back. 'I'll offer you £37,500,' I said. The seller was confused. 'I thought you couldn't afford any more,' he choked. I must have over-negotiated! 'The trouble is,' he explained, 'I can't sell it to you because the other guy has actually exchanged contracts. His lawyer, Mr Bullivant, completed everything in 24 hours.' Bullivant must be a good lawyer, I thought, if he can do a deal in 24 hours that Bob needs six weeks to do. Not to be defeated, I found out who'd bought the house and offered him a £5,000 profit to turn it on, which he accepted. The seller was furious and stripped everything including light bulbs and towel rails before he left.

Geoff decided he would ring Peter Bullivant and get him round to meet me straight away. Before I left Geoff's office we had a new lawyer! 'Who are your accountants?' Geoff asked next. 'Harold Smith? Never heard of them. You need Stainless Stephen at Arthur Young.' Geoff had him round in two minutes. This 'Liverpool Mafia' seemed to be a group of professionals all involved in the property world and who all knew each other and worked together. I was keen to join the club.

Changing auditors wasn't just up to me so Bernie and I went to meet the senior partner at Arthur Young who turned out to be Frank Taylor. Frank had sold us the Alpine shops when he was at Huntingdon's. They were later taken over by Arthur Young and later still became Ernst & Young. Frank was charming and explained how well they would look after us and why we really needed one of the 'big boys' in the accountancy world. We moved firms and Stephen Laing, or 'Stainless Stephen' as everyone called him in reference to his unbending integrity, became our audit partner.

Visits to Liverpool often involved lunch at Casa Italia. There wasn't much to choose from in the way of restaurants at that time, not just in Liverpool but the whole of the UK. Standards were uniformly poor. Casa Italia was a pizza restaurant run by an Italian called Julian. Pizza restaurants were still a novelty and Julian demanded unbelievably high standards in everything. The food was brilliant, the place was spotless and you never went in there without seeing him on the floor. As a consequence his restaurant was always packed out and he made a fortune. Peter and I liked the concept, we liked the 'buzz' about the place and we thought we should go into the pizza restaurant business ourselves.

Why we did it I don't know but we couldn't stop ourselves. We rented a shop in the High Street in Rhyl and employed Arthur Hapgoods to fit it out. We sent them to Liverpool to copy the style of Casa Italia and we created a rustic Italian restaurant the like of which had never been seen in Rhyl before. We could never hope to achieve the standards of Casa Italia but we thought we had a formula which would be simple to replicate and we could build a chain. Rhyl wasn't the best place in the world to start as it was dead in winter but we thought if the first one was on our doorstep we could refine the concept before we rolled it out.

The idea was not to be too serious: we were fun, 'tongue in cheek' Italian. We called the restaurant 'Cassanova' and the whole theme of the place was 'sex'. We employed good-looking waitresses dressed in jeans and tight T-shirts. Our pizzas were all given girls' names. Never mind Quattro Stagioni or Neapolitana, we had Pizza Sophia and Maria. Our logo was a heart with the words, 'You'll LOVE our Pizzas'. The wine list suggested 'A meal without wine – is like a night without love'. What a concept!

The concept was fast food and we didn't want the hassle of employing a proper chef, so we developed a menu which we thought would be idiot-proof for any member of staff to prepare! We used frozen pizza bases; the toppings, of course, needed no real preparation. Other items on the menu were designed round a few basic, common ingredients. Tinned chopped tomato, tinned minced beef and tinned red beans gave us the basics for Spaghetti Bolognese, Cannelloni and Chilli con Carne! Salads and most other things were easy. We photographed every dish and wrote down instructions for their preparation and put them on charts on the wall in the kitchen. All we needed now was a manager. We roped in Bernie Moore, the Iceland manager from Prestatyn.

It was great fun setting up Cassanova. In one way, Rhyl proved ideal for the first restaurant, as there were plenty of catering equipment suppliers in the town, all eager to offer help and advice. We allowed several days for staff training and for them to practise cooking everything. We explained exactly how we wanted them to behave with customers and exactly how we wanted the food served. On the Saturday night before we opened, we organised a big party and tested everything on our friends. The service was a bit slow but nobody noticed as the booze was flowing freely.

We opened for real in time for lunch on a Monday at the height of the summer season. All the locals had been watching for weeks as the restaurant was being fitted out and they were keen to try it. There was a queue outside when we opened the doors. We had room to seat 60 diners. The first 60 people walked straight in, 60 people sat down all at the same time and 60 people ordered their food within minutes of each other, and then they waited ... and they waited. Even today, if you look in a pizza restaurant, the oven, which is usually on show, will most likely be a Blodgett. They are the best pizza ovens available so we just bought a Blodgett oven without thinking much about its power or capacity. Ours was slow. I'm sure it could cook 60 pizzas an hour but maybe during an hour rather than all at once! The lunchtime trade on a normal day would be staggered but on the opening day everyone came in together. It was total chaos. People were complaining, the staff were in tears, Bernie Moore kept fiddling with the Blodgett, trying to speed it up. It was a complete nightmare and many of our first customers went without lunch that day!

Things did settle down and no permanent damage had been done to our reputation, but our new venture did seem to take up a disproportionate amount of our time. We would go to Cassanova almost every lunchtime and occasionally in the evening and usually ended up staying much longer than we intended to, in order to solve some problem or other. Visitors to the Iceland office in Ernest Street would sometimes offer to buy us lunch and we usually took them to Cassanova without telling them we were the owners. That would cause an enormous amount of stress for us when things didn't go exactly right! Bernie Moore did pretty well as an amateur chef but he was really just an 'assembler' of ingredients. It was actually all quite good fun but we soon realised it wasn't possible both to keep up standards at Cassanova and to run Iceland. We needed to delegate the building of our second retail chain. Alan Jones was not enjoying life working for Dick Kirk so we offered him the chance of a new career. He could take over Cassanova and expand the business. If he did well we would give him a share of the company. Ever the socialist, Alan insisted we give him a share of the business first. His reasoning was you could never trust a boss to honour a promise. We left him with Dick.

Rhyl in winter was a desolate place in the late 1970s. Cassanova had a retail shop window and, driving past at night, the sight of a single courting couple sitting in the corner of an empty candlelit restaurant didn't do a lot for my enthusiasm for the business. We tried hiring a country and western guitarist and sat him on a high stool in the corner but he turned out to be diabetic and Bernie or I had to drive him home half-way through each evening for his injection. One bright spot in our new venture was a private party for our friends on what turned out to be a wild New Year's Eve, but January and February were dire. We enjoyed another summer and then in autumn 1979 decided to get rid of the place. Miraculously, we got all our money back. We sold the business to a lecturer from the local catering college who turned it into a burger joint.

We had already outgrown our offices in Ernest Street and even bought a terraced house next door as an overspill office. The cold store was also many years old and suffered from 'frost heave'. Modern cold stores have a heater mat fitted under the floor to stop the ground beneath it gradually becoming frozen. The cold store at Ernest Street had no heater mat and the permafrost below it must by now have been several feet thick. As the ice in the ground freezes and expands it pushes up the concrete floor of the cold store so that it becomes impossible to run a pallet truck over it and the shelving tips over. We were forever drilling deep holes in the floor and putting heating elements down to melt the ice and lower the floor! We were also fast outgrowing the small cold store and opening new shops at an increasing rate. If Geoff Mason detected any hesitation on my part regarding a potential site, his standard response was 'Get it bought!' The problem was only going to get worse. We were also spending more money fitting out our shops now but our company was increasing its profits every year and new shops could be financed out of our cash flow. Our problem was that we needed to build a new office and cold store and we would need to borrow a lot of money to pay for it.

Cold stores are measured in cubic feet as opposed to square feet for conventional warehouses. Our cold store in Rhyl was 25,000 cubic feet and we needed to build one of at least 250,000 cubic feet. A rule of thumb at the time was that it cost about £1 per cubic foot to build a cold store. Peter wanted to build one in Rhyl; there was a site available on the old council rubbish tip! I think this decision was largely based on the fact he was now living in Rhyl and Jean didn't want to move house. There was, however, a big new industrial estate being built on the site of the old John Summers steelworks in Shotton, Deeside. This was a massive undertaking funded by the EEC as they were trying to generate new industry and jobs after the closure of the steelworks. Unemployment in the area was over 20 per cent. This was to my mind the ideal location as it was only about one mile from the start of the M56 and much nearer to the majority of our shops and any future expansion, while Rhyl was very much out on a limb. Shotton was a huge site covering 630 acres but it did look very bleak and windswept. No one had actually built a factory there yet, although the roads and infrastructure were already in place.

The NatWest bank refused to lend us the money we needed. Woodward's had less influence than we imagined and we realised the bank actually viewed Iceland and Woodward's as one borrowing unit. Woodward's was probably holding us back. We had to get the money from somewhere. Grants were available for everything in those days but only to manufacturing companies. There was a widely held belief, but a myth, that only manufacturing companies created 'real' jobs while service industries, particularly retailers, were parasites on society. Peter Summers (the son of Sir Richard Summers, who was Chairman of the family steelworks before nationalisation) was in charge of the Deeside Enterprise Trust and his job was to persuade companies to relocate to the site. He didn't really want us there, as we weren't manufacturers, but he was keen to get the first company on to the site and we were the only one showing any interest. He suggested the 'European Coal and Steel Community Fund' might lend us some money if we could create the right number of jobs and give preference to ex-steelworkers. I promised him we would create 25 new jobs. (Twenty years later there were around 2,000 people working on the site.) In the end we borrowed £160,000 from the Coal and Steel Fund and ICFC (the Industrial and Commercial Finance Corporation, now 3i), who administered the fund, lent us another £50,000. The NatWest eventually lent us the rest but only after we threatened to move back to Barclays. Our total borrowing requirement was for £350,000 but the net worth of Iceland at the time we were looking for the loan was only £160,000 so, looking back, I don't suppose it was ever going to be easy.

We wanted to build new offices as well as a cold store as we felt it was important to be based next to our warehouse so we could see the products as they came in. We decided, however, to put all the available money into building the biggest cold store we could afford and keep our offices in Rhyl. We moved into our new cold store in

1979 and, on the same day that we went 'live' with deliveries to our stores, we also went live with our first computer, an IBM 34. The computer was probably no more powerful than a calculator today but it was big and impressive and it handled all our product deliveries and store charging systems. It was only a matter of weeks before we realised it was not practical for our office to be twenty miles from the cold store so we bought a Portakabin, put it next to the cold store, and moved in. Our company sales for the year ended 1979 were £5 million and our profits were about £160,000. We employed 150 people. Our profits more than doubled the following year thanks to better buying prices because of our bigger cold store, and our sales increased to £8 million.

Once we had a proper base to work from we set about building our management team. We had already recruited Barry Glover from the refrigeration company that sold us our first freezer. Barry was in charge of shopfitting and drew up the store plans and managed the contractors. We recruited Janet Weinstein as our Personnel Manager and Derek Harris as Marketing Manager. Andy Errington joined us as our first buyer and later Nigel Broadhurst became our Buying Director. We tried to recruit the best people. Youth and above all enthusiasm were what mattered most. Everyone could see the potential for the company and we only recruited people we felt were capable of helping us to run a bigger business than we had at the moment.

8
Another Day, Another Deal!

Peter and I became good friends with Alan Birchall and John Murphy, from whom we had bought Alpine Foods. Colemans, their meat business, was now out of receivership and doing well. Peter was buying meat from them. The Alpine shops had proved to be a good buy for us and we found Alan and John both interesting and entertaining. They were always talking about lots of money-making schemes and wheezes they wanted to involve us in, but none ever came to fruition. It was always good fun planning, though.

John and Alan decided that Peter and I had never fully completed our business education because we hadn't been to America. There was so much we could learn from the Americans, they told us, particularly about customer service. They invited us to the Chicago meat exhibition. Like everything in America the scale of it was vast. The exhibition seemed to cover hundreds of acres and giant machines were on display where I imagined you drove a herd of cows in at one end and beefburgers came out of the other. None of this was relevant to us, of course, but the American experience was incredible. It was the first time I'd stayed in posh hotels and I thought the chocolate on the pillow at night was so impressive! I picked up a book of matches at the Marriott Hotel and they'd printed on the front cover 'We do it right!' That seemed to summarise our philosophy at Iceland so we adopted the slogan and used it extensively. We even used it as a headline on our first ever annual report as a public company.

Alan was a stunning singer. He was briefly in the 'Black and White Minstrels' and had an incredible and powerful bass voice. Many other people talented in that way might try to earn their living from singing and supplement their income with small business deals on the side. Alan did it the other way round. Business was his main interest but he remorselessly exploited his singing ability to further his business career and would burst into song at the slightest encouragement. Everyone wanted him around and singing opened a lot of doors.

One night we were having dinner at a mega restaurant, The Plaza, in Chicago. This was a formal restaurant with a classical violinist wandering round the tables. John decided Alan should sing. Persuading the restaurant manager was not easy. The last thing he wanted was some out-of-key Englishman making a fool of himself. Eventually John convinced him that Alan was a professional. The effect was remarkable. When Alan sings, the proverbial hairs on the back of your neck stand on end. He's better at singing 'Ol' Man River' than Paul Robeson. The whole restaurant was spellbound and within minutes Alan was surrounded by American businessmen making him all kinds of offers. 'Gee, Alan, can I fly you down to sing at my church in Clearwater, Florida?' This then became the pattern for the trip. Everywhere we went the challenge was to get Alan to sing. He sang in restaurants, hotel lobbies and also at the meat exhibition. I saw people in the Grand Hyatt Hotel walking backwards down the escalator in the Atrium so they could listen to him.

At breakfast John Murphy asked if we'd seen the TV news. The Chicago Bears football team was having an important match that day and George Hallas, the 84-year-old billionaire owner of the team, had just been on TV saying he planned to get Pavarotti to record the Chicago Bears anthem. 'We've got to get you to sing for George,' said John. Later that day we were at the gates of the stadium, without tickets, but John managed to blag his way in. 'We're from a radio station in Wales, England,' he told the staff on the gate. 'We want to do a programme on the match.' There were no seats left for us but we were let onto the roof of the building. We watched the first half looking down from the roof parapet with only a leather-jacketed policeman for company. He was more interested in the girlfriend he had on the roof with him than in enforcing security.

At half time we went down in a lift and, with John talking his way through layers of security, we ended up in George Hallas's private box. To a bemused George Hallas, John launched into a speech about Alan, a famous singer from Wales, England, who was responding to his TV appearance that morning and would like to record the Chicago Bears song. Alan clicked his fingers to start the beat and went unaccompanied into a powerful rendition of 'Ol' Man River'. George, as expected, was spellbound. Alan promised to record his song and we were let out through the other door into the stadium to watch the remainder of the match. Alan did record the song, accompanied by the Rhosllanerchrugog Welsh male voice choir but sadly, before he sent it to Chicago, George Hallas died.

I was getting increasingly frustrated with the Woodward brothers remaining as shareholders in Iceland. We got on really well together but they were completely passive investors, which suited me fine except that Iceland was growing and they were not able to help us any more financially. We'd moved back to Barclays Bank soon after the cold store was completed and discovered a huge difference in attitude. The local Barclays manager in the tiny branch at Mold, North Wales, had called to see us speculatively and, when we indicated we might be ready to change banks, he brought his boss round the very next day. David Lees was the local bank director based in Shrewsbury and he was a human dynamo compared with the NatWest manager in Oswestry. David insisted we take him round all our branches and he spent time getting to know Iceland and understand it. He was enthusiastic about our business. We changed banks to Barclays in Mold, which kept our account for the next 35 years.

I explained to Bill and Norman that I felt they had prospered well in their association with Iceland and they should now sell their shareholding back to us. They weren't impressed with my logic and couldn't see how we could afford to buy their shares anyway. I wouldn't let it go. I pestered and badgered them constantly but to no avail. David Lees of Barclays suggested that Barclays Development Capital might be able to help and he introduced us to Graham Williams. Graham explained how Barclays Development Capital invested in companies and provided cash to help them grow. He said that they might be interested in investing in Iceland. The idea was that we could sell Barclays a smaller stake than the Woodwards held and use some of the cash to buy out the Woodwards. This would increase our own shareholding and, at the same time, we would be bringing on board investors with real financial clout that could help us expand even faster. This all seemed like a good idea so we invited them to make a proposal.

Graham came up to Deeside and spent weeks in our Portakabin going through the numbers and making financial forecasts. We thought they were taking forever so we brought in ICFC who had loaned us the money to build the cold store. ICFC looked at us as an investment opportunity and would have been happy to share the deal with Barclays but again they seemed to take ages to come up with a proposal. We did, however, manage to get the local boss of ICFC to meet Bill and Norman and, once they indicated that they might be able to come up with some real money, Bill and Norman suddenly became interested in doing a deal.

The deal with Barclays and ICFC dragged on and on but one day I had a visitor to the Portakabin, a Mr Leslie Reich. Our receptionist said he was a 'financial broker' and did I want to see him? I invited Leslie in and he explained that his speciality was raising money. I told him we didn't need any money and enjoyed a good relationship with Barclays but he was persistent. We must need money for something. It was a 'cold call' and I didn't take him too seriously but then I asked him if he could find serious money to buy out our partners. He said this was his speciality and he worked with a number of investors who were keen to do deals of this kind. He introduced us to a company called Chesham Amalgamations who in turn introduced us to the British Rail Pension Fund (BRPF).

John McLachlan was the investment manager at BRPF and one of his responsibilities was to invest in private companies. He came up to Chester to see us. Peter and I met him at Chester railway station. (He didn't get a car with his job but unlimited rail travel instead.) We showed John and his pretty female assistant around some of the stores and took him to our head office to meet the management team. He came back to us almost immediately with an offer, subject to an accountants' report.

We had gradually seduced the Woodwards into selling and established that £550,000 would be the right price for their stake. We had kept them on the boil for months with continuous updates about Barclays and ICFC but suddenly the BRPF had come up with the goods. They offered us the necessary £550,000 for a 25 per cent stake in Iceland, which we later negotiated down to 16 per cent. They also offered us a further £750,000 by way of preference shares in Iceland (a kind of loan) to help us fund another new cold store, which we were already planning. Peat, Marwick, Mitchell & Co (now KPMG) started their investigation into Iceland during the autumn of 1980 and produced a 70-page report on 17 February 1981. They found remarkably little to criticise and the deal was done.

We had swapped our two original partners, owning 50 per cent of our business, for one new partner with only 16 per cent and the promise of additional funding when we needed it. We felt it was a remarkably good deal and the Woodwards were also delighted. They had turned £5,000 into £550,000 in only seven years, which was a 110-fold return. We remained good friends and they were happy for our continuing success. At the time Iceland had 37 stores and was making a profit of £374,000. Four more stores were in the pipeline and profits were forecast at £400,000 for the following year. In the event we made £537,000.

Exchanging the Woodwards' 50 per cent stake for BRPF's 16 per cent meant that the remaining 34 per cent would be returned to Peter and me. I had worked very hard on this deal and took all of the credit for making it happen. Nevertheless I expected to split the 34 per cent with Peter Hinchcliffe. When it was time to get the lawyers involved, Bernard Leigh and I went to visit Peter Bullivant to instruct him on the deal. Bullivant was sitting behind his desk and Bernie and I were facing him. I explained the deal in great detail. Bernie was there to deal with any technicalities. Bullivant decided to recap. 'So, let me see, I assume the three of you will increase your shareholdings in proportion to your existing holdings. It would also make sense if we were to tidy up Bernie's non-voting shares and make them ordinary shares. Is that what you want to do?' To which I replied weakly 'Er ... yes.' Bullivant had just made Bernie a multimillionaire and I was too soft to contradict him! As it happened I don't think Peter Hinchcliffe had even thought about the split so he wasn't particularly disappointed.

Iceland was on a roll. Morale was off the scale and the management team was totally committed. On Friday night most people finish work early but our stores were open until 8pm so everyone stayed late and went out for a beer afterwards. These Friday nights out were the one time everyone could get together after a hectic week and we could all relax. Conversation was still almost exclusively business and plans were made and strategy discussed. Adrenalin and energy levels were high and a 'few beers in the pub' evolved into 'business dinners' and got more and more high spirited and outrageous as time went by. Peter and I realised that it would be our management team who would make the business succeed and we did everything we could to encourage a fun and hardworking culture.

We decided to organise our first ever management conference. We brought all our staff together to play 'war games'. We decked out a conference room at a hotel in Manchester as a battlefield with camouflage nets and military hardware and the management team dressed up with tin helmets. The message was we were battling for our very livelihoods as Tesco and other food retailers would try to put us out of business. We introduced our unique weaponry as better products and systems, and we also unveiled a new battledress (staff uniform). Then we introduced our secret weapon, the Courtesy Contract. We got all our staff or 'soldiers' to sign up to it in return for a modest increase in wages!

Dick Kirk was now very much part of the team and the diversification bug must have bitten him too. He decided he wanted to try his own hand at a new venture and persuaded us that Iceland should go into the discount electrical business. Look out Comet, here we come! Iceland already sold freezers and microwave ovens, though not very successfully. However, Dick was convinced great riches lay in electrical retailing! We opened 'Iceland Electrics' next to our freezer centre in Connah's Quay. Unfortunately it only averaged about £3,000 per week in sales on wafer-thin margins and soon joined Hi-Speed Printers and Cassanova as might-have-beens.

We had surely learned our lesson about diversification by now and promised ourselves we'd stick to our knitting and do what we knew best, frozen foods. If only we'd put as much effort into Iceland as we had into failed ventures over the years, we'd have been a lot further on but it was hard to stop ourselves. One last venture proved profitable for a while and provided extra pocket money for Peter and me. Alan Birchall was supplying Kwik Save with meat and we persuaded him to try to sell them ice cream as well. It worked. We contracted a local manufacturer to make cheap ice cream under a label we invented called 'Buttercup Farm'. The name, I thought, was pure inspiration! Kwik Save bought container loads of it without ever knowing it came through us. Ross Foods eventually took over all frozen food supplies to Kwik Save and we supplied them for a while before we finally sold them the brand name.

Around the time of the deal with BRPF we were approached by Jimmy Gulliver who wanted to buy our business. Jimmy was a flamboyant character who enjoyed a spectacular career that culminated in the creation of Argyll Foods, which took over Safeway. One of his first deals in the mid-1970s was to buy Cordon Bleu, a Manchester-based chain of freezer centres that was a rival to Iceland. By 1980 he had moved on to bigger fish but he wanted Iceland to merge with Cordon Bleu. He eventually wrote and offered us £2 million for Iceland on condition we made at least £350,000 profit in the year ended 31 December 1980. It was nice to receive the offer but by this time we were well on with our deal with BRPF. We kept in touch with Jimmy and met him and his colleagues Alistair Grant and David Webster several times over the next few years. At first they wanted to buy Iceland but later we wanted to buy Cordon Bleu from them. We could never agree on anything and eventually Cordon Bleu disappeared and the majority of their sites were absorbed into Argyll's Lo-Cost grocery chain.

Jimmy eventually bid for the drinks company Distillers and fought a battle with Ernest Saunders of Guinness for control. He lost the bid and never quite recovered his confidence. Alistair Grant eventually took over control of Argyll and, although Alistair was a really nice man, it was sad to see history rewritten and Jimmy airbrushed from the scene. It was Jimmy who created that business but Alistair who got the knighthood.

Our Portakabin at Deeside grew longer and longer every couple of months. Portakabins were built in eight-foot sections and, as we expanded and took on more staff, we'd just add another slice. We had a separate meeting room by now and held a weekly management meeting where everything was discussed openly. We had no secrets from the team. The walls of this room were covered with full-page newspaper adverts for St Catherine's Freezer Centres, who were based in Bristol. Although Bristol was outside our territory we had slowly become aware of St Catherine's and Tony Palmer who owned the business. I could never understand how he could sell his products so cheaply. I would get more and more agitated at these adverts and accuse Peter of not buying products as well as Tony Palmer. I'd been in all Tony's stores and they were very busy. He obviously had something in his formula that we were missing. We followed his expansion avidly.

One day I was driving in the Bristol area with Peter and we decided to give Tony Palmer a call. I had one of the first car telephones and you had to go through the Vodafone operator to get a number. It was also one-way speech. We told Tony we were in the area and he invited us to see him. As soon as we walked through his office we knew he was in trouble. Paper and invoices were piled everywhere and there was an obvious lack of control. That first meeting didn't achieve very much with each of us trying to impress the other. We had a typical 'My Dad's bigger than your Dad' type of conversation but we'd made contact and I just knew Tony's business wasn't on a sound footing, however good his sales were. He had eighteen stores and his average sales per store were double ours but he had no management and, it appeared obvious, no financial controls. We decided to watch him even more closely.

I spent so much of my time site finding with John Prestt that I had by now acquired a brand new Rolls-Royce and also employed a chauffeur. The chauffeur idea was sensible as it meant I could work in the back of the car instead of just driving for eight hours a day as we toured the country. Given my constant speeding convictions it was also probably essential. The Rolls-Royce wasn't such a good idea. I knew it was vulgar but it was a lot of fun for a 35-year-old and it was a reward I had promised myself when the company profits broke the million pound barrier. Rolls-Royce boasted their cars were hand-made. That actually meant they couldn't afford the robots and technology of the Germans so every one had a host of different faults built in. Mine broke down so many times it was a nightmare and I eventually changed it, with a big cash incentive from Rolls, for a slightly less ostentatious Bentley!

We had already used the money BRPF provided for preference shares towards building a new 1 million cubic feet cold store. This was joined onto our first one and we had also started to build a smart new office block on the same site. (The length of the Portakabin was now getting ridiculous.) We were building up our management team and confident about the future. My mother was very proud of me!

Geoff Mason decided to introduce me to Albert Gubay, the Kwik Save founder. Albert was nearly twenty years older than me. After leaving Kwik Save he had set up a discount grocery chain in New Zealand which he called '3 Guys'. He sold it to the management a few years later when it enjoyed over a 30 per cent share of the New Zealand grocery market. He'd then set up again in Ireland and sold to Tesco, first a 50 per cent stake and then the whole company. Tesco had a very unhappy experience with Albert and pulled out of Ireland soon after they bought it. He had now set up 3 Guys in North Carolina in America and wanted to do a deal with us. His suggestion was that Iceland should merge with 3 Guys in America and then we should buy Lennons, the publicly quoted supermarket chain, which was based in the North West of England. We had several meetings to talk about this and one day Albert suggested we meet at his merchant bankers in London, Robert Fleming, to discuss the deal further. I turned up with Bernie and was staggered to be shown into a room with about twenty advisers sitting round a table all ready to finalise the terms of a deal! Some 'back of the envelope' calculations Albert had done in front of us at an earlier meeting had somehow been turned into a very impressive document, which everyone was now working from. We rapidly retreated and told Albert we didn't like being rushed.

Albert had a fearsome reputation for being totally ruthless and penny-pinching in the extreme. This mentality had made him extremely successful. Discount grocery retailing is all about tight cost control and he was the expert. The stories about him were legion. Alan Birchall knew him and told a story about Albert chatting with him in the yard of his depot. A driver walked across the yard and the sole of his shoe was hanging loose and flapping as he walked, making a noise. Albert said 'Excuse me' to Alan and walked across the yard to speak to the driver. He pulled a wodge of £5 notes out of his pocket but the driver's smile was short-lived. He took the elastic band off the bundle of money and said to the driver, 'Here, put that round your shoe!'

Albert invited Peter and me to visit his operation in North Carolina. We went there with Geoff Mason. Albert met us at the airport and drove us to the hotel. He'd checked Peter and me into a double room and Geoff was staying at Albert's house. We were paying for ourselves, of course, but Albert would never conceive that anyone could waste money on two rooms. As soon as he left we booked an extra room. His stores were much bigger than we expected but everything was designed for the lowest cost operation. In his warehouse he proudly showed us his latest idea for saving money on pallet-wrap. The rest of the world uses a kind of industrial cling film to wrap pallets of stock that have been picked and are ready to deliver to stores. This is to stop them falling over in transit. Albert had strips of car tyre inner tube knotted together, which his warehouse men would stretch over the boxes on the pallet. There were mountains of them ready to be used and they were returned by the stores to be recycled.

Our trip covered a weekend and Albert invited us to his house for Sunday lunch. Peter and I arrived to be shown in by Carmel, his Irish girlfriend. Albert was sitting in an armchair watching TV but there was a large stack of newspapers in front of him and he was clipping away at them with scissors. 'What are you doing?' I asked him. 'Oh, these Sunday papers cost 50 cents each but there's $3 worth of grocery coupons in them!' I was stunned. Not only would Albert the multimillionaire be spending his Sunday doing this but no doubt all his directors would have to be doing it as well.

We decided not to progress the deal with Albert. He was an incredibly tough character and had a habit of falling out with everyone he was involved with. We knew if we got involved with him our lives wouldn't be our own afterwards.

The next suitor was Alec Monk from the Dee Corporation. Alec rivalled Jimmy Gulliver in building a supermarket empire and, in a series of acquisitions, mopped up Linfood, Keymarkets and eventually Dee Stores, which later became Gateway and then Somerfield. Alec came to see us in February 1983. Our sales had increased from £8 million in 1980 to £24 million in 1982 and our profits had gone from £374,000 to £850,000. Alec made the most amateurish proposal I have ever seen anybody make. He was ill at ease as he spoke and shuffled bits of paper in front of him but eventually we concluded he was offering us £12 million for the company. Based on his performance we wondered how he could be so successful. We turned him down and our sales and profits more than doubled the following year partly due to the St Catherine's acquisition we had completed by then.

I went to see Tony Palmer again towards the end of 1982. This time I was with Bernie and Tony immediately started to tell me all his troubles. He was obviously very lonely in his business life with no management team to help him. I listened sympathetically to him and then asked when his financial year-end was. He said they'd just completed their half-year and he admitted he had made a loss. I suggested he might want to sell his business to us and he said for the right price he might. He said he wanted £18 million, which was one year's turnover! We invited Tony up to Deeside with the intention of impressing him and convincing him we had a better operation and would eventually put him out of business. It worked, we blew his mind with the professionalism of Iceland, our big cold storage facilities and our posh new offices! He knew he was losing money, he was under pressure from his bank but he still thought his business was worth more than it was. We talked about Tony becoming a millionaire rather than how much his business was worth. Eventually we half convinced him that he should walk away with £1 million from us and all his troubles would be over.

I had several more meetings with Tony, trying to pin him down on price. The longer it went on the more money he was losing and the less we could pay him. Eventually, just before Christmas, we had an all-day negotiating session in a hotel room in Bristol and we finally agreed a price of £899,001! This was on the basis that his loss for the year to 31 January 1983 would be no greater than £215,000 or he had to refund the difference. The deal was finally completed in February 1983 but almost collapsed at the last moment as we argued about the value of his car. In the end we gave it to him.

When the results of the stock-take at the end of January were worked out the loss was in fact £524,842 and Tony had to give us back £309,842. He didn't want to, of course, and even refused to accept the findings of two independent sets of auditors but he finally handed over the cheque on the steps of the High Court in Bristol.

The initial purchase price of nearly £1 million for St Catherine's was stretching our resources at Iceland so we had to raise more money very quickly. The obvious place to go was BRPF and we put our case to John McLachlan. Our relationship with BRPF was very good. We'd kept them fully informed of the company's progress and we were performing well. It came as something of a surprise, therefore, when John told us they wanted to increase their stake to 25 per cent if they were to provide the finance we needed. I was mortified at this and accused them of exploiting their position and demanded to see the trustees of the pension fund. This was just not done but I insisted and, eventually, one of their formal meetings was interrupted, much to the bemusement of the trustees, by Peter and me explaining our case and telling them not to be greedy! It worked, we secured the finance and they increased their stake by only 4 per cent to 20 per cent.

St Catherine's was now losing money at the rate of £15,000 per week and urgent action was necessary. We had a strong management team at Iceland and they were all now assembled at the Holiday Inn in Bristol, waiting for the call to say the deal had been signed. Within minutes of that call they were in St Catherine's stores and in just a few days we swept through the company and tightened all their systems and procedures. We closed down their loss-making butchery department and their head office and put new controls on their staffing levels. Crucially, we introduced the Iceland product range and a more sensible pricing structure. Sales did drop back a bit but profitability was soon restored and St Catherine's turned out to be a very successful acquisition that moved Iceland firmly into the next division.

I'd become reasonably friendly with Michael Weeks, the joint MD of Kwik Save, and we'd been opening a number of stores alongside and sometimes even inside Kwik Save stores. Kwik Save weren't very strong in frozen food at that time and they were happy to have us there. One of the stores I took from them was next door to their store on the Wakefield road just outside Huddersfield. It was only five miles from Grange Moor where I was brought up. It wasn't the best looking store in the world and not one I could be especially proud of but it was in my home town and something special was called for.

Since the store was out of town with no passing trade, we decided a grand opening was called for to 'put the store on the map' and raise local awareness. The *Huddersfield Examiner* ran the usual 'local boy makes good' type of story but we decided we should have a celebrity opening. I rang Bernard Hinchcliffe, a theatrical agent in Huddersfield who I had used to book groups during my days as a schoolboy impresario. He suggested we should book Terry Wogan. The only problem was that he didn't finish his morning radio programme in London until 9am so we decided to fly him up by helicopter and open the store at 11am or whenever he arrived.

We planned to land the helicopter at a rugby club ground just outside Huddersfield and then drive him to the store. We asked Norman Woodward if he would drive him in his open-topped Aston Martin. Bill Woodward wanted to bring along his vintage Bentley as well, and then we decided we might as well add half a dozen Iceland lorries to the procession and so it grew! We decided the Iceland shop would be too crowded for people to see him properly so we built a wooden stage in the car park for him and the whole event just grew in scale and ambition. By the time we'd finished we even had a children's dance troupe and a band performing for him as his helicopter arrived.

Terry Wogan was at the height of his popularity and, when he landed in the helicopter and I explained what we had arranged for him, he wasn't at all impressed. I told him we had a stage in the car park and when we arrived there he could stand on it to do his stuff. 'What do you mean: do my stuff? I'm not a stand-up comic, you know. I'm here to cut the ribbon and that's it!' He was not being cooperative and I was panicking it might all go wrong but we got him into Norman's car and started the drive into Huddersfield. We planned to go through the main street and hopefully attract some publicity. We had already distributed flyers around town and put an advert in the *Examiner* but we were totally unprepared for what followed.

It was like the Queen had arrived, or even more like her Coronation! Crowds lined the streets, traffic stopped. People were hanging from first floor windows to get a better view and everyone was screaming his name. Terry was gobsmacked and stood up in the car waving at the crowds like the Queen. The procession had grown and Peter, Bernie and I brought up the rear in a white Rolls-Royce we had hired. When we arrived at the store, a sea of cheering people covered the car park. Terry leapt onto the stage and proceeded to tell the crowd what a good company Iceland was and how he could recommend our products. The crowds were cheering and Terry was beaming with satisfaction. Alan Birchall had been roped in as Master of Ceremonies and he sang to the crowds. Terry then spent the rest of the morning in the store signing copies of *The Iceland Review*, our free customer magazine. The store was packed, but only with people queuing for his autograph – nobody was shopping.

The local police seemed just as big fans as anyone else and when it was time to go they provided a motorcycle escort with sirens blaring to accompany his car back to the rugby club. The amazing thing was we took hardly any money in the store. People had come to see Wogan, not to buy frozen food. When it was time to pay him there wasn't even enough cash in the till and we had to drive to the bank to get some money! Huddersfield never did do any good as a store and that taught us the value of celebrity openings!

Terry Wogan, however, was a changed man. He went on about Huddersfield for days afterwards on his radio programme. He had probably never realised just how popular he was.

9

Riding a Rocket

By the end of 1983 we had 75 branches, employed 600 people and generated annual sales of £50 million with profits of £1.8 million. We were growing fast and recognised that our staff, and particularly our management team, were the people who made it all possible. We had just given Dick Kirk a small equity share in the business (even though we told him we wouldn't when he joined) and had also given shares to 24 other senior and long-serving staff. Everyone felt involved and everyone was highly motivated. Our senior people recognised that their own personal financial success was linked to that of the company and they were therefore totally committed to the business. We all worked long hours and raced around all over the country but we also had a lot of fun.

Peter Hinchcliffe and I had a strange relationship. We never socialised outside work and had little in common but our partnership worked very well. It worked because we wanted it to. I used to enjoy shocking people in later years by saying 'I've known Peter for 25 years and never been to his house!' Actually, that wasn't strictly true, but it nearly was. We were very different people but complemented each other well and in the time we were together we'd never really had a row. That was probably unhealthy but for most of the time Peter concentrated on the buying side of the business and left me to get on with everything else.

Iceland was the most important thing in my life, except of course for my family. Ranny and I were happily married and by now we had three children: Alexia, Caroline and Richard. I worked long hours but Ranny never questioned it and always supported me. Having said that, I never worked weekends (after the first couple of years) and never took work home. I never missed a birthday, sports day or school play. At home I would also spend my time working, developing the house and garden, but when I was at Iceland I gave it 120 per cent to the exclusion of all else.

People often tell me they wish they could be successful in business and I always tell them they can if they want to but they don't really want to. When they ask what I mean I say you have to *really* want to. How many people will give up everything for business success? Football, hobbies, nights out in the week, a social life, you only succeed if you are driven by that burning desire to succeed. My burning desire was fuelled by financial insecurity. I had a nice house, a good car and a successful business but what if it all went wrong tomorrow? I had no money in the bank and I am a born worrier. I can only think that insecurity was behind our decision to seek a public flotation for the company and 'cash in some chips'. With hindsight I'd have been a lot richer and a lot happier in the longer term if we'd stayed private! At the time, though, I thought a flotation was an achievement in itself and also public recognition and confirmation of our success.

In early 1983 a journalist on London's *Evening Standard*, Hugh Sharpe, telephoned me out of the blue to ask about Iceland, its growth and success. This led to a long and complimentary article, which in turn led to a number of approaches from merchant banks. We saw them all. The pattern was always the same. They'd fly into Manchester airport to be met by Peter and Dick who'd show them a couple of stores on their way to the office. I would give them a tour round the Deeside office and cold store and then Bernie and

I would have a discussion with them about how they might help us float the company. This carried on for months and then Bernie read an article in the *Financial Times* about the rising stars in the banking world. N M Rothschild was tipped for great success now that Michael Richardson, later Sir Michael, had joined them from Cazenove. Michael himself made the journey north and came to see us. We were very impressed. Michael had an aristocratic bearing about him and was a great smoothy. He commanded a lot of respect. Michael was also a director of the Savoy Hotel group and later entertained us to lunch in one of their private dining rooms. He was also a compulsive name-dropper and when he left us after lunch he asked, 'Any message for the Prime Minister?' He was going to see her next!

To float the company we would also need a firm of stockbrokers to work with the merchant bankers. We favoured a company called Scrimgeour Vickers but Michael Richardson explained that it was important to have a firm Rothschilds had confidence in and suggested Hoare Govett. We used Hoare Govett! Richard Westmacott was the senior partner at Hoare's and although he confessed to not having been north of Lord's in ten years, he also made the journey to Deeside and therefore passed the test! It was also suggested that, as we were a northern firm, we might need a firm of regional brokers to generate a following of local investors. We knew Kit Jackson and Mike Orsborn, known as 'Ossie', stockbrokers from Tilney in Liverpool, and so we appointed them. Richardson and Westmacott were serious big hitters and legends in the City. I can't imagine either of them had ever been in a supermarket before but they made a brave effort of going round the cabinets in Iceland and showing an interest in frozen pies and beefburgers. Peter Bullivant was our company lawyer, and by this time a personal friend, but we needed one of the big London firms to handle the complexities of the float. Richardson suggested Herbert Smith and introduced me to Edward Walker-Arnott who later became senior partner. We certainly had the 'A Team' in place.

The first stages of a company flotation are to commission an exhaustive (and that means expensive!) accountants' report and also to write a 'long form report'. This is the definitive document on the company, which gives every detail of information and has to be verified by the accountants and checked and double-checked by the lawyers for accuracy. From this is distilled the information which goes into the offer document for distribution to anyone who may want to buy shares. The process involved many meetings with lawyers and bankers and soon I was out of my depth and found the detail beyond me. You just put your faith in the people you have appointed and hope they look after you. We intended to float in October 1984 and this was close enough to the end of our financial year (December) for us to have to make a profit forecast. This again needed much verification and checking as it just had to be right. We forecast profits of not less than £2.8 million for the year to December 1984 and in the event we made £2,969,000.

In early October we had to fix the price for the company flotation. We had to decide how many shares we would divide the company into, and how much each share would be worth, which would then put a value on the whole company. The usual way to do this is to work out a multiple of the expected profits, which is known as the 'price earnings multiple' or PE. I honestly didn't have a clue about this at the time and I had never even heard of a PE.

Iceland was by now the second largest freezer centre operator in the UK but based mainly in the north of England so few people in the City had heard of us. Bejam were our southern rivals, already a public company and very much larger than Iceland. Being based in the south they were also well known by their presence on the high street to the bankers and financiers in the City. Bejam were highly regarded by the City and they were already trading on the stock market at a PE of sixteen. All I knew was that if they were on a PE of sixteen, we were a better company and should therefore have a higher PE. I now realise there is always a conflict between the bankers and brokers floating a company and the company directors who are effectively selling their shares. The directors want as high a price as possible

Malcolm the budding entrepreneur, aged seven.

Malcolm and Rhianydd
on their wedding day, 1969.

Sex sells! The strawberry stall on the Horseshoe Pass, North Wales.

The first Iceland shop in Oswestry, November 1970.

For frozen food—shop here and save

ICELAND

COMES TO OSWESTRY
NOW OPEN AT 19 LEG STREET

WHY PAY FOR FANCY PACKAGING WHEN YOU CAN BUY

LOOSE FROZEN FOOD

AND SAVE UP TO HALF ON NORMAL PACKET PRICES

PEAS 2'-lb. CHIPS 1'9lb. SPROUTS 1'5

SLICED BEANS		SWEET CORN		CAULIFLOWER FLORETS 1/6 ¼ lb
STRAWBERRIES	2/1 lb	RASPBERRIES	84 each	X-QUOLLS	8d each
FISH FINGERS	5d each	FISH CAKES	5d each	PLAICE PORTIONS	1/10 each
COD IN BREADCRUMBS	1/3 each	CHICKENS		TURKEYS for Xmas at LOW PRICES

THIS IS JUST A VERY SMALL SELECTION OF THE NORMAL RANGE WHICH ALSO INCLUDES SEAFOODS AND OTHER EXCITING DELICACIES

GOOD FOOD AT ROCK BOTTOM PRICES

SUPPLIED BY **ROSS** The good ONE in frozen foods

SAVE EVEN MORE BY CUTTING OUT AND USING THESE COUPONS

3d. OFF LB PEAS	2d. OFF LB CHIPS	1/- OFF KRAFT COOKING OIL	2d. OFF ONE PLAICE PORTION	4d. OFF ½ LB STRAWBERRIES
Valid until November 30	Valid until November 30	Valid until November 30	Valid until November 30	Valid until November 30

ALL ITEMS SUBJECT TO AVAILABILITY   SEE YOU IN ICELAND

Iceland's very first press advertisement.

Malcolm and Peter outside Iceland's second shop in Rhyl.

Iceland in Rhyl, the night before the opening.

Loose frozen food in Rhyl.

The Takeaway: 'better eating for less'.
The prototype for Pret A Manger?

Iceland's first head office, cold store and cash and carry in Rhyl.

Cassanova: 'Rhyl has gone to pizzas!'

Malcolm and Peter study the plans for the new Deeside cold store with Peter Summers of the Deeside Enterprise Trust in 1978.

W/ENDING 24.10.73	N° 14	OSWESTRY		RHYL		FLINT		MOLD		CHESTER		HES
SALES		WEEK	PERIOD	WEEK	PERIOD	WEEK	PERIOD	WEEK	PERIOD	WEEK	PERIOD	WEEK
MONDAY		132.61		91.15		44.45		45.85				
TUESDAY		99.82		105.10		43.81		44.65				
WEDNESDAY		309.00		102.20		33.40		108.66				
THURSDAY		181.85		64.40		49.60		35.38				
FRIDAY		502.61		338.68		183.12		156.48				
SATURDAY		489.61		229.15		123.56		224.21				
TOTAL SALES THIS YEAR		1653.50	16404.18	803.68	15149.32	509.94	8978.26	621.23	12186.38			
TOTAL SALES LAST YEAR		1013.21	9994.03	449.80	1012.06	859.03	5491.02	—				
% INCREASE		62.30	39.51	44.82	33.19	49.00	38.84					
STOCK PURCHASES		1263.63½	11992.36½	592.43½	10639.19	404.63½	6230.08	441.58½	8798.08½			
GROSS PROFIT £		4644.76		211.27		452.01	103.31	2748.19	159.65	3388.30		
'G' %		280.13	28.12	260.78	29.83	20.21	30.61	28.70	27.80			
EXPENSE												
RENT 1/52ⁿᵈ		14.42	245.14	17.30	294.10	14.42	248.14	28.85	490.45			
RATES 1/52ⁿᵈ		5.00	85.00	5.97	101.49	6.11	816.87	4.96	84.32			
ELECTRIC			91.94		136.57		716.11		112.78			
WAGES		48.63	849.44	48.86	959.17	44.69	646.59	40.06	769.32			
NAT INS		3.36	44.15	3.82	61.44	2.31	33.68	2.31	37.23			
TAX + GRAD PENS		6.84	96.61	4.74	88.19	3.51	58.69	4.56	63.16			
PHONE			58.28		14.19		9.41		1.52			
INSURANCE 1/52ⁿᵈ		99	16.83	85	14.45	68	11.56	64	10.88			
BAGS + WRAPPING		12.24	42.19	12.24	63.27	6.00	28.37		40.68			
CLEANING		5.17	18.70	12	7.85	16	10.42	40	8.74			
STATIONERY + POSTAGE			10.07		9.42		10.29	21	9.44			
ADVERTISING												
PRINTING + PRICE LIST		15.28	38.28	15.28	38.28	15.28	38.28	15.28	38.28			
REPAIRS + RENEWELS			14.89	27	6.08				12.18			
CAPITAL		1514.30			22.25		22.25		131.29	85.25		
SUNDRY												
OPENING EXPENSES		184.11	184.11									
DEPOT CHARGE		56.65	1003.25	56.65	1003.25	56.65	1003.25	56.65	1003.25			
TOTAL EXPENSES		168.10	2633.73	144	2900.34	149.41	2214.61	153.92	2498.23			
NETT PROFIT £		379.79	1981.04	44.73	1119.65	046.10	473.48	8.43	700.07			
% NETT		22.90	12.07	5.64	11.86	9.07	5.27	.92	5.74			

EXPENSE ITEMS NOT SHOWN AS A 52ⁿᵈ WILL TEND TO DISTORT THE NETT

NO ADJUSTMENT HAS BEEN MADE FOR S.O.H.

Wales's largest cold store.

(*below*) Tight financial controls from the very beginning: an early Iceland Directors' Report.

DEPOT RUNNING COSTS — WEEK No 14

	ERNEST ST. CASH + CARRY		FREEZERS ALL BRANCHES			WEEK	PERIOD
PERIOD	WEEK	PERIOD	WEEK	PERIOD			
	123.57		66.00		VEHICLE MAINTAINANCE	22.85	243.85
	84.46		132.00		PETROL + OIL		500.34
	102.35		65.00		ROAD TAX	1.91	32.47
	240.41				VEHICLE INSURANCE 1/52nd	3.10	82.70
	329.98						
	306.84						
	1187.41	24417.62	263.00	2344.84	REFRIGERATION MAINTAINANCE	5.30	90.10
	812.14	19661.20					
	31.62	19.47					
	213.78	4395.13					
	18.00	18.00			PETTY CASH	44.49	233.87
	19.23	326.91			RENT 1/52nd	38.46	653.82
	8.53	94.01			RATES 1/52nd	11.06	188.02
					ELECTRIC		
	32.17	397.57			WAGES	115.06	1746.90
	2.15	35.14			NAT INS	9.62	150.07
	3.51	62.44			TAX + GRAD PENS	23.02	245.16
					PHONE		169.74
	1.33	27.61			INSURANCE 1/52nd	7.00	119.00
	1.61	28.41			BAGS + WRAPPING		1.00
		2.10			CLEANING		
		53.84			STATIONERY + POSTAGE	1.36	107.77
		7.50			ADVERTISING		50.30
	15.28	38.28			PRINTING		284.72
		18.24			REPAIRS + RENEWELS		137.00
		398.10			CAPITAL	16.41	2042.99
					SUNDRY		
	86.65	1003.25					
	137.46	2240.32			TOTAL EXPENSES ✱	283.23	5016.83
	96.37	2104.91			DIVIDE BY No OF BRANCHES ✱ 5		
	6.42	8.62			FOR DEPOT CHARGE £56.65		

The board in the early 1980s. L to R: Dick Kirk, Peter Hinchcliffe, Malcolm Walker, Bernard Leigh.

At the Chicago Bears stadium. L to R: John Murphy, Peter Hinchcliffe, Alan Birchall and Frank Taylor.

but the bankers and brokers want a price low enough to ensure that all the shares get sold. This is not only because their own credibility is on the line but also because the brokers have to 'underwrite' the offer. This effectively means they agree to buy the shares themselves if nobody else does.

The directors who are selling their shares also don't want the offer to fall because although they would still get their money (as the brokers have underwritten it), a public offer that gets off to a bad start often blights the share price for a long time to come. It's a balance and you have to rely on your advisers to get the balance right. Michael Richardson made a big speech at the pricing meeting and persuaded us that Bejam was much better-known than Iceland and, in order to ensure a successful after-market in our shares, we should float on a multiple of 12. I wasn't happy but I accepted it. We split the company into 14.3 million shares and priced each share at £2.10, which valued the company at £30 million. I've since seen this pattern so many times. A bank will promise a company that intends to float a high share price but days before the float, when everyone is committed and the company has spent money on fees, every excuse will be brought up as to why the price should be lower. Schroder's merchant bank tried that on with my pal Graham Kirkham of DFS. I'd already warned Graham what was likely to happen so he simply stormed out of the meeting and pulled the flotation. I was due to become a non-executive director of DFS, and a very worried Alan Jacobs of Schroder's rang me on holiday in Mexico to ask if I thought Graham really would pull the float. I assured him he would. Graham got his price!

As with selling any other product (the product in this case being Iceland) you need good marketing and we had to take on a firm of financial public relations consultants to ensure favourable press coverage. We chose a company called Streets Financial and Michael Sandler and Keith Hann were assigned to our case. With all these professionals involved, the fees they charged for organising the flotation added up to over £400,000. The 'offer document' went out, we received a lot of favourable publicity and the *Financial Times* described the pricing as being 'on the cautious side'. The closing date for people to apply for shares was set for 9 October and we all went down to London to see the results. Rothschilds insisted we travel separately because if we were all killed in a plane crash they would be financially exposed! To apply for shares you had to fill in a form and enclose a cheque for the full value of the shares applied for. In spite of the fact that the miners' strike was still on, the economy was improving and the stock market was rising. Investors would often apply for more shares in a company than they expected to get on the basis that the application would be oversubscribed and people would be scaled back. Investors known as 'stags' would complete multiple applications to increase their chance of getting shares. This was all done on the assumption that shares in a newly floated company would soon rise and they could then be sold for a quick profit. Multiple share applications became illegal soon after our flotation.

You could either post your share application form or hand it in personally at Barclays Bank in Farringdon Street. The application forms were then taken upstairs to be sorted out. We wandered into the ground floor office at Barclays and were nearly killed in the scrum. It was worse than any half price sale you'd ever seen. People were fighting and pushing to get to the counter where they would dump dozens of application forms onto the piles already on the counter. There seemed to be lots of people, many of them Orthodox Jews for some reason, with their black hats and ringlets, carrying armfuls of forms. They would go along the counter dropping a few here and a few there to ensure their multiple applications were well mixed in and wouldn't be spotted and excluded. We went upstairs and saw eight large tables with piles of application forms being sorted by value. We were only selling £8 million worth of shares (most of the money was for new shares we issued for the company) but many of the cheques were for applications of £1 million and several had applied for the entire issue of £8 million. Almost £1 billion had been sent in cheques and the issue had been 113 times oversubscribed. A British record! At first I was delighted but then it slowly dawned on me we had been seriously underpriced by Rothschilds.

I asked what would happen to the £904 million in cheques we had received and couldn't believe it when I was told that the money would be banked for a few days until they worked out who was getting how many shares, and then the balance would be returned to the share applicants but we could keep the bank interest on the money. The bank interest for those few days amounted to £748,000, which more than paid for the expenses of the float!

Share trading started the following Tuesday. We were very excited and couldn't wait to see what price our shares would open at. The whole day was something of a celebration and we had been invited onto the Stock Exchange floor to see trading take place. Now of course the 'floor' doesn't exist and trading is carried out by computers and television screens. In 1984 it was still done face-to-face on the floor of the Stock Exchange amid a great deal of shouting. We decided to take our wives to join in the fun and booked in at the Dorchester Hotel. We hired a Lear jet to take us down from Manchester. I had sold 777,777 shares at £2.10 but was both horrified and delighted when within minutes of trading starting the price soared to £3.44. I'd lost a fortune on the shares I'd sold too cheaply, but the shares I had left were already worth over £10 million. One year later the share price had doubled again. The day after our flotation Ranny was withdrawing money from our bank in Mold and the cashier asked rather disapprovingly if we were expecting any money to come into the account as we were very overdrawn. The float wasn't a moment too soon! Our management team were also thrilled with the day's events. We had made many of them wealthy.

After the float Peter and I decided we should reward ourselves for all our hard work, so we decided to buy an aeroplane. We'd occasionally hired one from Northern Executive Aviation in Manchester so we asked them to find us one. They came up with a second hand 'Golden Eagle', which is top of the range for a twin engined propeller job and only one step down from a jet. The plane was for sale in Stockholm so we flew out to see it and bought it for £350,000. We registered it in the UK with the letters G-FROZ. When Stephen Laing at Ernst & Young found out, he reminded us we would have to pay VAT on the price when we imported it into the UK. We were buying this plane personally and hadn't budgeted for this. 'How can we avoid paying the VAT?' we asked him. The only way seemed to be to set up a charter business and we duly registered the name 'European Air Charter'.

The consequence of this was, if we wanted to use it ourselves, we had to pay for it. Every time I wanted to go to London I'd decide to take the plane but then calculate the trip would cost me nearly £1,000 so I'd decide to drive. As a result we hardly ever used the plane. Vladivar Vodka hired it once for a nude calendar photo shoot, which caused a great deal of excitement! Stephen was nervous about us renting it to Iceland at anything other than a bargain price so that we couldn't be accused of profiting from the transaction. After a year or so we sold it. Iceland by this time was using the plane quite often but Stephen didn't want us to sell the plane to Iceland because it would be a 'related transaction' since we were directors of both Iceland and European Air Charter. In the end we sold it to a slot machine operator and Iceland bought a second hand Citation jet.

The success of the Iceland flotation encouraged other people to invest in the frozen food business. Orchard Foods was a retail chain with 37 small frozen food stores based in Essex and owned by the Carr family. They had brought in Brian Baylis as Chief Executive. Brian was an experienced retailer who had worked at Cordon Bleu. He had no trouble at all in raising money from six City institutions within days of the Iceland flotation. In spite of this Orchard was struggling by the following year and in August 1985 Peter and Dick made a tour of their stores and found most of them had serious stock shortages. Even though their store managers claimed they had 'a drivers' strike', we could only conclude they weren't paying their suppliers. Brian persuaded his institutional investors to put in more money and things improved for a while. I found out who their investors were and decided to try to talk to some of them but they were having none of it. Eventually though, the inevitable happened and Orchard went into receivership.

Stephen Whitam of Thornton Baker was appointed as the receiver and I flew down in the Golden Eagle to negotiate a deal with him, taking with me Bernie, Peter Bullivant and John Berry our Company Secretary. We intended to close a deal that day and we took with us several banker's drafts totalling £400,000. We were not sure exactly how much we would have to pay but we only wanted twelve of the 37 shops and decided £400,000 was our top price. We were with him until 2am but eventually concluded a deal and handed over £400,000, which was the agreed price. After a lousy Chinese meal at 2.30am we took a taxi to Heathrow to find our 'hired' pilot had decided he was too tired to fly and had gone off to bed! We rented a car and drove back to Manchester with me vowing to employ our own full-time pilot. I rather childishly parked the hire car so close to the office door at the Northern Aviation office that they would be unable to get in. I was still seething about their work-to-rule pilot.

Next morning we had a bombshell. Stephen Whitam had reneged on the deal and was now talking to Bejam who wanted the same twelve shops. He effectively ran an auction and the price went up. I would have preferred to tell him to stuff his shops but we really needed this deal as it gave us a foothold in what we considered to be the soft and prosperous Bejam territory of the South East. I thought the price was getting much too high but Peter insisted it didn't really matter what we paid as the purchase price in reality had little effect on the break-even of the deal. He was right. When you looked at Bernie's numbers, even double the price didn't really seem to kill the deal. It was only our pride that was being hurt in paying more than we had initially agreed but the strategic benefits of this deal would be enormous. We decided to put in a knockout offer that would blow Bejam out of the water. We bid £910,000. Luck was on our side. John Apthorp, the boss of Bejam, was out shooting, the board couldn't get hold of him and they didn't top our offer. We now had twelve shops trading in Basildon, Dagenham, Dover, Faversham, Gillingham, Grays, Harlow, Harold Hill, Ramsgate, Sittingbourne, Witham and Worthing. The takeover was completed on 4 December 1985.

We'd learned a lot from the St Catherine's escapade and we had our management team all ready to go into the stores as soon as the deal was signed. One enthusiastic area manager went to the wrong address and spent most of the morning reorganising a privately owned freezer centre before his mistake was discovered! Bejam meanwhile were devastated that we'd infiltrated their territory and allowing us to buy those shops was a big mistake on their part.

I can't imagine why we did it but once again I was tempted into diversification. On my site finding travels I couldn't help noticing the number of shops springing up in every town selling bulk dry goods. In essence this was no different from loose frozen food but for items such as flour, raisins, cornflakes and sugar. The attraction was the same, you bought exactly the amount you wanted and saved a fortune on the price by not paying for packaging. The problem was that all the shops were one-off, dirty and badly run local operations but they were all busy. Even Fine Fare, a large supermarket chain at the time, had a loose dry goods section.

We decided there was a niche business opportunity here and set up two experimental shops called 'The Food Factory'. The shops were attractive and stylish in a 'Habitat' kind of way. We imported oak barrels from America to display the products and everything looked set for an ambitious roll-out of the concept. We even made a video of the shop to send to property agents as we felt we would be able to open dozens of units every year. The two shops were very busy and we thought successful until we realised the price of everything was so low we couldn't take any real money. It was OK for a husband and wife team to run this kind of shop just for wages but we spent too much money fitting them out to a high standard and there wasn't going to be the return for us. It wasn't worth the effort. Once again, a good idea was abandoned and we resolved yet again to stick to frozen foods.

After Orchard we picked up several more small chains of freezer centres that were all verging on bankruptcy to add to our empire. The frozen food market was growing but it wasn't that easy to make money out of it as everybody else was finding out. We believed that we had the magic formula, however, and it wasn't rocket science. A motivated management team that was well rewarded, a desire to keep things simple and an absolute focus on what we were doing made it all work. We bought Fulham Frozen Foods which was based in Doncaster, AJ & M Freezer Foods in Newcastle, and Igloo and Freezeway, also in the North East.

Growth in Iceland continued unchecked but in spite of that my old insecurity had returned soon after the flotation. I had sold more shares since the float but I still worried about the company whatever our current success. By the end of 1988 we had 106 stores and enjoyed sales of £200 million per year and our profits were approaching £10 million. We might not believe retailing was rocket science but it really felt like we were riding a rocket and I knew the only way to survive was to cling on and keep expanding!

Ranny and I had been looking for a new house since before we floated the company. We'd travelled over a wide area but found nothing we liked. We wanted a large family home with land and I hoped we could find something of sufficient substance so that we could be there for the rest of our lives. Ranny saw an advert for an impressive Elizabethan manor house called Broxton Old Hall and as we drove up the drive on our first visit we both knew this was the one. It was situated on the top of a ridge with a magnificent view over the Cheshire plain. Location, location, location! The problem was we couldn't afford it and, although we agonised, I didn't dare risk it, as undoubtedly a lot more money would need to be spent on the house and even furnishing it would cost a fortune. It was sold within the week for £500,000.

After we floated I stepped up the house search but could find nothing to approach Broxton Old Hall. I rang Graham Adnitt of Jackson-Stops & Staff, the property agent who had sold the house, and asked if the guy who had bought it, Nat Meek, would turn it on for a profit. I think Graham thought I was barmy but in the end we bought the house, eighteen months after it was sold the first time, for £750,000. I was making a habit of overpaying for houses! When Nat moved out, the house looked quite sad and we left it empty for almost a year while we considered what to do with it. I had six different architects prepare schemes for improvements and repairs but nothing seemed right. The house was actually in poor repair and very little of the original Elizabethan building remained – most of it was poor quality Victorian additions. In the end a London architect called Chris Carnell came up with the perfect solution. Knock it down and rebuild it. I'd just paid £750,000 for a building plot!

The house was Grade II listed but, with the full blessing of the planners and the Cheshire conservation department, we embarked on a massive project to rebuild, keeping as much of the original house as we could (about 15 per cent) and using all the authentic materials, an Elizabethan manor house. It wasn't our original intention but it took over our lives and cost many times more than our original budget. It is however one of the things I'm most proud of and in 1989 the *Sunday Times* voted it the best 'traditional house' built in Britain during the last ten years. The house has continued to mature and we have developed the gardens into something truly special.

10
'Let's Go Hostile'

John Apthorp started Bejam in 1967. His father had a potato business and John worked for the company, which they later sold to
Ross Foods. John managed the business for Ross but disagreed with
the way they wanted to run things so he decided to set up on his own.
He'd worked for a while in supermarkets in America and had seen the
growth in freezer ownership over there. As a freezer owner himself
he had difficulty in buying bulk meat and other products and decided
there must be money in supplying freezer owners. He famously invited
three friends to dinner and served them smoked salmon, steak and
ice cream – all from the freezer. The four of them – Bill Perry, Peter
Hearth, Jim Elfick and John – decided to set up a small butchery in
Burnt Oak, near Edgware, and deliver meat to freezer owners. After
six months they opened a shop in Edgware and soon a second one
in High Wycombe. Bejam Freezer Foods was born, and named after
members of the Apthorp family: Brian, Eric, John Apthorp, Millie.
Eric and Millie were John's parents, and Brian was his brother.

John started the company with £20,000 he had borrowed from
his family and, just as Peter and I brought in the British Rail Pension
Fund to provide extra finance, John had sold 20 per cent of Bejam
to Williams & Glyn's Bank to do the same job. Bejam floated in 1973
and by the end of 1987 they had 251 stores and were making profits

of £24 million. John had also found diversification irresistible and at various times owned farms and factories which supplied Bejam. His biggest mistake was to go into hamburger restaurants and even fish and chip shops. 'Trumps Hamburgers' and 'The Hungry Fisherman' soon went the same way as Cassanova and Hi-Speed Printers! He also bought a discount grocery chain called 'Victor Value' from Tesco and started a chain of wine warehouses called 'Wizard Wine'. John was a brilliant businessman but rumour had it he was bored. He spent most of his time shooting and Bill Perry was the driving force behind the business for many years until he became ill with a brain tumour.

I first met John in the early 1980s when he flew up to Deeside to see me (Bejam also had a company plane). We were talking to Argyll at the time and I think John wanted to see if there were any opportunities for him. It was a brief meeting (John has no time for small talk) and, after telling him we wanted to remain independent, I suggested we should cooperate by keeping out of each other's way. John told me in no uncertain terms that when they could find a site in Chester they would open there. They did too, a purpose-built flagship store just to demonstrate they had the muscle!

The frozen food market was changing. We'd started out in 'loose' frozen foods and then evolved into freezer centres, which was Bejam's marketplace. Iceland was changing again, however, and 'value added' or recipe dishes were becoming a more important part of our range. Bejam wasn't adapting to this and their sales were beginning to flatten off. In the spring of 1986 I received a letter from John congratulating me on an excellent set of recent results. I thought this was very strange and took it as a signal that he wanted to talk. I rang him and we agreed to meet at his flat in Mayfair. On the way down I was working out how I could engineer the conversation round to some kind of merger with us coming out on top. Bejam was much bigger than we were and any kind of full-blown takeover was out of the question, although were it possible I would dearly like to have tried. Maybe in a few more years we would manage it but clearly John had something in mind.

John invited me into his flat. Sandwiches were set out on the coffee table and he opened a bottle of wine. He started the conversation by saying, 'You're coming south and we're going north, it seems like we are going to be more and more in competition with each other.' I agreed with his observations and was feeling my way in the conversation when he said, 'If you can raise the money you can have it.' I was shocked by the way he came straight out with it. 'How much?' was my instinctive response. Bejam's share price had been around £1.60 for ages and didn't seem to be moving. John said he wanted £2.50, which seemed like a big increase but I said I would go and see Rothschilds. I asked John if he still used Kleinwort Benson but he said he didn't want his bankers involved. He then stood up and the meeting was clearly over. I'd taken one bite of a sandwich and a sip of wine but it was obviously time for me to go!

Peter, Bernie and Dick were waiting for me round the corner in the Hilton Hotel on Park Lane. I explained what had happened and then we went to see Russell Edey at Rothschilds. The standard form at a Rothschilds meeting is to be ushered into a plush meeting room where uniformed butlers will serve tea. Russell, as the big boss, would arrive and sit opposite with two colleagues. Tony Allen, Russell's junior, would speak only occasionally and scribble the odd note on a single sheet of paper. A very junior 'scribe' would also be there with a stack of files and he would write feverishly without daring to utter a word. Russell would talk most of the time but never make a note. I became good friends with Russell but, just as we viewed him as a pompous, arrogant, posh and condescending 'City' man, he viewed us as a couple of 'northern lads' who needed keeping in check. He would also always imitate my accent. It usually made for great sport and an entertaining meeting.

Russell was happy about the prospect of a deal but felt £2.00 would be the right price. He was also surprised at John's approach and confused as to whether John was talking to us as the Chairman of Bejam with the authority of the board, or as a major shareholder with a 30 per cent stake. Either way John was in a position to deliver us the company if he wanted to. Russell invited John to come and see him, which he did, but John was still adamant he didn't want Kleinworts involved, he wanted to agree a deal first. Russell felt the only way to do a deal at the right price was for the bankers to talk to each other because once that happens the deal gathers its own momentum. To my intense frustration the deal fizzled out over the summer.

In an attempt to resurrect the situation I wrote to John and suggested we get together again 'before the shooting season started'. John rang me immediately he received the letter and invited me to meet him at his house in Radlett. His brother Brian, who was also a Bejam shareholder, was there. Brian lived in Hong Kong and worked as a doctor specialising in venereal disease. I could appreciate his sense of humour when he told me about a boat he kept out there which he had named *Dirty Dick*. We spent some time chatting in John's study, which was covered in animal heads, guns and game trophies. John then decided to show me his wine cellar. He took me down a spiral staircase in his study to the cellar, which was stacked floor to ceiling with expensive wine. I asked him how much it was all worth and he told me 'more than the house'. But we couldn't agree anything on the price for his shares so I left downhearted.

The press however knew something was going on. Every time I spoke to John the Bejam share price would go up and there was lots of speculation about a possible approach from Iceland. In an effort to keep things moving I wrote to Laurence Don, who was now the Managing Director of Bejam, and suggested a meeting. I got a negative response but tried to talk to him on the phone anyway. He was very cool towards me but one night I was in north London and decided to pay Laurence a visit at the Bejam head office in Stanmore. Laurence was courteous and showed me round but was at pains to assure me everything was going well for them and that John Apthorp was still very much a hands-on Chairman. When I left my chauffeur, who had been chatting to Laurence's chauffeur in the car park, was able to tell me that John hardly came into the office any more!

Bill Perry then rang me out of the blue. I'd met Bill before when he was Managing Director at Bejam and liked him a lot. He was a charismatic person and very highly thought of by his staff. He'd partly recovered from his brain tumour by now although he'd retired early from the company. He felt it was sad that Bejam was no longer a 'happy ship' and encouraged us to buy the company. I had lunch with Bill at the Savoy but he died soon afterwards. Bill Perry had lived life to the full and I remember reading a glowing and moving tribute to him by John in a trade magazine. He wrote: 'Not only did Bill Perry burn life's candle at both ends, it also glowed in the middle.'

Around this time Paul Judge pulled off a management buyout from Cadbury Schweppes of many of their well-known grocery brands. It was stunningly successful and after their first year of trading in spring 1987 Premier Brands, as he called the company, invited 30 or so people from the grocery industry to help them celebrate at Brocket Hall. I saw Mr and Mrs Apthorp on the guest list so I accepted the invitation. We arrived in the late afternoon and after changing into black tie we went down for dinner. I was discussing with Ranny how we should arrange to 'bump into' the Apthorps and work the conversation round to a possible deal when they came up right behind us in the queue to shake hands with Paul Judge on the way into dinner. Never one to waste words, I had barely introduced Ranny to John and his wife Jane when he said, 'If we're ever going to do anything we ought to be getting on with it.' He suggested that when we left Brocket, after the weekend, I should follow him in his car to Radlett. Before we'd even sat down to dinner I'd got the result I wanted. We avoided speaking to each other any more, much to the amusement of all the other guests who thought they might see us hatching a deal.

Back in John's study again I told him we could not pay £2.50 per share.

'OK, what about £2.30?' he asked.

'Done,' I said and we shook hands on the deal.

'Are you happy to have Kleinworts involved now?' I asked him and he said he was. 'What about your other directors?'

'Don't worry about them, the only one who might be a problem is Don and I'll take care of him.'

John asked me if I'd close down Stanmore and I said I wasn't sure. He clearly didn't see this as a 'merger'. I asked him if he'd keep any of his stake in the business and he said he wouldn't but he offered to stay on and help to smooth the transition, even as Chairman if I wanted him to. I obviously wasn't keen on that idea as I was sure it would lead to problems.

On Monday morning I rang Rothschilds and spoke to Philip Swatman as Russell Edey was unwell. He was sceptical but said he would ring Kleinworts. When he rang me back he was bubbling. John had already briefed them. Philip suggested we prepare a press release, which would form the heads of agreement, with a view to announcing the deal on Thursday morning. After years of trying I couldn't believe the speed at which things were suddenly moving. I had several telephone conversations with John and agreed to meet him at his flat on Wednesday afternoon to sort out more of the details. We met and chatted for a few minutes about how the deal would work when I asked him what his board thought about the deal. John said, 'You can ask them, they'll be here in a minute.' As if on cue the doorbell rang and they all trooped in. They all looked worried except Laurence Don who seemed to look quite smug. I wondered how John had 'taken care of him'.

Nobody spoke and after an uncomfortable minute of silence I decided to give the big speech. I explained that although we were buying them and this was technically a takeover, we must all view it as a merger; we wanted to keep the best talent from both businesses and we should all work together. I explained our board structure and said it was open for change but I would be Chairman and Chief Executive. Nobody spoke and I wondered if John had even told them about this deal or if it was a bolt from the blue. After a while I suggested I would go for a walk and get some coffee and leave them to chat. I rang Peter, Dick and Bernie and filled them in on the conversation. I suggested it might be a good idea if they came down to London straight away and perhaps we should meet up with the Bejam board that night.

I went back into the meeting and nothing much else was said but we agreed that since the deal was being announced in the morning the two lots of directors should meet for a drink at 9pm in the bar of the Piccadilly Hotel where we were staying. I had to go straight round to Rothschilds to sort out some details of the deal. What I didn't know was that the Bejam board was in complete disarray. There were major differences of opinion on strategy, John had lost all interest in the business and wanted out and he and Laurence Don had a major boardroom row which culminated in them authorising John to discuss the possibility of a merger with Iceland but with me as the Managing Director and Don as Chairman.

At Rothschilds a big problem had arisen which centred on John Apthorp's reluctance to give us a binding undertaking to sell his shares. This meant that once the deal was announced, if a higher offer came along and John accepted the higher offer, we would be left with underwriting fees of several million pounds. We argued about this with Kleinworts until about 9.30pm when it was clear that John would not budge. This was totally unreasonable but something was clearly wrong at their end and the deal wasn't going smoothly. I left to go to the Piccadilly with this issue unresolved and met Peter, Dick and Bernie who had already had a few beers. John rang me at about 10pm to say they had a few problems but he was still keen the two boards should meet. The Bejam board arrived at midnight without John or Laurence. The meeting didn't go well. We'd been in the bar for three hours and were in high spirits. They were clearly in a state of shock and very nervous. We tried to give them reassurances but in our usual jokey way, which wasn't appreciated. When John Edwards, the Bejam Finance Director, asked who would be Finance Director of the new group, him or Bernie, Dick suggested the best way to sort that one out would be for them to go outside and have a fight! We all thought that was hilarious but somehow they just didn't see the funny side of it.

They left us at 3am but, after I'd gone to bed, Peter knocked on my door and said he was worried. Taking over Bejam would mean issuing new shares and our own stake would be diluted so that we were no longer in control. Apthorp was being unreasonable in not giving us the undertaking we wanted and the whole thing was too much risk. We decided to toughen our approach in the morning. In the twenty-minute taxi ride to Rothschild's offices we agreed not to do the deal unless Apthorp gave in.

We were met by a frowning Philip Swatman who told us there was a problem. 'Basically, the Bejam directors have got the shits. Rosalind Hedley-Miller at Kleinworts is saying they will only agree to do a deal if we appoint an independent Chairman.' I was obviously not happy with this but we started to discuss the matter. Philip then told us that the Bejam share price was starting to rise, there had obviously been a leak and the Stock Exchange had been on to Kleinworts already and asked them to put out a statement either confirming or denying that a deal was being discussed.

Michael Richardson came into the room to give us a pep talk. 'Now then you boys,' he said, 'these opportunities in life come but fleeting by and you have to grab them with both hands.' He told us an independent Chairman wouldn't be such a bad thing and he suggested we should consider Professor Roland Smith, Chairman of House of Fraser and British Aerospace. I suggested I should ring John Apthorp at Kleinworts and try to reason with him. I dialled their number. 'John, why do you want an independent Chairman, you never mentioned this before?' He told me he didn't want to see his people disadvantaged and asked for my decision. He also said the Stock Exchange had now telephoned three times and they had to put out a statement immediately. I asked him to hang on for one minute and I put him on hold. I looked at the others. I didn't want them to think my ego was stopping the deal. 'Shall we do it?' I asked them. They nodded in agreement.

I pushed the button to reconnect. 'Hello John ... John? John? Oh fuck, I've cut him off!' It took me a minute to redial. John said, 'I'm sorry, we couldn't wait any longer, we've put out an announcement to say there's no truth in the speculation that we are in talks which might lead to a bid.' I was devastated. I'd lost the deal of a lifetime because I couldn't work the bloody telephone properly. 'They've stopped him selling,' I said. 'How can that be right when he owns 30 per cent of the company?' Philip replied, 'John Apthorp is sitting on a desert island surrounded by cash but his directors have got the canoe.' We left for a very gloomy lunch at Green's, the seafood restaurant in Duke Street, where I just kept apologising for messing up.

Iceland continued expanding. We were the 'darlings of the City' and consistently produced big increases in sales and profits. Food retail analysts wrote admiringly about our business and the financial press were always very kind to us. We had already won all kinds of business awards and had been confirmed as one of the 100 Best Companies to Work For in the UK. By early 1989 Iceland was valued on the stock market at over £100 million. Bejam was valued at about £200 million but they were fast falling from favour and their profits were declining. We kept our operation very simple but embraced computerisation and had already started to link our checkout scanning system to the head office for automatic reordering of stock. We were very unusual among food retailers in that we provided a national distribution service to our stores from our single cold store and distribution centre in Deeside. We believed this was an important factor in the low cost and simplicity of our operation. We had commissioned a new £9 million cold store to be built at Deeside, which would be linked to the other two and take our capacity up to 3 million cubic feet. While our cold store operation until now had been extremely low-tech we had decided to build one of the largest and most modern semi-automated box picking stores in Europe.

I'd been to Sweden to look at automated box picking systems in cold stores but was sceptical about their flexibility and cost-effectiveness. The automated handling of full pallets of stock was already well established and robotic trucks already worked in darkened cold stores retrieving and putting away pallets without any human participation. Our operation was different. Products were delivered to us and put away in the racking in full pallets, but boxes for delivery to our stores were picked singly. I could see no other way but the attractions of minimising labour in the hostile environment of a cold store at minus 30° Celsius were obvious.

Peter Williams, our Systems Director, had visited America and come up with a solution, which involved semi-automatic racking, a computerised picking system and two miles of electrically powered conveyors. It came from three different suppliers who had never even worked in Britain before. Nevertheless, we were all enthusiastic and went to the States to look at similar systems. Even though our cold store was half-built already, we decided to go for it. We had never had any problems with our computerised systems or with commissioning our previous two cold stores. We had probably become far too cocky about our own abilities and thought we could walk on water!

The Iceland Annual General Meeting was usually held in May at 10am in Deeside. We always hoped no one would turn up but inevitably two or three local people with a couple of hundred shares would come along for a three-minute meeting with coffee, and sometimes we'd give them a tour round the office. On 12 May 1988 we decided to make the AGM later, at 12 noon, so more people could attend and also to make it a high-profile affair. We invited as many analysts, financial journalists and major shareholders as we could. We put up a small marquee in the staff car park and after the AGM we provided a tour round the site and a preview of our new cold store in operation. The system hadn't yet been commissioned but it was advanced enough to provide an impressive 'simulated' display of 64,000 boxes per shift whizzing round the conveyor system and being sorted by bar codes and scanners into sixteen palletising stations where the boxes were stacked, shrink wrapped and dispatched to stores. The results were rapturously received. Our credibility with the analysts and financial press was at an all-time high. We were now thinking of launching a hostile bid for Bejam and we needed the full backing of the City.

On Monday, 23 May our cold store picking system was due to go live. We'd not really tested it because we couldn't in a live situation; we just had to assume it would work. The process was non-reversible in that once we'd switched it on there was really no going back as the whole layout of the cold store would change. The day was stop and start as various teething problems emerged but eventually it went live. It did all work, very well, except for one major problem; nobody else in the industry scanned outer box bar codes. Suppliers by now almost always printed a bar code on the product but not on the outer box. We spent months organising and educating them to do this and by the time we went live 99 per cent of our outer boxes had bar codes but they'd not all been properly tested. The quality of print on a corrugated cardboard box, with maybe a shrink wrap or plastic band round it, is not always best suited to be picked up by a sensitive scanner. The boxes were due to be electronically sorted at great speed and sent down dispatch lines for loading onto the lorries for delivery to stores. Any boxes that for any reason couldn't be successfully scanned were sent down a 'dump line' at the end of the conveyor. We anticipated just 1 per cent would go down the dump line. In the event 30 per cent of the boxes went down the dump line and piled up on the floor in seconds. Chaos ensued as cold store men became buried in boxes and the conveyors had to be stopped while the mess was sorted out. Occasionally an overhead conveyor would malfunction and boxes of frozen chickens would rain down 30 feet onto people below.

It was an unmitigated nightmare. Our cold store men were in the middle of negotiating a pay rise so they all decided to go home at 6pm and leave us with it. We roped in office staff, secretaries and store managers and worked through the night to try to get the system to work and stock delivered to stores. This went on for three days and many of us didn't get any sleep for those three days and nights. Our stores were running out of stock, sales were suffering and we were no nearer to solving the problem. Everybody 'mucked in' and I spent three nights driving a forklift truck and trying to cause as little damage to the cold store as I could. It was not possible to revert back to the old manual system but in the end we had to or we would have bankrupted the company with no stock being delivered to the stores.

It took months to sort out the problem and convince our suppliers of the need to print proper bar codes on their outer boxes. Russell Edey knew about our problem, of course, and refused to discuss a bid for Bejam until we could prove that the 'Hurdy Gurdy' system, as we called it, worked properly. I didn't want to go to Rothschild's offices any more as I was paranoid about being seen and the Bejam share price rising. So I arranged to meet Russell in the autumn of 1988 in a bedroom at the Intercontinental Hotel. I showed him a video of the cold store Hurdy Gurdy system in full and flawless operation and asked him, 'Now can we go hostile on Bejam?'

Many changes had been made at Bejam in the last year and Rosalind Hedley-Miller of Kleinworts was now a non-executive director. Laurence Don was Deputy Chairman and Tim How was the Managing Director. John had officially taken a step back and gone part-time. I'd telephoned Tim several times through the summer to ask for a meeting but he didn't want to know.

Peter Hinchcliffe had been slowly winding down since our flotation four years earlier and was now officially working only three days per week at a reduced salary, but he still saw buying as his territory and was possessive of the department. Dick and I felt there were a lot of problems in the buying department and were anxious to get involved. We were on the verge of suggesting that Peter should become non-executive when things started to happen with Bejam. Russell at last conceded that Rothschilds would support us in a hostile bid. This seemed the only way we could ever win control of the company but it was almost an impossibility. The Apthorp family owned 30 per cent of the shares. Five per cent of the shares were almost certainly in the hands of 'tracker funds' who would try to follow the FT Index and would therefore take a passive role and support the incumbent management. Five per cent of shareholders would never bother to vote and therefore we had to win over 50 per cent of the votes from just the remaining 60 per cent of shareholders. This was asking a lot! A failed attempt would lose us credibility and cost us a fortune in fees.

We had a discussion in the boardroom about everything that was involved. Peter was lukewarm about the idea and Bernie said he didn't 'particularly want to work any harder'! I was furious with him. Dick was as enthusiastic as I was and we decided to go for it Peter and Bernie were soon caught up in the excitement, however, and we became a united team.

One final hurdle we had to clear was to seek the view of our major institutional shareholder. The British Rail Pension Fund was still a big shareholder in Iceland and the shares were managed by Mercury Fund Management. Mercury also owned shares in Iceland on behalf of other clients and owned Bejam shares too. We had to go and see them and seek their blessing. This was of course highly confidential and in doing so we made them 'insiders' so they wouldn't be allowed to deal in our shares for a while. We were in the middle of presenting to Carol Galley and Bill Baker when the uniformed butler brought in the tea. I stopped talking and covered my papers. 'Carry on,' said Carol, unconcerned. I did, but I couldn't help noticing the butler's Rolex!

We had to produce reams of planning papers for Russell about why it was all a good idea, how we could improve Bejam's performance, and also market statistics to show why they were underperforming and we were doing well. It was of course all supposition and conjecture on our part because we had no hard information on Bejam except what our spies were telling us and what we could glean by going round their stores. Eventually we came up with enough to convince Russell and we set D-Day as Friday, 28 October 1988. We went down to London the day before and were all shown into a basement room at Rothschild's offices known as 'the bunker'. This was equipped with office furniture and telephones and was to be our headquarters for the 60-day period that is allowed as the timescale for a takeover bid.

Russell explained that we would launch the bid in the morning with me telephoning John Apthorp at about 8am to give him the news. We would then hold a press conference and an analysts' meeting at about 9.30am where we would go through the slide presentation we had put together to show why the Bejam shareholders would be better off with us running the company. We would then mail out that night an 'offer document' which we had put together. This gave all the details of the offer and an explanation as to why we thought Bejam's management was performing badly and why we would do better! The shareholders would really have to believe in the strength of the Iceland management for us to succeed because we were not offering cash for the Bejam shares but asking them to accept new Iceland shares which we would issue in payment. Our 'paper offer' valued Bejam at £240 million or £1.90 for each Bejam share. This was a long way short of the £2.30 price we had agreed only eighteen months earlier but better than the £1.60 they had been trading at for most of the last four years.

That night I could hardly sleep. Peter, Bernie and I still owned over 40 per cent of Iceland so we effectively controlled the company and we certainly felt as if we owned it! By issuing new shares to pay for Bejam we would reduce our stake to just over 15 per cent. We would become managers instead of proprietors. It didn't matter. I knew I would always feel as if I was the 'owner' of the business and it was absolutely the right thing to do for the future. Iceland and Bejam had about 450 stores between them but we only overlapped in twelve towns, so if we won the bid there would be hardly any store closures. We would of course close down their head office and probably one or two of their depots and this would give us massive cost savings. We would also be a much stronger company with better buying power while eliminating our biggest future competitor. Many takeovers are launched for reasons of ego: management ambition, the desire to run a bigger company, a bigger salary for the boss. There was some of that, of course, but this one also made sound commercial sense!

Next morning I was very tense and excited. I had to make the phone call to John. How would he react? I thought in one way he would be pleased but he would be very unhappy with the price. I was rehearsing in my mind what I was going to say. I sat down at a desk and dialled his home number. Peter, Dick, Bernie, Russell Edey and Tony Allen were all standing behind me waiting for the fireworks. No reply. I tried his mobile. No reply. I rang his office.

'Good morning, I want to speak to John Apthorp.'

'Sorry, he's not in today.'

'Laurence Don?'

'Not in.'

'Tim How?'

'Sorry, no reply from his phone, he's not in yet.'

'Brian Jackson?'

'Sorry, he's not in either.'

'Look, this is really urgent, I have to speak to someone important. Who's the most senior person in the building?'

'Er, Jim Rainey.'

'Who's he?'

'The Administration Services Manager, I'll put you through.'

'Hello, Jim? This is Malcolm Walker from Iceland, I just want to let you know I'm launching a takeover bid for your company this morning.'

Jim just laughed.

John rang me a couple of hours later and his first words were, 'You've cost me a day's shooting!' John had been having breakfast in a Little Chef when he got the call. He was on his way to a partridge shoot so he went straight to Kleinworts and spent the day there in his plus fours and shooting clothes.

Streets Financial Public Relations had ceased to exist and we needed a 'heavyweight' financial PR guy to help us with the bid. The press would be so important in determining the result and it was important to try to get them on our side. A friend of mine recommended Brian Basham. Brian was a veteran of many takeover bids and later hit the headlines himself in the scrap between Lord King of British Airways and Richard Branson. Brian was a likeable guy but for one major fault. He never wore a watch and had no concept of punctuality for meetings. He would often turn up more than an hour late and this drove Russell insane. The rest of the team were Rothschilds and Hoare Govett. It was by no means certain we'd win this bid with the Apthorp family owning 30 per cent and, if we lost, the abortive fees could make a serious hole in our balance sheet so I negotiated a deal whereby we would pay a bigger fee if we won and hardly anything if we lost. Everyone had an incentive to win.

The day passed in a whirlwind and that night the plan was to meet with all the rest of the board at the Piccadilly Hotel for a meal and a few beers. I was in the shower when the phone went.

'It's Brian here.'

I thought, 'Brian? Brian?' It must be Basham. 'Oh hello Brian.'

'You sound as if you were expecting this call?'

I realised it wasn't Basham but instead of saying, 'Who is it?' I just said 'Er well, yes, sort of.'

The mystery caller then asked if I could meet him at his flat in an hour and gave me an address in Hampstead.

I went down to the bar and asked the others if we knew anyone called Brian in Hampstead. 'Brian Jackson, Buying Director of Bejam, where does he live? Brian Basham? Dunno.'

I went to Hampstead for Brian Apthorp to open the door with his brother John waiting inside.

'Make it a cash offer and you can have the company,' he said with his customary directness.

'I can't. We've no money. I can't borrow that much.'

'Well, we'll have to fight it then. Have a glass of wine.'

I lived in London for most of the next two months and spent my time either plotting our next move with Russell in the bunker, or visiting shareholders. Bernie was with me for most of the time and Peter for some of the time. The battle raged, with each side accusing the other of being poor managers. Bejam said we were inexperienced and would not be able to run a bigger company. We highlighted their declining performance against our success. We accused them of having lost their way. 'Bejam have consultants in the business, at Iceland the expertise lies within the company!' We pointed out they were experimenting with different formats, always a sign that management has lost confidence in their business. We each sent circulars to all the Bejam shareholders arguing these points and highlighted rafts of statistics which best suited our own case and urged them to support our side. We each lobbied the press and both sides made presentations to most of the Bejam shareholders. The difference was that John's heart wasn't in it but we were desperate to succeed. John had built a fantastic business over the last twenty years but now he was fed up with it and he wanted out. For him, the fun had gone out of it.

Halfway through the bid we were able to announce we'd won the Business Enterprise Award, conferred by the CBI. This was a prestigious award for wealth and job creation and was a timely bonus. The press were on our side but had by now decided the battle was 'vicious' and 'acrimonious' and a personal battle between John and me. Certainly it was hard fought and each side pulled out every trick in the book but it really wasn't personal.

The bid had been deliberately timed so that the closing day for the offer was Friday, 30 December but, because of Christmas, we could claim the 23rd was effectively the last day and if we had still not received enough acceptances by then we had the option to fight on to the 30th. The problem was that nobody sends in their acceptance until the last minute in case a higher offer materialises. In the last few days before Christmas the acceptances started to come in but we only got to 42 per cent. Normally a company will raise its offer price during the course of a bid but we had not done that. The Bejam share price had dropped back to £1.50, which was lower than before we started, and that said the market thought our bid would fail. We could start spending money and buy shares in the market but we needed at least another 8 per cent to win. Nigel Mills of Hoare Govett was only confident of being able to buy 6 per cent. His market intelligence had to be good. If we started buying and couldn't get 8 per cent we would have a big problem. The bid would fail, we would be stuck with millions of pounds worth of Bejam shares and the price was sure to drop. Peter, Bernie and I had dinner at the Four Seasons Hotel and we realised we had lost the bid.

However, as the meal progressed we rallied each other and decided to have one last big push. The next day we went to see the Prudential, Postel and the Pearl. These were virtually the only big institutions which had decided to support Bejam. The Pearl always backed the incumbent management and would not budge. Postel (the Post Office pension fund) had a strange argument. They owned Iceland shares as well as Bejam and agreed we were the better management but thought that we would grow faster without Bejam so they would not support the bid. I had been to see them three times before to try to persuade them. The fund manager, who made the decision, was a young woman with hair down to her waist called Ingrid Kirby. I thought something was wrong with the system when the result of the bid was virtually in her hands. What did she know about running a company? The Prudential listened to our case for the third time and said they would let us know.

We returned to the bunker and waited ... and waited. If we could secure the Pru's support, we would have enough acceptances to risk going into the market to buy shares, but it was a big risk. The Pru rang and said they were going to support us and would accept our offer. We were jubilant! It was just a few days before Christmas and Nigel Mills of Hoare Govett got to work and bought every Bejam share he could lay his hands on. By Christmas Eve we had 49.5 per cent acceptances but only 45.5 per cent of those were valid i.e. with the share certificate attached. The others said the share certificate was in the post or lost. The Pru had let us down. They only accepted our offer for half their holding and sold the rest in the market. I was furious with them. It was close enough to fight on until 30 December but we were getting desperate and left no stone unturned. Barry Owen, of Mason Owen, spent two days on the telephone ringing everyone he knew to ask if they owned any Bejam shares. I picked up a certificate for 1,000 shares from my local newsagent on Christmas Eve and we even sent the company jet to St Austell in Cornwall to pick up the certificate from someone with 2,000 shares. One of the most bizarre incidents was when one of our area managers was sent to Batley in Yorkshire to collect a certificate for 100,000 shares after the owner said he would sell. They went to the bank together to collect the certificate but the bank wouldn't release it as it was held as security for a loan. The only way to get it was to pay the bank in cash. After many phone calls the money was paid and the area manager flew down to Heathrow to deliver it.

The time between Christmas and New Year is very quiet in the City. No one is doing much business but Hoare Govett had to strain every muscle to buy every last Bejam share they could get their hands on. This was going to be perilously close. An accurate count of the acceptances was crucial. Not long before, Hoare Govett had been party to a fiasco when they declared Blue Circle the winners of a bid for Birmid Qualcast but the acceptances had been miscounted! This time no one was taking any chances. The company registrars, Lloyds Bank in Worthing, who were responsible for doing the count, were being slow and not keeping us informed of the count minute by minute. John Berry went down to their offices in Worthing to wind them up. We did everything we could to increase our chances.

By 30 December we were able to announce we had 50.09 per cent valid acceptances. This was an amazing victory and we hadn't even increased our offer price but we had only just scraped through by the thinnest of margins. Ranny had taken the children skiing to Kitzbuhl the day before and I flew out on the company jet to join them in time for some extra special New Year celebrations. On my return from the holiday I had to spend a lot of time in London and on a spare half day I went to the boat show, which is always held at Earl's Court in the first week of January. We had owned a house in Spain since before the company flotation and I kept a small boat there, which was due to be replaced. I treated myself to a 37-foot Sunseeker which to everyone's puzzlement I called 'Point Nought Nine!'

11

Conquering the World

I met John Apthorp on 30 December after we announced the result of the takeover battle. We were alone in a small office at Rothschilds. He was courteous and congratulated me on our victory. John had just picked up £70 million worth of Iceland shares, which he sold in the market straight away. I thought he was a bit rash as the winner's share price always drops back after a bid, but for him it was a matter of principle. He was no longer in control so he didn't want the shares. He suggested there were 'a few housekeeping points to sort out' and asked me what I intended to do about his company car. I asked him what he had and he told me a Bentley Turbo. I said I would give it to him. John then said, 'Right, how can I help you?' I think that gesture was important to him. He then couldn't have been more helpful in talking me through the problems and personalities at Bejam. We have remained friends ever since and John's wife Jane has more than once introduced me to her friends as 'the man we have to thank for our lifestyle'!

I met Tim How, the Managing Director of Bejam, and John Edwards, the Finance Director, soon afterwards in the same office. I made a big conciliatory speech about this really being a merger, not a takeover, and how we wanted to take the best from both companies. I explained that we had made no decisions about the board and had no fixed plans about what we would do with the company. We would wait and see what we found over the next couple of weeks. Tim's reaction couldn't have been more different from John's. He stunned me by saying that he wasn't surprised we had no idea what to do next but he thought the shareholders would be! I thought his approach to my olive branch showed a gross lack of judgement when I would be responsible for his future pay-off!

On Monday, 9 January 1989 the Iceland board walked into the Bejam head office at Honeypot Lane, Stanmore. I was both scared and excited at the prospect but I guess it was even more stomach churning for the Bejam staff. We sat down briefly with their board and Kit Farrow from Kleinwort Benson, their bankers, to complete the handover formalities. After that we were on our own. We felt like army officers in occupied hostile territory. Peter, Dick and I made John's office our base and we spent the next couple of weeks familiarising ourselves with what we had acquired. The first shock was their sales position. Because we had made a hostile bid we had no information on Bejam other than what was publicly available or what our spies told us. We had estimated their sales would be 5 per cent down on the previous year but found to our horror they were down 13 per cent. This meant a loss of £35 million in budgeted sales and possibly £5 million in profit. This would make the £40 million combined profit, which the analysts had pencilled in for the year, even harder to achieve. Iceland, on the other hand, was performing well and sales were 15 per cent ahead of the previous year on a like-for-like basis. This was a huge difference in performance. Iceland and Bejam were in the same business, and customers would not easily spot a great difference between our stores, but this illustrated very well how small differences in operation and management enthusiasm could impact on sales. We had a big task in front of us.

The Bejam directors were still in their offices, trying to keep busy but obviously worrying about whether they still had jobs or not. I was constantly hassled by most of them who wanted to know what our plans were and I began to worry and feel perhaps we hadn't done our homework properly. I mentioned this to Russell Edey and he suggested I should have lunch with a friend of his, Peter Harper, who was a main board director of Hanson Trust. Hanson were respected and feared takeover specialists at the time and Russell thought I might learn something from the experts. Lunch was set for Monday, 6 February but before it came round we had finalised our plans and started to act with a speed the Bejam directors found bewildering. They then started to complain we were being too hasty! Lunch with Peter Harper was then not so necessary but it was entertaining. He said, 'Let me guess, you looked at Bejam and thought, they're in the south, we're in the north, there are not too many overlaps, we'll give it a crack.' I admitted that wasn't far from the truth. Peter said the world imagined that Hanson prepared a huge and detailed plan prior to any takeover but the reality was they didn't. Their takeovers were made on much more broad-based assumptions. You never knew what you would find until you got in there and decisions had to be made as you went along. He assured me a two-week familiarisation 'do nothing' period was the right way to do it. I felt greatly relieved we were not complete amateurs!

The only part of Bejam we really knew nothing about was their appliance division. Bejam sold more freezers and microwave ovens than anybody else in the UK and they also ran a national repair service. Charles Rathgay ran the division quite autonomously and I had telephoned him halfway through the bid to reassure him that his job would be safe if we won. We'd actually have a real problem if he left! Every other part of the company was no problem for us and we viewed the task ahead as one of simple integration. Simple, that is, except for the staff. We had to close down their head office in Stanmore and make 600 people redundant but we had to do it in an organised way and gradually transfer all the operations to Deeside. This was going to take about nine months and we had to persuade all the staff to leave when we wanted them to and not to make a mass exodus. We had to buy Portakabins and stack them two high on the car park at Deeside to accommodate the 300 extra staff we would need there. Recruiting and training that number of people was no easy task. It was nine months of organised chaos but it worked. Our biggest worry was that Bejam had an ageing mainframe IBM computer which we thought would fall over at any time, but it didn't. We gradually closed down their office, section by section, yet managed to maintain morale and the goodwill of the staff.

We mixed up the retail teams and put Iceland area managers into Bejam stores and Bejam area managers into Iceland stores and pretty soon we had a unified team. The only problem area was the cold storage and distribution centres, where we suffered unrest and disruption from a much more militant workforce. Bejam had five old-fashioned and inefficient distribution centres, which took us several years to sort out. A new product range, taking the best from both companies, and also major changes in distribution and store operation, were planned to be introduced in a 'big bang' fashion on 'D-Day', Thursday, 18 May 1989. We organised a dinner the night before for 50 of our senior people and invited John Garnett, the president of the Industrial Society and the best motivational speaker in the world, to address us. He inspired everyone for the task ahead and likened the next day to the Normandy landings. It was like a war for a few weeks. The Iceland lorry drivers went on their first ever strike for more pay and parity with the Bejam drivers and chaos reigned for some time. Gradually, though, order was restored, the new systems settled down and slowly sales improved.

We were keen to keep as many senior Bejam executives as we could but no one was prepared to move to Deeside and gradually they all left. All the directors were made redundant except Charles Rathgay and Jill McWilliam their Marketing Director. We persuaded Jill to go back into public relations, which had been her forte at Bejam for many years and she was outstandingly good at it. We made her our PR Director and she stayed with us for about seven years. We tried to keep Brian Jackson, their Buying Director, and he moved to Deeside for a short while but the cultural differences were too big for him to cope with and he soon left. Iceland was very informal, even our internal telephone directory was printed in alphabetical order of first names. My home phone number was on the wall in the office of every store and we prided ourselves on our approachability and our unambiguous and straight-talking style with our staff. We were very open and honest in our communication. Bejam by contrast were very formal and hierarchical and no one would dare to jump a reporting line of communication let alone ring me at home with a problem.

In addition to the Bejam stores we also inherited two other businesses, part of Bejam's attempt at diversification. We had 46 Victor Value discount stores, which were a Kwik Save look-alike operation, and also a number of retail wine warehouses which traded as Wizard Wine. Tempting as it was to keep these, we decided we had to be focused. The stakes were too high to be distracted by other ventures and we decided to sell these businesses as quickly as possible. We offered Victor Value to the highest bidder and were disappointed that Kwik Save was the only interested party. We didn't tell them that, of course, and we ran a make believe auction between Kwik Save and nobody else and finally agreed a price of £15.75 million. We also kept eight property freeholds. It was interesting to see how Graham Seabrook, the CEO of Kwik Save, approached the sale. He made such heavy weather of it and had a negotiating team of six or eight people versus just me and John Berry. Discussions went on for weeks. It seemed like they couldn't make any decision but eventually the deal was signed.

Wizard Wine was altogether more interesting. John Apthorp rang me and asked if I would sell him the business. He arrived at Deeside with Tim How, who was to be his new Managing Director, and in typical John style we had agreed a deal within the hour. I sold him the company for £1.2 million plus a case of 1970 Chateau Petrus for me! Chateau Petrus is one of the most expensive wines in the world. I'd only tried it once before, in the middle of the bid, at the Four Seasons Hotel with Bernie. We had decided for some reason to treat ourselves but the wine was off! John reneged on the deal. He sent me a case of

1970 Chateau Haut-Brion plus one bottle of Petrus. I've still got the Petrus and am waiting for the right celebration to drink it! I didn't rate Tim How when he was at Bejam, particularly after his attack on me at Rothschilds, but he did a fantastic job at Wizard Wine, which is now known as Majestic Wine. John floated the company in October 1996 and they now have over 180 branches.

Soon after the takeover battle was won, we decided to host a party as a 'thank you' to all our professional advisers. Nigel Mills from Hoare Govett, Mike Orsborn from Charterhouse and Russell Edey from Rothschilds were all invited as was the great man himself, Sir Michael Richardson. We held it down in the wine cellar of the Café Royal, which was a great venue and also very private. We had champagne, of course, but also a barrel of beer as a token of our 'northern roots' and gave everyone a commemorative silver tankard. Michael Richardson always came across as a flirt with the ladies, so we decided it would be good sport to set him up at dinner with a very attractive waitress who was actually a stripper. It worked a treat. She became ever more familiar with him as the meal progressed and eventually took off her clothes – all of them. Michael didn't bat an eyelid and posed happily with his arm round her as we took photographs.

A few weeks later I asked our art studio if they could do a special project for me. I bought a copy of *Private Eye* magazine and asked if they could reproduce the front cover using the photo of Michael and the nude stripper under the headline: 'City banker in sex scandal, Thatcher asks questions in the House'. The end result was indistinguishable from the real thing. We sent it to Russell Edey who took it in to show Michael. Michael completely fell for it in a big way and for about 90 seconds was close to a heart attack and a very worried man. He did appreciate the joke, however, and I understand the magazine was framed and had pride of place hanging in his toilet at home!

Nothing goes entirely to plan and since sales at Bejam were so much worse than we had anticipated, they took a little longer than planned to recover. By July 1989, in the half-year result figures, we were able to show sales for the combined group that were just 1 per cent ahead. We had to work hard to convince the doubters in the City that we could cope with a bigger business and all would be well. We had emerged from the takeover with high borrowings and interest rates were now at 14 per cent. Expectations in the City were that our profits would be around £37 million. Our share price had been about £3.90 but by November it had dropped back to £3.19. We were not confident of making the expected number and Hoare Govett and Tilney, our brokers, moved to a lower forecast of £35 million. Our shares were marked down to £2.80 and drifted even lower to £2.46 by January but we eventually posted profits for the year of £35.4 million and our shares rose to £2.69 in relief. It was still an increase of 17 per cent in earnings per share, which I thought an outstanding performance, but the City was expecting more.

Peter Hinchcliffe was now back into the job 100 per cent and back on a full salary. The Bejam integration took less than a year and we were refitting Bejam stores into the Iceland style at the rate of one every four days. We were also opening new stores at a record rate with 26 new stores opened in 1989 and 41 new store openings in 1990. Her Royal Highness the Princess Royal had opened the 250th Bejam store and we felt it appropriate to ask her to open our 500th store in Clapham on 15 March 1991. Our earnings per share for the year ended December 1990 showed an increase of 16 per cent with profits of £40.3 million. We now employed 11,000 people. This was the company's 21st birthday year. The country by now was in a deep recession, but for us it didn't seem to matter.

One of the first things I discovered soon after the Bejam takeover was the environmental problem created by discarded household appliances. Bejam were market leaders in the sale of fridges and freezers but most people already had one so it was largely a replacement market. After every delivery the customer would usually ask the driver to take away their old freezer. On a tour round the Bejam appliance warehouse I saw a mountain of scrap freezers in the yard outside. 'What do you do with these?' I asked. 'Oh, we give them to the scrap man who takes the copper out and then I suppose he dumps the rest.' CFCs were just coming into the news and the damage to the environment caused by the gas released from just one discarded freezer was reckoned to make a hole in the ozone layer the size of a double decker bus. Bejam scrapped 100,000 freezers every year. Nobody seemed bothered.

I asked if there was a way of recycling the gas from inside the freezers and after a lot of worrying about the likely increased cost, we set up a simple extraction unit for the scrap man to operate. Nobody else was doing this and so we cashed in on the publicity value to great effect. 'Buy your freezer from Iceland and help to save the world' was one of our more modest slogans. We had a unique advantage over other appliance retailers in that we operated our own delivery service and could guarantee that the customer's old freezer would be returned and safely degassed. This initiative won us great acclaim from the press and environmentalists and we began to realise you could often 'do the right thing' and also profit by it. We won an award for this initiative, which was presented by Princess Diana. I went up to receive it at a special lunch, with the acceptance speech Jill McWilliam had written for me safely in my pocket. I shook hands with Princess Di, turned to the microphone and promptly forgot what I was supposed to say. The audience swam before my eyes and all I could say was, 'In the commercial world ... er ... I'm sorry, I've forgotten what I was going to say!' I sat down at the table with Jill and other ex-Bejam staff to thunderous applause from the room but also great embarrassment from our table that their new boss had let them down. After that I always wrote my own speeches and then I could remember them! I did get a return match with Princess Di when I presented a cheque for £1 million that Iceland staff had raised for the Petö Institute, an organisation that helps children with cerebral palsy. I think I acquitted myself OK the second time. Charity fundraising became a team building morale booster for our staff and while Iceland had always given substantially to charity (nearly £3 million between 1990 and 1998, which had grown to more than £11.5 million by 2013) our staff would always raise many times more every year for a variety of causes.

Staff morale and enthusiasm was everything to us and Peter and I went on a trip to Disney World in Florida to look behind the scenes at how they managed to keep such enthusiasm among their employees. We brought back a million ideas, we implemented as many as we could and then we sent over Dick Kirk and Janet Weinstein, our Personnel Director, so they could benefit from the opportunity.

Iceland made another acquisition at the end of 1990 with the purchase of twelve Freezerite freezer centres for £1.8 million. There was really nobody else left to buy now and while we did mop up one or two other small chains over the next year or two, our future development could only be by organic growth ... or by going overseas. I had been over to Northern Ireland with Tim Yates our Property Director and we were very excited at the opportunities we saw over there. There was still a war on but I thought we would trade well. Peter and Dick went over and were less convinced. They really didn't want to do it and I didn't argue. However, we did go into Northern Ireland two years later and after that into the Republic. Northern Ireland proved to be the most successful area in the UK for Iceland with sales per store double the company average.

Our increased profile through the flotation meant we were now getting all kinds of approaches and opportunities put before us and several of them were to acquire businesses in France. Britain is the only country in the world where freezer centres exist except for, funnily enough, France. This would seem unlikely with their food culture but several chains had been developed. They tended to specialise in much better quality products than we could sell in the UK. Commodity items like fish and meat were a big part of their business and their ready meals were very expensive but of good quality. The stores themselves in France were much more basic than ours, and their sales were much lower. They tended to survive only because of much lower running costs. A store would typically have only one member of staff and would close for lunch!

We looked at a couple of chains that were for sale but in the end we seconded Belinda Lavenstein, one of our area managers who was French, to research the project. We came up with the idea in 1991 of approaching a small company based in Lille, northern France, called 'Au Gel', which traded from twelve stores. It was run by a father and son, Francois and Olivier Bequet. The idea was that we would buy a 50 per cent stake and let them continue to run it, but they would benefit from our ideas, expertise and scale. We were well aware of the pitfalls and cultural differences of this new market but on a joint venture basis we thought it might work. We resolved not to put too much money into the company and to pull out if we had problems. We successfully negotiated a deal but played it down from a City point of view as we knew there would be a great deal of cynicism about the venture.

It was good fun, for a while. I visited Lille almost every week but the big difficulty was keeping the rest of the Iceland management team away. Everybody wanted to be involved and most people found an excuse to make the trip. (When it started to go wrong nobody wanted to have anything to do with it!) I couldn't speak a word of French, the Bequets couldn't speak English, or at least they pretended they couldn't, and Belinda, who was now living over there, had to translate every conversation and argument. During the honeymoon period I tried really hard with the Bequets. We had them over to Deeside several times, we entertained them and they stayed at my house and even enjoyed one of our parties. I had countless heavy lunches in Lille because no matter what was on the agenda everything really did stop for a two-hour lunch.

I had forgotten, though, that the French national sport is ripping off the English and I think the Bequets were awkward as a matter of principle. The cultural differences were just insurmountable and in the end we had no option but to buy them out in order to make any progress at all in developing the business. If ever a lesson was needed on why John Major negotiated us out of the social contract then people should try running a business in France. The bureaucracy was mind-bending and crippling and eventually we closed down the business in 1994 with a loss of £8 million. We had no criticism from the City for pulling out!

The year 1992 was a good one for Iceland. We were opening new stores at the rate of one every week, our new extended office accommodation at Deeside was nearing completion and we were at last due to get rid of the Portakabins where we had been 'camping out' since the Bejam acquisition.

Early in the year Peter Hinchcliffe had a visitor. His name was Peter Merrikin and he used to be in the frozen vegetable business but had now retired. Peter vaguely remembered him. Merrikin explained that he was involved with three other individuals who were trying to buy a state farm in Hungary! Communism had just collapsed and privatisation of state assets was about to happen. Merrikin wanted to know if Peter and I would be interested in joining them. I felt we had enough to do at Iceland. It was a long time since we'd learnt the lessons of diversification and we'd recently started a small travel agency business. (We thought it would be useful with our growing need for travel and hotel bookings!) We were busy in France, busy opening new stores, we were planning a new £30 million distribution centre in Swindon and our office was a building site. I didn't want to waste time dreaming about a farm in Hungary that would never happen.

Merrikin kept coming to see Peter and I grew increasingly irritated with them both. Merrikin was in fantasy land. They had identified a farm of 20,000 acres called the Kiskunsag State Farm and were trying to buy it. There was no way I would invest any money in a project like that but Merrikin said they didn't need any money. They intended to buy the farm with all borrowings and wanted to cut us in for equal shares because they felt our name would lend credibility to their efforts. They also thought Iceland would be a possible customer for the vast amounts of vegetables they planned to grow. Merrikin introduced us to his partners, Tom and Mark Cherrington and John Hobbins. Tom Cherrington ran an antiquarian bookshop in London and was going to be the Chairman of the new venture, while his brother Mark and John Hobbins were farmers who planned to go and live in Hungary and run the business. They were very keen for us to be involved and assured us it would cost us nothing. In the end, out of deference to Peter, I agreed to go along with it, as we had nothing to lose, although I was convinced we were wasting our time.

Sometimes an idea is so ridiculous, so absurd that people do take you seriously and it comes off. How they did it I don't know but in July 1992 they completed the purchase of the farm. Peter Bullivant, our lawyer, set up a company based in Jersey called Bronze Investment Co. Ltd with the six of us as equal shareholders. We each subscribed £2 for our share in the company. The company then bought the Kiskunsag State Farm from the Hungarian state property agency for 50 million Hungarian Forints (about £5 million). A complicated funding arrangement was put in place, which involved borrowing all the money, mainly from the Bank of Budapest, with the state providing a bank guarantee. The six of us now owned a 20,000-acre farm in Hungary and all it had cost us was £2 each! Merrikin and his colleagues I now considered were all financial geniuses. If only we could find people of their calibre to help us run Iceland we could conquer the world.

We called the Hungarian farm company 'Danube Farms kft'. Our partners were well established as the new Barons of Kiskunsag by the time Peter Hinchcliffe, Peter Bullivant and I went out to inspect the estate in early July. We flew into Budapest and stayed there for the first night. It was a wonderful old city just waking up to the western world. The next day we travelled to the farm. Twenty thousand acres is a lot of land. We owned a village with several hundred houses, and also the hotel where we stayed, which Cherrington and Hobbins had made their base. We also owned the second largest indoor riding arena in Hungary, with hundreds of horses kept in training, which was famous throughout the world for its teams of display riders. We visited the cattle station where thousands of beef cattle were being reared and went to the arable fields in time to see a fleet of combine harvesters appearing over the horizon. I'd wave my arms to an incredulous Peter Bullivant and tell him we owned everything as far as the eye could see, all for two quid! We were feudal lords. The local villagers feted us as their new landlords, they put on a riding display just for the seven of us and we even had our own village gypsy band to play for us. Hungarian music is so beautiful but melancholy and I fell for it in a big way. I was keen to bring 'our band' over to England to play at one of our parties!

The Russians had not long vacated the area and part of our land included an old Russian army barracks and even a sinister looking chemical dump with hundreds of rusting 40 gallon drums oozing green and yellow sludge. It was going to be expensive to clear but grants were available! We even owned an old shooting lodge in the forest, which the Russian officers had used for rest and relaxation, but it was unattractive and cheaply furnished with Formica tables and plastic chairs. On our return to Budapest we had dinner at 'Gundel', a famous old restaurant that had been bought by a wealthy American-Hungarian and restored to its former pre-war glory. The setting was magical, the traditional food was heavy but of course appropriate and the resident gypsy band all combined to make me feel I was on a film set for *Doctor Zhivago*. We spared no expense at the top restaurant in Hungary but struggled to spend more than £5 per head. We really felt we would make millions when Hungary became fully accepted as part of Europe. I couldn't wait to take Ranny and the children and soon did a rerun of the trip in the October half term holiday. My two daughters were mad on horses at that time and most impressed with the riding school and all the horses Dad owned!

We left our four genius farming financiers to run the operation and wouldn't have dreamed of interfering in any way. A fortune was spent on an irrigation system and sending various experts and consultants out from the UK. Seeds and fertiliser were ordered and an ambitious planting schedule was planned for the following year. Iceland was to benefit from hundreds of tons of cheap vegetables being grown for us and we were also going to be able to import enough pork at amazingly low prices to wipe out our competitors.

Then our farming financiers ran out of money, the company went bankrupt and the government repossessed the farm. Peter and I were just left wondering what might have been and if we would ever be allowed into Hungary again.

Our colleagues in Iceland were unaware of these adventures and growth continued unchecked. By the end of 1992 we were able to report we had increased our annual sales to over £1 billion and our profits were up 20 per cent.

One day in conversation with Dick he mentioned that he had heard from an ex-Woolworth's colleague about A.V. Green (our old boss from Woolworth's who had fired us); he had long since retired but was fit and well. We wondered if we could track him down and thought what a nice idea it would be to get in touch and let him know there were no hard feelings. Dick managed to get hold of him and he said he was pleased for our success and showed a lot of interest in Iceland. We decided to invite him to the office for a reunion. It was a really enjoyable day. We entertained him to lunch in the boardroom and gave him a tour of the offices and warehouse. We presented him with a coloured cartoon drawing of him booting us out of Woolworth's front door and he posed happily for photographs. He wasn't the ogre I'd remembered but I still couldn't bring myself to call him by his first name. He was Mr Green!

12

Killing the Sacred Cows

In late 1992 I heard that Littlewoods stores were closing down their food operation and were looking for food retailers to bid for the space. If they weren't able to conclude a deal they intended to give the space back to textiles. I thought this presented a great opportunity and envisaged Iceland running a kind of 'poor man's Marks & Spencer' food hall operation out of Littlewoods. Bernie and I went to see the board of Littlewoods on 6 January 1993 and made a presentation outlining our proposal. We had artist's impressions of what the stores would look like, we gave them a list of 48 of their stores where we felt the concept would work and we also gave them a 'roll-out' timetable for doing it. We anticipated spending about £20 million on the project so we suggested a trial first of ten stores before we committed to the full roll-out. We proposed a rent of 4 per cent of sales to include all overheads, including electricity. This would be a very good deal for Iceland but we also convinced them that, apart from the rental income, it would also benefit Littlewoods by increasing the traffic flow in their stores and thereby increase their own sales. We planned to copy the Marks & Spencer food offer with fresh fruit and vegetables, a large range of chilled food, selected groceries and a reduced offering of frozen foods. Littlewoods' directors loved the concept of 'an affordable M&S' as we called it and, apart from asking for an extra half a per cent on the rent, they agreed to our proposal in its entirety.

Following the Bejam takeover, our share price suffered because many people thought we would run out of cash and need a 'rights issue'. Much as we tried to explain that Iceland was a very cash generative business and we would soon repay our borrowings, the idea persisted. A rights issue is when a company raises money by issuing more shares but this has to be done at a discount to the market price. It's not something a company wants to do, as more shares in issue means the company has to increase its profits even more in order to keep its earnings per share growing. The Littlewoods deal looked like it would be very profitable for Iceland and, although we could easily afford the £20 million it would cost us, we also planned to open 60 new Iceland stores at a cost of £30 million and spend another £20 million during the year on building a new distribution centre in Swindon. Our planned capital expenditure for 1993 was likely to be £110 million in total. I was concerned that the City would worry and the suggestion of a rights issue would return to haunt us. The way to kill the idea, I thought, was to have a small rights issue and get it over with. Only three weeks after our first meeting with Littlewoods we announced our deal with them and on 1 February 1993 we issued 4,297,520 new shares in Iceland which raised £27.3 million. The City loved the Littlewoods idea and our share price reached new heights, valuing the company on the stock market at £750 million and making us the 180th largest company in the UK.

The first 'Iceland at Littlewoods' was opened in Wrexham and John Moores, the son of Littlewoods' founder Sir John Moores, attended the opening. Littlewoods was not exactly a stable business. The stores division was on its tenth Managing Director in ten years, Brian Mayo. He was an internal appointment having been moved over from the IT department. He didn't profess to know much about retailing! Sir Desmond Pitcher was Chief Executive of the Littlewoods group but as a privately owned company it must have been a nightmare for him to run, with the constant interference of the family. John Moores was a nice man who for some reason took a shine to me and seemed to regard me as a great retailing expert. Much to the annoyance of some of their senior people he listened to any suggestions I made and I developed a good relationship with him. On that first meeting we walked round the Wrexham store together and I soon realised they hadn't a clue about running a retail business. Littlewoods survived by its own momentum but it wasn't going anywhere. John interfered with the business but he didn't have a commercial bone in his body and was much more interested in his charity work. At that very first meeting an audacious idea began to grow in my mind that maybe we could take over their stores division.

Over the next year I made a great effort to get to know John, I spoke to him often and supported all his charities. Iceland at Littlewoods had proved a great success and John's confidence in me grew. By this time Bob Willett had taken over from Brian Mayo and Barry Dale had taken over from Sir Desmond. I got to know them both and gradually the idea of Iceland buying Littlewoods was introduced and accepted. John's prime concern was that there would be no redundancies, we would keep their name over the stores and we would look after the staff well. A deal was eventually put together and I agreed to buy the Littlewoods chainstore division for £200 million plus £200 million for the freehold properties. I instructed Rothschilds and Littlewoods instructed Kleinworts and a timetable was set. We knew nothing about running downmarket department stores but our whole rationale was that we couldn't do any worse than they were doing! I had agreed with Bob Willett that he would be the Managing Director. He was as keen as I was for it to happen.

Nothing is ever straightforward and at about the same time I was contacted out of the blue by an Irish lawyer and invited to go to Dublin to meet Ben Dunne. Dunnes Stores were a privately owned retail business that dominated food and textiles in the Republic of Ireland and also in Northern Ireland. They were really a 'rip off' of Marks & Spencer and they had copied the M&S store design and layouts exactly. Even their product range was sold under the

'St Bernard' label, which looked uncannily like M&S's 'St Michael'! Ben was a larger than life character who had run the business for years under the watchful eye of his father who had founded it. His father had died and there was rivalry and squabbling between Ben and his brother and sisters. This culminated in him being thrown out of the company after a well publicised incident in America when he was caught threatening to jump off a hotel balcony after a cocaine-fuelled session with a prostitute.

Ben had been paid off by the family but he wanted to buy the company back and he thought we could help him. Ben judged the timing was right and felt that somehow there was a deal to be done with Iceland and Dunnes Stores. Ben had put me up in the Conrad Hotel and given me the presidential suite, which seemed to cover half of the top floor and even contained a full size grand piano. It was all very bizarre. The next day Ben showed me round some of the stores. I decided to tell him about Littlewoods. Potentially, there was the deal of a lifetime to be done here by putting the two companies together. I went to see Russell Edey. He was very suspicious of the whole idea and didn't seem to think that the combination of buying stores in the Irish Republic (Outer Mongolia as far as Russell was concerned) and the name Ben Dunne were somehow institutionally acceptable. Throughout all my dealings with Rothschilds I have found them to be reactive and not proactive. They would always look for reasons why a deal shouldn't be done. It was very frustrating.

I managed to get Russell over to Ireland to meet Ben Dunne and we also instructed Mason Owen & Partners to carry out an 'under cover' valuation of all their properties. I met Ben several times and found him to be hugely entertaining, larger than life and like all his countrymen, full of the 'blarney'! He was a great storyteller and very upfront about his past misdemeanours. He was kidnapped once by the IRA and held to ransom. I'm not sure how easy it would have been to work with him but I enjoyed the adventure, which ran for months but, in the end, just fizzled out.

Problems by now were starting to emerge at Iceland. Although we managed to increase our sales and profits every year and made it look effortless to the outside world, Iceland was in fact a very volatile business and had long since given up the monopoly it once enjoyed in the frozen food market. We only prospered by constantly evolving our formula and always adding new and innovative products to the range. Every year we would have periods where sales were good and then periods where sales were flat, depending on the success of our promotional activity, but we were used to this and learned to live with the constant uncertainty. Iceland was always a business where you felt it could all go wrong tomorrow. In 1993 the supermarkets were introducing cheap 'value packs,' price wars were talked about constantly and we had just lost the 'Keep Sunday Special' campaign.

Sunday trading was not something we wanted. I didn't believe it would be good for business as it would just spread six days' sales over seven days and increase costs. Socially it was also wrong. Retail managers work phenomenal hours as it is and I didn't believe we should follow America and turn Sunday into just another working day. It wasn't done in the rest of Europe and the only beneficiaries would be the superstores and out-of-town retailers. I didn't believe the high street would ever fully open on Sunday but people would drive to superstores and retail parks. Marks & Spencer, John Lewis and Iceland were all opposed to Sunday trading and we funded and supported the 'Keep Sunday Special' campaign. The superstores and DIY operators were already breaking the law and opening. A free vote was allowed in Parliament but, at the last moment, and after a lot of pressure from the big retailers, the shopworkers' union USDAW, which had always opposed Sunday trading, changed their mind on the issue. A young, up-and-coming MP called Tony Blair also did a U-turn on the subject and voted in favour of Sunday trading, having previously been against it. We lost the vote by a whisker.

All this meant that like-for-like sales were slowing down. In 1993 we achieved 7 per cent growth in the first half of the year but only 3 per cent in the second. Our Littlewoods stores were performing well but our core Iceland stores were struggling. The City for some reason had made their mind up that Littlewoods wasn't working and we just couldn't convince them otherwise. The competition from supermarkets was intense but our number one competitor was … Iceland! Our new store opening programme had been so successful and we were opening so many stores that our new stores were taking sales away from existing ones. In many ways all this underlined the need for major diversification. How long could we keep Iceland growing for? We needed another business but we also needed to concentrate our energies on Iceland and get sales growing again.

I knew diversification would be a huge risk. Russell wasn't keen on being involved with Dunnes but by now the clock was ticking with Littlewoods and a timetable for the acquisition had been set. I was still arguing detail with Barry Dale and we had a difference of opinion over how we were going to finance the £200 million of properties in the deal. This wasn't an insurmountable problem but it had become a sticking point and it was with some relief that I took a call from Barry on my car phone, while driving into work one morning, to say the deal was off. I didn't argue with him. I felt we could always resurrect the deal but just at that moment we couldn't handle it, it looked increasingly likely that the City wouldn't like it and we needed to concentrate all our resources on Iceland.

My relationship with Peter Hinchcliffe was at an all-time low. We didn't argue, we just saw very little of each other and didn't speak very much because neither of us had much to say. We had nothing in common and even polite conversation was now a struggle. However, Peter now started working more and more hours in the business. This seemed to coincide with me pulling back from day-to-day operational issues and I became out of touch with what was going on in the stores as Peter became more hands-on. We'd drifted further and further apart in our ideas. Furthermore, factions, cliques and politics had developed within the business. He would be away overnight a lot and made frequent trips to America with other directors to look at IT software (and play golf). Supplier hospitality was abundant and 'jollies' were all some of our directors seemed to care about. I felt the business was getting out of control. I had this uneasy feeling that we were heading for trouble and no one seemed to care. I felt I was losing my influence on the business but I also felt incapable of stamping my authority because I'd lost touch with day-to-day operations. Any issues or concerns that I raised were always explained away as no problem.

I seriously considered leaving the business but our share price had halved over the previous twelve months and I was desperate to try to get the company back on track. The problem, though, was that we needed radical change. In mid-December 1993 my frustration boiled over. I didn't know much about management consultants but I remembered reading about Bain and their involvement in sorting out Guinness years earlier. One particular article which I remembered well gave them a near mythical status and described them as almost clones of each other, all with top university degrees, wearing identical dark suits, with identical haircuts and all in their late twenties. I rang directory enquiries for Bain's number. I asked for the managing partner but was put through to his secretary. She explained Robin Buchanan was in America but was due to fly back on Monday 13th and I could see him as soon as he arrived in the office.

I didn't know what to expect but Robin looked the part. He was probably younger than he looked but had grey hair and wore rimless glasses. He spoke with a 'mid-Atlantic' accent and somehow inspired my confidence. I spent half an hour telling him the Iceland story and he listened intently and never interrupted. At the end of my story I told him I didn't know if we had a problem or not. We were after all about to show an increase in profits that year to over £65 million. Maybe it was just me, but I was uneasy about the future. Robin explained that my approach was not unusual and suggested the way forward would be for him to send a team of people to Deeside to carry out a seven-week 'diagnostic'. Then they would tell us if we had a problem and if we did they would help us fix it. The cost of the seven weeks' work would be £350,000.

I went back to Deeside and told Peter, Dick and Bernie that I

Iceland Electrics.

Buttercup Farm packaging.

Iceland REVIEW

The newsmagazine for customers of ICELAND FROZEN FOODS LTD — **Opening Edition**

At one o'clock Tues 22nd July...

MEET TERRY AT ICELAND

A NEW KIND of food store has come to town. An Iceland Freezer Centre, superbly laid out with scores of clear topped display cabinets, packed with over 600 frozen food products and with its wide aisles and beautifully finished interior, giving shoppers a taste of what 80's shopping really means. Brightly lit and with clearly marked displays it is a joy to visit and the centre is guaranteed to be as enjoyable to shop in as it is economical.

As Britain's largest and fastest growing privately owned frozen food retailer with over 30 stores Icelands buying power is immense, and this is reflected by the fact in the last year the average price throughout their entire range of products, (around 600), only increased by eleven per cent.

Exclusive special offers

Featuring prominently in the centre are pretty well every brand name in frozen food - and a few others. Walls, Lyons Maid, Findus, Birds Eye, Youngs and

Seafoods, Kraft, are among many who regularly promote special offers exclusive with Iceland.

You don't need a freezer to shop at Iceland either. Scores of popular main course convenience foods and vegetables are available in small packs to enable purchases to be made for the 'meal ahead'.

The Iceland policy on pricing is simple - one which makes competition beat a retreat - and customers beat a track to the centre. Come and have a look for yourself. Try Iceland and treat yourself.

TV star opens new freezer centre at Wakefield Rd.

SHOPPING HOURS

Mon-Sat 9am - 5.30pm
Late night Thursday and Friday
till 8.00 pm

Iceland Frozen Foods Ltd.
Wakefield Rd., Huddersfield.

The Iceland approach to freezer centres. Wide aisles, clear-topped cabinets for ease of selection, well-lit and spacious. Everything, in fact, to make shopping a pleasure.

BACK PAGE
£1.18
worth of COUPONS

SPECIAL OPENING OFFERS

Terry Wogan comes to Huddersfield.

In the new Huddersfield store: Bill Woodward, Terry Wogan, Norman Woodward and Alan Birchall.

Iceland Frozen Foods Limited

STAFF DANCE
Saturday, January 12th 1980

To be held at the

Hawarden Suite
Deeside Leisure Centre
Queensferry

8.00 p.m. to 1.00 a.m.

Staff and first guest £1 each
Gentlemen-Dinner jacket or Lounge suit
Free transport provided from all shops and back.

Disco, cabaret, bar, buffet with seasonal fare.
REG COATES EXPERIENCE SHOW BAND
PLUS
BIG E DISCO

Iceland: always up for a good party.

Malcolm and Rhianydd Walker with Peter and Jean Hinchcliffe enjoy a staff party.

ABRIDGED PARTICULARS

Application has been made to the Council of The Stock Exchange for the ordinary shares of Iceland Frozen Foods Holdings plc to be admitted to the Official List

ICELAND

Iceland Frozen Foods Holdings plc

(Incorporated under the Companies Acts 1948 to 1980)

Offer for Sale

by

N.M. Rothschild & Sons Limited

of 3,835,928 ordinary shares of 10p each at a price of 210p per share, payable in full on application

SHARE CAPITAL

Authorised		Issued and to be issued fully paid
£1,700,000	in ordinary shares of 10p each	£1,430,887
£860,000	in 8.4 per cent cumulative redeemable preference shares of £1 each	£860,000
£2,560,000		£2,290,887

Iceland is a multiple retailer of frozen foods and also sells a limited range of groceries, chilled products, domestic freezers and microwave ovens.

Its 81 stores are organised into 9 geographical divisions and each sells a wide range of products covering between 600 and 1,000 lines depending on store size. Iceland operates a central cold storage and warehousing facility and its own distribution fleet.

The application list will open at 10 a.m. on Tuesday, 9th October, 1984 and may be closed at any time thereafter.

Copies of the prospectus (on the terms of which alone applications will be considered), with application forms, are available from:

N.M. Rothschild & Sons Limited,
New Court
St. Swithin's Lane,
London EC4P 4DU.

3 York Street,
Manchester 2.

Hoare Govett Limited,
Heron House,
319/325 High Holborn,
London WC1V 7PB.

Tilney,
385 Sefton House,
Exchange Buildings,
Liverpool L2 3RT.

Barclays Bank PLC, New Issues Department,
P.O. Box 123, Fleetway House, 25 Farringdon Street, London EC4A 4HD.

and from the following branches of **Barclays Bank PLC:-**

Stock Exchange Branch, 8 Angel Court,
Throgmorton Street, London EC2R 8HT.

90 St. Vincent Street,
Glasgow G2 5UQ.

P.O. Box No. 34, 63 Colmore Row, Birmingham B3 2BY.

37 Park Row, Leeds LS1 1HS.

P.O. Box No. 207, 40 Corn Street,
Bristol BS99 7AJ.

P.O. Box No. 107, 4 Water Street,
Liverpool L69 2DU.

P.O. Box No. 69, 121 Queen Street,
Cardiff CF1 1SG.

P.O. Box No. 357, 17 York Street,
Manchester M60 2AU.

35 St. Andrew Square, Edinburgh EH2 2AD.   P.O. Box No. 2, 30 High Street, Southampton SO9 7AB.

The prospectus was advertised in full, with an application form, in the Financial Times and Daily Telegraph on 4th October, 1984.

Iceland goes public.

Malcolm and Peter at the London Stock Exchange on the first day of dealings, October 1984.

Food Factory: it seemed like a good idea at the time.

Hall of history

Manor work helps firm win top award

● *Broxton Old Hall – restoration award for Carnell Green*

THE Carnell Green Partnership of Nottingham has won a major award for the restoration and reconstruction of an important Elizabethan manor house, Broxton Old Hall, near Chester, parts of which date from 1590.

Broxton Old Hall showed the best use of traditional skills and carried off first prize in the Large Country House category of the prestigious Jackson Stops and Staff/Sunday Times Country House Awards, ahead of 133 other entrants.

Occupying a spectacular site in the Bickerton Hills, with extensive views towards Wales, the house was purchased by Malcolm Walker, chairman of Iceland Frozen Foods, in 1985.

Although a listed building, much of the house was in poor repair and had extensive Victorian additions. Chester planning department and conservation office was very enthusiastic at Carnell Green's proposals which involved removing three-quarters of the house and recreating an Elizabethan style manor house of almost 20,000 sq ft.

A showcase of traditional crafts, Broxton Old Hall has a green English oak strutural timber frame with decorative brickwork in two inch Tudor quality bricks from Holland, lead rainwater pipes, handmade leaded glass windows, York stone flagged floors and extensive use of English oak for joinery work.

Carved

The stonework used in the plinths, window and door surrounds has been hand-carved in local red sandstone.

Although 16th century traditional construction has been faithfully followed, the house has been designed for 20th century living and features an indoor swimming pool in a Florentine Baroque style, an orangery, garage block for four cars, all served by "state of the art" heating, ventilating, electrical, audio and communications services.

Outside, the extensive grounds have been landscaped to include a gazebo, lake, wild flower meadow and a large traditional barn.

Broxton Old Hall, bought by Malcolm and Rhianydd in 1985.

A Bejam store.

Malcolm making the phone call to tell Bejam Iceland is bidding for them, 28 October 1988.

Bejam
Chairman
John Apthorp.

In the bunker at Rothschild's:
Russell Edey and Dick Kirk share a joke.

HRH The Princess Royal opens Iceland's 500th store in Clapham on Red Nose Day, 1991.

Dumbstruck by meeting Princess Diana to receive an award for Iceland's CFC recycling initiative.

Malcolm and Peter reunited with A.V. Green, who booted them out of Woolworth's in February 1971.

Iceland at Littlewoods.

Malcolm collecting his CBE in 1995.
L to R: Richard, Rhianydd, Malcolm, Caroline and Alexia Walker.

wanted Bain to come in to the business. Bernie supported me, Dick was undecided but Peter was dead against it. I could normally get my own way at Iceland on just about anything but the Bain issue proved a real problem. Peter just didn't want it to happen and put every obstacle in the way.

Late one night, after a session in the pub with Peter and Dick, Peter finally agreed. I asked him why he had objected for so long and his reply was prophetic: 'Because things will never be the same again.' Next morning Peter was waiting for me in the office. He'd changed his mind. He'd obviously been up half the night and prepared sheets and sheets of foolscap paper, full of arguments as to why it was a bad idea. It was too late. I made the call to Robin.

The Bainies arrived in late January and did indeed all look the same. They took over several offices and worked every day until the early hours of the morning, crunching numbers and analysing the business. They were briefed to look at every aspect of the business but the one thing they didn't want to be involved in was commenting on management ability or structure. Nevertheless, our senior executives and directors sensed change and there was great apprehension in the business from the day they arrived. Since the mid-1970s if you asked any of our management team to describe the management style and culture at Iceland, they would all have come up with the same answer: 'We are young, lean, hungry, aggressive and ambitious.' They would still have said those same words now but they were meaningless. We were overpaid, overcar'd, overweight and complacent. The hunger had gone.

When we took over Bejam, John Apthorp knew what was wrong with his company but he couldn't kill his own sacred cows. He hadn't the energy left. The day Bain walked through our door I woke up. I knew what had to be done. We had exactly the same management team in place now that we had had in the mid-1970s. Back then we turned over £5 million per year in sales, now it was £1.5 billion. Not surprisingly the company had outgrown some of our people (even me probably) but we were all still in place. Before Bain had finished their diagnostic we had acted. We had a radical appraisal of all our management team and fired a number of senior people including several directors. Peter and Dick were very much involved in the decisions about who should go but I had to do the deed. It was the hardest thing I'd ever had to do. Many of the people we were getting rid of had helped to build the business but were now holding us back. We owed them loyalty but I felt it was about the survival of the business and ultimately everybody else's job security. We looked after everybody as best we could; we paid them lots of guilt money and kept our eye on them to ensure they all got other jobs.

Bain finished their diagnostic and they presented a whole list of problems they thought the company faced but at the same time proposed a load of other work they could do for us which, they assured us, would turn round the fortunes of the company. The next lot of work would cost us £1.5 million but we were hooked.

We had made some progress in addressing our management problems but Peter and I still had fundamental differences in ideas and style and this would not be resolved while we were both there. We needed clarity of leadership and I believed one of us had to go. I held the title of Chairman and Chief Executive and Peter was Joint Managing Director with Dick Kirk. I was regaining my confidence, Peter was on the back foot and at a dinner to discuss the future he asked me if I would ever split my role with him. I said I wouldn't until I was confident we were back on the right track. By now Peter was spending more and more time away from the business and it didn't take too much effort to persuade him he should leave. I was sad the way our partnership had ended but it had simply died over time as opposed to being killed in some dramatic way!

At least I could now look forward to a period in the business without the politics. In one way I envied Peter being out of the daily hassle and aggravation of a business we were struggling to keep afloat but, in another way, I was relieved at having a clear run. Peter officially resigned at the end of 1994 and then carried on for another eighteen months as a non-executive director although I saw very little of him. He has since made a great success of growing a hotel chain. In spite of all our problems we kept profits moving ahead and reported a figure for the year of £70.2 million. Sales were nearly flat, however, and we knew we wouldn't be able to go on squeezing profits much longer unless we could get sales growing again. This was a real problem with 2 per cent deflation in food prices and unprecedented competitor price activity.

One brighter interlude occurred one morning in mid-November. I was looking through the post at home before leaving for work and I saw an envelope marked 'The Prime Minister's Office'. Somehow I guessed what was inside it so I walked away from the hubbub in the kitchen to open it. 'The Prime Minister is minded to recommend that you be awarded the honour of Commander of the Order of the British Empire ... please inform us if you would be prepared to accept.' As if I would turn it down! I'd not the slightest idea that this would be forthcoming but a few years earlier I had been 'sounded out' by an official from the Welsh Office who obviously planned to put my name forward then. It was a 'coded' type of conversation but I suggested that whatever was being put forward should include Peter as we were partners. I never heard any more.

The announcement was made on New Year's Day and the award ceremony was held in May at Buckingham Palace. Prince Charles carried out the investiture. You are officially only allowed to bring two guests but fortunately Iceland had sponsored The Duke of Edinburgh Award Scheme that year and I was able to wangle extra tickets so Ranny and all three children could be there. While waiting to go in you are held in roped off 'pens' in an anteroom. CBEs, MBEs, OBEs and Knights, all separated according to rank. His Grace the Duke of Westminster was there at the same time. He lives in Chester and asked me over to chat. 'You outrank me,' he quipped. 'I've only got an OBE!'

We went to the Savoy Hotel for a celebration lunch afterwards. Just the family but I also invited Jill McWilliam, our director of public relations, formerly from Bejam. I suspected she might have had something to do with it all!

Mark Hudson was the Bain senior manager, and later partner, responsible for the Iceland project. I rated him and all the Bain people very highly. They were doing a lot of work on product strategy and also developing a system of 'supplier partnering'. This was something we were convinced would put several percentage points on our profit margin. It involved our buyers understanding our suppliers' manufacturing processes better and being open about raw material costs. The idea was we would work together with suppliers to lower costs rather than the traditional buyer/supplier adversarial approach. I saw a lot of Robin Buchanan and regarded him as a wise 'sage' who would advise, guide and counsel me. I'd introduced Robin to Russell Edey, who regarded him totally differently. Russell's view of management consultants was characteristically cynical. 'They are past masters of getting inside a Chief Executive's trousers and once they're in a company you can never get rid of them!' On one occasion I'd invited them both on a shooting party and over dinner they both put on an amazing display of petty sniping and petulance with each other to the great amusement of all the other guests.

Over one late dinner with Robin and his colleague, Stan Miranda, Robin was explaining the benefits of networking. 'There's a retail mafia out there and it's all based in Marylebone Road, London, and you're not part of it, you are isolated and remote up here.' The general thrust of the conversation was that our senior people would be more effective if they mixed more with other business people. 'Why aren't you encouraging your directors to take up non-executive positions with other companies? It would broaden their outlook.' When, by coincidence, a director from Rothschilds rang me soon after to explain they were looking for a non-executive director for a private retail business they had an investment in, called Peacocks, I said 'I've got just the man!' I went to see Dick Kirk. 'Look, you need to broaden your interests, I've got you an interesting part-time job.' It was an offer I later came to regret.

I seriously wondered whether Iceland had outgrown my own capabilities. Our original management team, like me, had no great educational qualifications. We survived and were held together by enthusiasm and experience. The Bainie guys were the brainiest people I'd ever met and Iceland was becoming an increasingly complex business to run. Once upon a time I could do every job in the business and there was no job that I hadn't done. Now there were large parts of the business I just didn't understand. Peter was gone and I was on my own. I needed a successor and although Dick was very much involved in running the business, particularly retail operations, he was, like me, full of 'old ideas'. We needed some new blood. Dick agreed with me, perhaps it was time for the next generation.

We instructed Whitehead Mann, the headhunters, to find us a new team of people. On my first phone call Anna Mann, the boss, said in a posh voice, 'We are very expensive, you know.' I thought this was a strange reaction to a potential new client but perhaps she thought a northern company like us couldn't afford their rates! I recruited several new key people, high flyers, MBAs and rocket scientists! I also poached Mark Hudson from Bain as my successor. That went down like a lead balloon with Robin. I'd known Mark for over a year and although we interviewed many other people (including Angus Monro who later went to Matalan) I thought Mark was a low-risk choice, as he knew the company inside out by that time.

Gradually we pulled the new team together and, although our sales performance wasn't getting any better, I started to feel more confident about the future except for one small incident which I tried to put out of my mind. Mark Hudson joined us on Monday, 22 May 1995 and on Wednesday I went to sit with him in his office to see what his plans were. He told me he'd prepared a list of his top priorities and pulled out a sheet of paper with at least a hundred different items on it. I went cold and felt a sudden shiver of alarm. What was the man doing?

During 1995 we opened our 750th store in Glengormley, Scotland. Littlewoods had yet another change of policy and decided they wanted some of our food space back to extend textiles. There was constant horse-trading going on as we endlessly swapped stores.

They were a nightmare to deal with. Barry Dale had left Littlewoods as Group CEO and surprised everybody by announcing he was going to put in an offer to buy the company. The Littlewoods family extended to over 30 members and shareholders. They received no dividend and many were rich on paper, with their Littlewoods shares, but poor in reality. The family was riven by squabbles and politics and many shareholders would no doubt be keen to cash in. All the same, Barry's approach was unwelcome to the more senior members of the family and no one really believed he could raise the money.

I had a call from Victor Blank, now Sir Victor and until recently Chairman of Lloyds TSB. Victor was Chairman of Charterhouse bank at the time and his claim to fame that made his fortune was putting together the deal to buy Woolworth's from its American parent. He put Sir Geoff Mulcahy in place to run the company. I knew Victor, as Charterhouse owned Tilney, our joint brokers. Victor was a gentle giant and a nice man whom I liked a lot. He told me he acted for Sir David Alliance, who among other things was the majority shareholder in N Brown, a mail order company. He said he was putting a syndicate together to buy Littlewoods and asked if I was interested. The idea was to bid £1 billion for the company and split it between Iceland who would take the stores, N Brown who would take the mail order business and Ladbrokes who would take Littlewoods pools. Of course I was interested!

Even though I liked and trusted Victor, he was acting for David Alliance and I had to have my own representation. I went to see Russell Edey.

As usual Russell gave me a list of reasons as to why this idea wouldn't work, which really boiled down to the fact that it wasn't his idea! Russell obviously knew everyone involved and in particular he knew David Alliance and warned me that he was a tough guy to deal with and a hard negotiator. David was incredibly wealthy, entirely through his own efforts having arrived in this country as a child, a penniless refugee. He said David would never stop negotiating right to the end of a deal and would move the goalposts at every meeting. He did it for sport! I had many meetings with David to put the deal together, which provided rich entertainment. He proved as good as Russell's prediction and started each meeting with a different recollection of what had been agreed at the last one. Russell and Victor were even more childish in each other's company than Russell had been with Robin Buchanan. At one dinner at the Four Seasons Hotel, Russell was baiting Victor in the most appalling way but David was preoccupied with his own thoughts. Suddenly he looked at me and out of the blue, in his heavily accented voice, he said, 'Have you ever seen a cat playing with a mouse?' 'Pardon?' I said. 'The way the cat catches the mouse and then lets it go, catches it and lets it go, catches it and lets it go. Why do you think it does that?' 'Er, I dunno,' I confessed. David beamed, 'Because he enjoys it,' was his reply!

I knew that if we managed to pull off this deal we would need a stronger management team than we currently possessed and this fact was not lost on Russell. I decided the deal was potentially big enough to attract some serious talent so I made two approaches to people I considered were 'heavy hitters'. To my surprise they were both interested on a 'provisional' basis, so I proposed that they should run Littlewoods as a partnership and promised them a share of the equity.

I'd met Alan Smith when he was a main board director of Marks & Spencer but he had now moved to Kingfisher as Chief Executive. It was common knowledge he was unhappy there. Geoff Mulcahy was a difficult man to work for and there was widely reported friction between them. I approached Alan while he was still at Kingfisher and we met several times to discuss the deal. He left Kingfisher soon after our first meeting and therefore became available but I think his experience there had knocked his confidence. M&S was a 'well-oiled machine' at that time and running any other company was an uncomfortable step into the real world! I think he doubted his own ability. On one occasion when we met at his house he explained that his management style was not hands-on. He said, 'You see, at

Marks & Spencer, someone in my role was more like a Cardinal in the Church! I'm more of a strategist.' I was still keen for him to join us and got to know him well. He was still highly regarded at that time although since then he has made a habit of becoming involved with companies in trouble.

Peter Davis, now Sir Peter and later Chief Executive of Sainsbury's, had a few years earlier invited me to join a government quango, which he chaired, called 'The National Council for Education and Training Targets'. It was mind-numbingly boring but we met every month to agree on the national target levels we were charged with setting for the number of people who would pass their A-levels, GCSEs and NVQs. It all seemed a bit pointless to me (as if setting the targets would make any difference to the number of people passing their exams!) but I was in good company. The other council members were all serious academics with Carol Galley from Mercury as the only other non-boffin. I felt quite at home with my O-level in woodwork! I did get to know Peter Davis quite well. He was the Chief Executive of Reed Elsevier at the time and our meetings took place in their offices. Peter lost his job soon afterwards so I approached him with the Littlewoods proposal. We had several meetings which included a trip to an Iceland store. At least Russell was impressed with my headhunting abilities and Peter Davis was an inspired choice if the deal had come off. He later went on to run the Prudential.

I worked very hard in trying to make the deal happen this time. I shuttled between David Alliance and Victor and Russell. I courted John Moores and went to see his niece Donatella, who had a big shareholding. She promised her support. We motivated the Littlewoods family into action and they brought in a financial adviser to consider the interests of all the family. The end result was a big family meeting and a vote on the future. Should they sell or should they continue to run the company as a private business? In the end they voted to keep the company private but they did make a lot of changes. They started to pay dividends and adopted a more professional management structure, which reduced family interference. However, our interest had been leaked to the press and we had to make a statement in our next annual report giving the reasons for our approach. We couldn't say we thought it was because our existing business had run out of steam!

13
Losing Sleep

When the inevitable happens, it's sometimes a huge relief. So it proved to be in July 1996 when we warned of our first ever drop in profits in the company's 25-year history. The first half of the year was a complete nightmare. I was desperately trying to turn round our slowing sales but nothing seemed to work. Morale was at an all-time low and good people in the business were looking elsewhere for new careers.

In April Dick Kirk returned from holiday and telephoned me to ask if we could meet for dinner. It didn't take long for him to get to the point. He told me he felt he was becoming stale at Iceland and needed a new challenge. Mark Hudson had effectively taken over as Managing Director and Dick told me he felt he was redundant. This was partly true but I wanted Dick to help me in a more strategic role and in any event I was already having uneasy feelings about Mark Hudson. Dick was very high-profile within Iceland and our store staff and managers saw him as the boss. If Dick left it would be seen as final confirmation by a great number of our people that the company was now beyond all hope. I was devastated by this news, which was just what I didn't need at that time. I asked Dick where he was going and he told me to Peacocks. That was the company where I had suggested him for a non-executive role the year before!

I couldn't really blame Dick, he was looking after himself but I still saw his resignation as 'jumping ship' and the ultimate betrayal at my moment of need. He'd been handsomely rewarded during his time in Iceland and, apart from his salary, the shares Peter and I had personally given him and the options he'd cashed amounted to £3.7 million. For the first time in my life I had sleepless nights which were caused by worrying about the business. I seemed to have a constant knot of anxiety in my stomach.

I was furious with James Stewart at Rothschilds. A few years earlier I had been invited to become an adviser to one of their venture capital funds. We met every few months to discuss various investments they wanted to make in private companies. My suggestion to Rothschilds that Dick should join the board of Peacocks, one of their investments, was meant to be of help to them. I didn't expect them to repay my help by poaching him as their new Managing Director without even a phone call to me first. I telephoned Russell and told him what I thought of their ethics but the damage was done.

I had to appoint a new Stores Director to replace Dick and offered the job to his number two, David Brown. I then tried to do as much damage limitation as I could in respect of staff morale. In reality Dick was soon forgotten but our sales problem continued to get worse and in any retail business morale is always driven by sales. I was getting increasingly desperate and decided to launch a very aggressive price cutting campaign which we called 'Price Check'. We slashed hundreds of prices which we expected would cost us 5 per cent off our profit margin but we thought it would give sales a kick-start. Unfortunately our in-store marketing and launch advertising was half-hearted due to lack of funds and also because Andy Brent, our new Marketing Director, was not fully bought-in to this kind of activity. Coming from Procter & Gamble, he was more interested in 'brand advertising'. All we succeeded in doing was reducing our sales by the 5 per cent that our prices were reduced by!

I had handed over the running of our weekly management meeting to Mark Hudson and one of the first things he did was to take the board away overnight for a brainstorming session, to come up with new ideas and also to set down the strategic direction for the company. On his return I was told the trip had been a great success and their prime achievement had been to set a new profit target for the company of £100 million by the end of 1999. I thought he was bonkers. It was becoming increasingly obvious we would have trouble hitting this year's forecast. Any fool could set a target but I was more interested in how we were going to achieve it. I remembered a few years earlier having a conversation with a former secretary of mine about her divorce from her first husband. I asked her when she realised she had made a mistake by marrying him. She told me I might find it hard to believe but she swore it was when they were having their wedding photographs taken! I remembered my conversation with Mark about his priority list on the third day after he'd started.

Just before Easter, Tesco had really worried me by launching a major 'customer service' campaign. They claimed they were putting 5,000 extra staff into their stores who would wear distinctive blue waistcoats and their sole job would be to help pack customers' bags at the checkouts and push their trolleys to the car park. They even promised that if there was one customer in front of you at the checkout they would open another one. 'Store wars' were now moving way beyond just price. We had recently launched our own customer service campaign but Tesco blew us out of the water.

I went into Tesco in Chester on Easter Saturday and saw with dismay the 'bluecoats' in action. There appeared to be dozens of them. I then went across the road to Iceland and wondered what on earth we could do to counteract the superstores' growing dominance. Perhaps it was too late and, in our company life cycle, we were now in unstoppable and terminal decline. Bag packers were hardly an innovation but they were a cost we just couldn't even contemplate. If we put just one extra full-time person in all our 760 stores it would knock over £7 million off our profits. How could we ever hope to compete? I was chatting to one of our staff members in the Chester store and I asked her if she thought it would increase sales if we employed bag packers. She didn't know but she knew customers would like it. Our Chester store was a flagship building we had inherited from Bejam. The sales in that store were about company average at £32,000 per week and declining. I reasoned that since Chester was our home town, and had visitors from head office in there every day, it should take £100,000 per week. Chester should be run at a loss if necessary but it should have every innovation and experiment going in order to generate sales.

I decided I would experiment with a bag packer, or even two, in our Chester store and see what it did for sales. The trouble was I knew that, whatever our intention, as soon as any head office visitors had gone the store manager would use the bag packer as just another staff member and take them away from the checkout for more important duties. For that reason I suggested they should wear a red sweatshirt and red baseball cap so they were easily identified. We would recruit someone to start immediately. I then started to wonder what else we could put into Chester that would help customer service. The bag packer would carry goods to the customer's car but what about offering to deliver it home for them if they didn't have a car? A stupid idea but why not? That had to be the ultimate customer service idea that even Tesco couldn't match but it would cost a fortune. Still, it didn't matter. We should do everything we could in the Chester store at whatever cost, just to see what it would do for sales. Why not install a mini-kitchen in the centre of the sales floor and offer product sampling? I went back to the office after Easter with a list of daft ideas. The first 'redcap' started a few days later.

Our company Annual General Meeting was held on 16 May. It was the last time I saw Peter Hinchcliffe until years later. He was still a non-executive director and he came up to attend the AGM. Afterwards I took him to see the Ellesmere Port store which we had set up early for the Price Check campaign, which was due to go live on the 20th. On the way there Peter asked me about Mark Hudson and the £100 million profit target. My embarrassment was obvious and when we saw the poor marketing effort in the store for Price

Check it didn't get any less. It was obvious from what we saw that the price cutting campaign wasn't going to work, but I was still hoping against hope. I told Peter about the home delivery idea in Chester and this probably just confirmed to him he'd made the right decision to leave the business!

In order to operate the home delivery service we had to find a miniature refrigerated vehicle. We had 20-ton trucks and 40-ton trucks but I wanted something the size of a little van, smaller even than a Transit van. It didn't exist, so I got our technical people to buy a small Vauxhall van and adapt it. It had to be insulated inside, have a special door fitted and a fridge unit installed on the roof. This took several weeks and was the subject of great ridicule and humour among my colleagues. I considered whether to charge for the new home delivery service but decided to offer it free within a ten-mile radius of the store, provided customers spent £25. The idea was customers would do their shopping in the normal way but then leave their bags at the checkout and we would deliver them to their home at an agreed time.

The redcap bag packer had no noticeable impact on sales during the weeks he was there, but I then transferred him to driving the home delivery van. We launched the service with an advert in the local paper and posters on the shop window. The result was immediate and undeniable. Sales increased 10 per cent in the first week. I couldn't believe it had worked so well but I thought it would be costing us a fortune. Apart from the cost of the newspaper advert (the *Chester Chronicle* is very expensive) it looked as if it might be viable. Customers were spending on average £40, not the £25 minimum and, while we offered a ten-mile delivery radius, the average journey was actually only about one-and-a-half miles. I decided to extend the test and chose Portsmouth as the test area. The reason for this was that we had about twelve stores in that area, all covered by one local newspaper, which meant advertising would be very cost effective.

On 6 June I flew down to Portsmouth and held a store managers' meeting. I explained about the Chester home delivery experiment and the trial I wanted to do in their area. I told them how important it was and asked for their personal support and enthusiasm for the project. We bought another twelve vans and had them converted and recruited twelve redcaps as drivers. We invited the redcaps up to Chester for a two-day training and motivation session. They collected their vans and drove them back to Portsmouth. Apart from one driver filling his petrol van with diesel on the way back it all went well. Maybe our training scheme was missing something! In addition to offering a home delivery service in Portsmouth, I planned to offer a telephone ordering service by printing a price list in the local paper. Customers would telephone their local store with the order. We launched the service and it immediately increased sales by about 12 per cent. Operationally it was a nightmare. We had no proper systems or procedures, storage of customers' shopping bags that were awaiting delivery was a problem, and separating the temperatures of ambient, chilled and frozen goods was difficult. Ice cream was arriving at the customers' homes melted and lemonade frozen solid! Nevertheless I knew we were onto a winner. We had to refine our systems, analyse the impact on profitability and then move to a bigger trial.

However, none of this could save us from the final realisation that we wouldn't be able to meet the City's profit expectations for the year. Over the years we'd had lean periods before and always been able to pull a rabbit out of the hat, but not this time. The price cutting campaign had not worked and had seriously damaged our profit margin. On Wednesday, 17 July we issued a profit warning and watched our share price collapse from about £1.60, where it had hovered for the past three years, to an eventual low of 73p. This meant Iceland was valued on the stock market at only £160 million but our profits (we eventually reported £56.2 million, down 22 per cent on the previous year) plus our depreciation (that's money we make as profit but is set aside for future equipment replacement) of £46 million meant we still generated over £100 million in cash.

You could buy the company with only eighteen months' cash

generation but our very low share price indicated something more fundamentally wrong. The retail analysts had long since felt Iceland had passed its sell-by date and couldn't see any reason for us to exist. With superstores catering for one market and discounters the other, where did we fit in? What was the point of a specialist frozen food retailer in today's high street? Our unbroken 25-year record of profit increases counted for little and, now that had gone, the stock market saw our continued decline as inevitable. Three years earlier all the superstores had reported a drop in their profits. That was out of the way and now forgotten. If only our profit warning had happened then, we'd have been lost in the pack but we were on our own now and highly visible. The financial press were savage in their reporting with the headlines predictable: 'Profits freeze at Iceland.' 'Iceland chills the City.'

In spite of this, I felt a great sense of relief. I'd worried for three years that this would happen and now that it had we could finally take a longer-term view of things. We could start spending money again! In our efforts to prop up profits we had cut down on store maintenance and made a lot of penny-pinching decisions over the past couple of years that were wrong for the business. Now we increased our staff training budget. We started painting the stores again. We started refurbishing staff canteens, something we could never have contemplated spending money on before. Our store refit programme was accelerated and we finished the year with 131 stores refurbished and 31 new store openings (hardly a company going out of business). We built a new product-testing kitchen next to our store in Chester and we started a determined and long-term project to upgrade the quality of our own-label food products.

There was a different atmosphere among the board now the pressure was off but there was still widespread gloom in the stores. Sales were getting worse and our staff were bound to be affected by the bad press comments and the low share price. David Brown, our Stores Director, decided we needed a store managers' conference to raise morale. Our half-yearly results would be announced in late September and we knew the press would just rerun all the bad news.

We decided the best time for the conference, and when it would be most needed, would be a few days after the results announcement. We settled on 2 October. David put the conference together with Alan Wight, my PA's husband, who ran his own production company.

We'd never had a full-scale conference before, as the cost would be enormous. Involving all 760 store managers, plus area managers and field staff, meant 1,000 people would have to be transported and accommodated overnight. We held it in the International Convention Centre in Birmingham and managers arrived for coffee from 9.30am onwards having travelled that morning from all over the UK. As people gathered you could sense the gloom and almost resentment that we were wasting money on such an event when the company was in such trouble. Everyone filed into the auditorium at 10.30am in a sombre mood.

The content of the conference was almost irrelevant. It just had to be an evangelical, morale-boosting event to give our staff confidence and let them know we still believed we had a future. And it was! We started with the news headlines from the previous week about our profit collapse but then gradually built up the tension through the day using audio visual, powerful music, special lighting effects and rabble-rousing speeches from the management team. The result was electrifying. At the end of the day our staff were cheering and convinced they worked for the best and most successful company in Britain. We had dinner and a big party that night and then next morning 1,000 supercharged managers and staff went back to their stores ready to conquer the world. It worked. That day, I believe, was the turning point in our fortunes.

Home delivery still looked like the most likely way to turn round our sales problem and I decided on another, larger trial before risking a national roll-out. Advertisers often use the Tyne Tees television region as a 'test area' because it's a discreet as well as discrete geographic location. I was paranoid about keeping the home delivery project secret. I didn't want the analysts to find out until I had proved it would work but, more importantly, I didn't want any of our competitors to copy the idea. Iceland had 35 stores in the Tyne Tees region and we decided to launch home delivery there and support it with a TV advert instead of local press. Telephone shopping was proving more difficult to manage so we decided to continue developing that service in Portsmouth and, if we could get it to work, we could add it later as a second phase. The launch was as successful in Tyne Tees as in Chester and Portsmouth. We put 12 per cent on our sales overnight. Sales in Chester and Portsmouth were still strong and even starting to grow more as the service attracted new customers. We'd improved our systems by now and even developed bigger and better delivery vehicles.

I was still preoccupied with our share price, which stuck stubbornly at around 73p. Sentiment for Iceland in the City was at an all-time low and I couldn't see it improving. The analysts had written us off. Bernie was the only other director with a shareholding and I discussed with him the idea of trying to take the company private.

Apart from Richard Branson and a couple of other cases where they still owned a big slug of their company shares, this hadn't been done very often at that time. Bernie and I now owned 17 million shares between us, which accounted for just over 6 per cent of the company. It would be a tall order. I invited the Royal Bank of Scotland to come and talk about the idea and was greatly encouraged when they indicated they might lend us the money (£165 million) provided we could raise about £40 million in new equity on top of our own shareholding. This appeared to be not too difficult but in reality it proved impossible. We saw several bankers and venture capitalists and many of them were not interested because of the poor City sentiment for Iceland but some of them were also openly hostile to the very idea. To take a public company private in 1996 was considered to be somehow immoral and cheating the shareholders! The directors would be suspected of trying to buy the company 'on the cheap'. How times change, now it's all the fashion.

Another problem was that whoever was going to invest £40 million in the company would need an 'exit'. How were they going to get their money back? Normally their exit would be a flotation or a sale but in this case we would want to take the company private to keep it private. We explained we had a brilliant cash flow and it would be very easy simply to repay the money over, say, five years. The trouble is, a venture capitalist expects a 30 per cent compound return on his investment and the numbers just wouldn't allow for that. They were too greedy. We tried for months but maybe we just didn't try hard enough. Although morale was getting better and home delivery looked promising I wasn't totally certain, in my heart of hearts, that we could sort the company out. Our final 'pitch' was to 3i in Manchester. They had a couple of independent advisers present at the meeting but, although 3i also turned us down, Paul Deakin, one of the advisers, came to see us with an idea. Paul had worked for Rothschilds some years earlier and now worked for a much smaller operation called Hawkpoint.

Paul's idea was that we could increase our own stake in the business by the company buying back and cancelling a big chunk of its own shares, say as much as 50 per cent. That would then have the effect of doubling our own stake. I explained the idea wasn't really attractive as, even if our stake doubled, it still wouldn't be large enough for me to feel like the owner again and we would still be a public company. The more we talked, however, the more the idea developed. If we halved the number of shares in the company the earnings per share would double. In theory that should double the share price! Suddenly this seemed like a good idea, although we had bought back 10 per cent of our own shares already, in spring 1996, as a 'demonstration of confidence' and also to increase earnings. It had had nil effect on the share price. This was different: buying back such a large amount of shares had only ever been done once before and it would be bound to have a much more dramatic result. A company normally has powers to buy back up to 10 per cent of its own shares but, for something on this scale, it would have to be done as a major capital reconstruction that would need the approval of not only all the shareholders but also the Court.

We decided to go with it. Organising the bank borrowings was not easy and Barclays took some convincing at the highest level. In the end we decided to buy back 35 per cent of our shares which, on top of the 10 per cent we'd bought earlier, would nearly halve the number of shares in issue. As usual, an army of advisers was involved: Herbert Smith, our expensive City lawyers, Rothschilds and Hoare Govett (or ABN Amro as they were now called) and of course Paul Deakin who'd had the idea in the first place. After a big row with Hoare Govett we fixed the offer price for the buyback at £1.05, which I thought was far too generous as the shares were still trading at 73p. Russell Edey made it very clear that the directors would not be allowed to sell any of their own shares as it would not show confidence in the company and might look like we were only doing it to get a higher price for ourselves! We didn't want to sell anyway.

This was an innovative step for the company to take. It gave shareholders a chance to sell at a price higher than the market and, for those who stayed in, we were at least doing something to improve earnings in the medium term even though some of the immediate benefit would be eaten up by higher interest charges on our increased borrowings. We decided to announce the capital reconstruction at the same time as our 1996 year-end announcement on 12 March 1997. We would have to confirm our first ever profit drop at that meeting but that was expected anyway. We also intended to announce our home delivery success and company-wide roll-out at the same time. This really would be a new beginning for the company.

Many of our staff had share options in the company, which were issued at £1.80 and even £2. Now the share price was languishing at 73p these options were worthless as option holders only benefit by the increase in share price over the issue price. I asked if it was possible to cancel these options and issue new ones at the current price. Our staff had a lot of hard work in front of them; I wanted to retain our good people and the options needed to be a real incentive. Options take three years to mature anyway before they can be cashed so if new options were issued they would have to start the three years all over again. It seemed a fair request and after a lot of discussion with all our advisers it was agreed. Russell again had a strong view on things looking right and said that, since the share price was expected to rise after the buyback, any new options issued for main board directors including myself should not be issued for three months to allow the price to settle down at a new higher level. I wasn't bothered, I'd never had any share options anyway until recently. Since I'd always had a large shareholding in the company I'd never even asked for any for the first twelve years after we floated.

The March analysts' meeting was as upbeat as I could make it. We'd grown sales and profits for 25 years in a row, we'd had only one setback, and now here was the solution for our recovery ... home delivery! At first the analysts were quite receptive, the idea of home delivery appealed but they'd misunderstood. As soon as the penny dropped that I wasn't talking about telephone shopping they were horrified. 'You mean, you have to go into the store and do the shopping yourself and then you deliver it? What's the point of that?' They could understand their own situation – married probably to another busy professional, eating out a lot, cash-rich time-poor – the ability to order groceries by telephone would appeal to them. 'Look,' I tried to explain, '60 per cent of UK households have only one car or no car. If they have only one car, the old man takes it to work, so in the real world like Oldham and Wigan the average housewife goes shopping on the bus. Home delivery is a godsend; their only other alternative is to visit the superstore in the family car on Sunday. It's how we can fight back.' It didn't cut any ice. They'd made up their minds and there was no shifting them. They couldn't understand the arithmetic of home delivery anyway and thought it was a recipe for bankruptcy. I was still reluctant to give away too much information, even to the analysts, as some of them were bound to pass it on to our competitors and I didn't explain about the higher than expected spend and shorter journey times. It didn't help that for the year so far sales were only half a per cent up. The bit about 60 per cent of British housewives not having access to a car Monday to Friday I'd made up but I found myself repeating it quite a lot and it's funny how since then it has turned into one of those statistics I've seen requoted a hundred times! Nevertheless, it's probably not far off the mark.

Our shares rose to about £1 on the news of the share buyback. It was generally welcomed, except by one analyst called Frank Davidson. His reasoning was that the company had no future and we would have too much debt after the buyback so he advised his clients to reject the proposal. I was stunned and couldn't understand his logic. If you thought the company had no future surely you should vote for the offer anyway so you could sell at least some of your shares at a higher price? Bernie and I went down to London to see him. I really didn't want him to put out a note with that recommendation, as I was worried about the effect it might have. We worked very hard to persuade him but I was constantly undecided whether to carry on sucking up to him or throttle him. He didn't change his recommendation but the capital reconstruction went through with virtually every shareholder except Bernie and me tendering the maximum number of shares to be bought back at £1.05. On the afternoon before trading started with the new share structure, I was sitting in the offices of our financial PR company Hudson Sandler and speculating what the share price might rise to the next day. I thought maybe £1.20 or £1.30 and persuaded my PA, who was sitting next to me, to buy some of our shares that day at £1. You can sell them straight away and make a profit, I explained. If they go down I'll pay you for them. Trading started next day and the shares slowly sank back to 73p. I had to give her a cheque for £10,000!

In spite of the minor problem of the stock market valuing our company for petty cash, things were actually looking up. Home delivery was being rolled out across the country by TV region and was working miracles for sales. It was quite a logistical challenge. We had ordered over 1,000 refrigerated vans made to our own specification. This was probably one of the largest orders for vans ever placed. We had to recruit 1,000 new drivers and set up all the systems and controls to run a complicated home delivery operation from the stores.

Our confidence was growing, our product quality was improving and we'd started a 'legendary customer service' campaign, which we were determined to drive forward to the extent that our customers really noticed a difference. Success feeds on itself. The more sales improved the more morale improved, the more we were prepared to try new ideas which all seemed to work. I went to America to visit Schwan's, a privately owned and very secretive company that ran a national frozen food home delivery service. The big difference was it was based on 'van sales' but the principle was the same: frozen food melts and it's better being delivered to your door by a refrigerated vehicle! In Germany, 40 per cent of frozen food is home delivered. I copied lots of ideas and became more convinced than ever that we were on the right track.

We had also diversified by buying Woodward's. A frozen food wholesale company that supplied the catering trade, Woodward's was based in Rhyl and was run by Jeremy Woodward. He owned the company with his Dad Norman, one of our original partners in the mid-1970s. Frozen food wholesaling was dominated by Brake Brothers in the UK but we reckoned we had the buying scale and muscle to start a new and complementary business to Iceland that could compete with Brakes. We left Jeremy in charge of the business and felt he would be capable of growing the company with our support. Woodward's was turning over £12 million per year in sales when we bought it and only three years later this had grown, partly organically and partly by acquisition, to nearly £100 million. The decision-making process to buy Woodward's caused a lot of argument in Iceland.

My relations with Mark Hudson and most of the new breed of MBAs and rocket scientists were becoming ever more strained. We argued constantly and it was always hard work to get my ideas accepted because of what I thought was a 'not invented here' syndrome. I'd come to realise that brainpower is no substitute for 'flair' (which doesn't exist in their book) or being streetwise when it comes to running a business. I'd come to the conclusion that, for all my earlier love affair with Bain, they'd contributed nothing to our business. I didn't regret having them in though; the £2 million we paid them was money well spent for the wake-up call their arrival brought us! The concept they introduced of supplier partnering, which Mark followed like a religion, was flawed. In theory, like communism, it was a good idea. But it just didn't work. Our buyers could never hope to understand a supplier's business as well as the supplier could and that's what we were asking them to do. Once we had agreed the principle of 'open book' it meant that if a supplier had a price increase on a raw material he could come to us for a cost price increase and we couldn't reasonably refuse. Under the old system we could just tell him to piss off, it was his problem not ours! A supplier could never be relied upon to own up to a price reduction, either! The suppliers ran rings round us and we got into all sorts of contractual arguments, the details of which our buyers couldn't hope to follow.

Price Waterhouse, Herbert Smith, Accenture and the like spend fortunes recruiting the very best graduates from the top universities. Everyone wants to be a lawyer or an accountant or a management consultant. There is no such thing as a career path for food retail buyers. Consequently buyers often end up in the job almost by accident and many of them are not very good. A skilled buyer has a unique combination of intelligence and flair and is also a hard negotiator. He is worth his weight in gold to a company but even second-rate ones command high salaries. A problem they often suffer from is an industrial disease that develops with the job, called arrogance. A junior buyer can hold the livelihood of a small manufacturer in his hands and so they are feted and flattered to the point where they develop a false impression of their own worth, popularity and capability. Most of our buyers were out of their depth with supplier partnering.

Mark could never accept the existence of intuition and every decision had to be researched and evaluated to death. He had correctly identified frozen food wholesaling as an area where we would have strength and expertise, but he thought we could run the business out of our existing shops. I couldn't even conceive how anybody with half a brain could think that for one second but we had to spend months analysing the situation before finally settling on the obvious, buy Woodward's. Mark brought in another ex-Bainie, Ed Hyslop, to run the evaluation project and he turned out to be very capable. We eventually put him alongside Jeremy to work as his partner. They complemented each other well.

Andy Brent, the former Procter & Gamble marketing manager we had brought in as our Marketing Director was also a big problem for me. Life was becoming one constant argument about which marketing approach we should take. Brand management for Fairy Liquid required different skills from those of a deal-driven retailer. I felt that we were on the verge of a great sales recovery but there were several bottlenecks (in terms of people) holding us back. More changes would have to be made.

Russell Ford had done a great job as the Appliance Director since Charles Rathgay retired. The appliance division was based in the original Bejam premises in Stanmore, north London, and consequently was left alone or even ignored unless there was a problem. Russell enjoyed the autonomy and effectively being his own boss and he thrived in that situation. He'd transformed the division's profile within Iceland and also its profitability. A major change he made that was difficult to implement was making the sales staff commission-based. We employed over 100 fridge engineers who offered a national breakdown service to support the after-service of our own freezer sales. This was a big overhead for us, which Russell converted into a stand-alone company that also worked for other retailers and manufacturers. It was well on its way to becoming a profit generator.

I was very keen to replace Andy Brent as quickly as possible but another outside appointment would be time consuming and a risk I didn't want to take. After discussing it with Bernie, Mark and Andy Pritchard (the Finance Director of the Iceland trading company, who was increasingly becoming a sounding board for me) we all agreed that Russell was innovative and commercially minded and, although he was not an obvious choice, we felt it would be a great idea to offer him the marketing job. Andy even commented that Russell could be our next MD. I arranged to meet Russell for dinner so we would have plenty of time to chat. He was not wildly enthusiastic about the idea and didn't want to report to Mark Hudson. He said he enjoyed the autonomy he had in appliances and described the marketing job in Iceland as a 'poisoned chalice'! I persuaded him he should take the job and even hinted it might lead to better things. Russell made clear his need to be allowed a free hand and I promised him Mark Hudson would not interfere with him. I arranged with Russell he would take over just as soon as he could replace himself in appliances. He said he had somebody in mind already!

John McLachlan was our sole non-executive director and had been since we floated. We were not a politically correct company because of that and also because I combined the role of Chief Executive and Chairman. I reasoned that as founder and a major shareholder in the company, my own interests were the same as the shareholders' and I was not going to be pressurised into 'window dressing' as I called it. However, I was beginning to wonder by now whether an independent outside director, someone I respected who could provide sound advice and wise counsel, might not be a great asset. I was even willing to give up the role of Chairman if we could find the right person to replace me. I'd asked Alan Smith repeatedly to join our board but he could never make up his mind as he always seemed to have something else on the horizon which might conflict. I'd been to see David Jones, the much respected Chief Executive of Next plc, but he turned me down. I'd had lunch with Ronnie Goldstein, the founder of Superdrug, but he wanted to come as a pair with his brother Peter and then only if they acquired a chunk of shares in the company.

For years I'd belonged to a Chief Executives' club called The Young Presidents' Organization (YPO). I rated it very highly and derived great benefit both socially and in business through my involvement. Graham Kirkham, now Lord Kirkham, was an enthusiastic member. We met through the club and became good friends.

He'd invited me to join the board of his company, DFS, when he floated it on the stock market, not because I was his pal but because he knew I would bring value. Iain Sharp was a member of the club and he'd founded and still ran Target Express, the parcel delivery company. Target Express was an extraordinary success story and hugely profitable in an industry where most of its competitors lost money. I thought Iain could be of great value to us, particularly in view of our venture into home delivery. He was not a 'name' that the City knew but I thought he would be ideal. He joined our board in May 1997. At first Iain showed a great interest in the business and started to familiarise himself with the operation. Unfortunately, soon after joining he sold Target and pocketed £70 million. He went to live in Jersey and understandably lost some interest in Iceland!

Two years later I invited Tom Knowlton, also from YPO, to join our board. Tom had been the CEO of Kelloggs in Europe for several years but had gone back home to Canada to run the whole of North America for Kelloggs. He thought he was in line for the top job but didn't get it and left Kelloggs soon after. Even though we had the cost of flying him over for board meetings I thought we were lucky to get someone of his stature.

Sales were improving, we were sorting out our management problems and we were even becoming 'respectable' with a full quota of non-executives! In spite of the success of the home delivery roll-out so far, it was not enough to affect our total like-for-like sales and for the first half-year of 1997 we were still only 1.1 per cent ahead. However, we were very confident of the future and our share price started to move up ... just a little!

14
Flying Again

We had a department in the office called 'customer services'. That was code for customer complaints! We received hundreds of letters and phone calls each week. Some were complimenting us on our good service, some were general enquiries and some were complaints, but they all had to be dealt with. Compliments were always passed on to the store with a bottle of champagne and a handwritten note from me. I saw complaints as an opportunity to win over a customer by trying really hard to satisfy them. Refunds were automatic but we'd often send an area manager to visit a customer and sometimes I'd even send flowers. Suppliers were always informed in the case of product complaints and we'd 'charge' them for having to handle the complaint. The department actually made a profit! Most customers were genuine but our computer system would pick up those with 'previous' and we could soon identify the professional complainers who tried to make a living out of us. We'd tell them to shop somewhere else!

Many letters would arrive addressed to 'The Chairman' but if any were addressed to me by name, I always read them and would answer personally. One day I had a letter asking about 'genetically modified soya beans'. I hadn't a clue what they were but I asked Bill Wadsworth, our technical boffin, to draft me a reply. I couldn't understand his letter but basically he was fobbing them off. I asked him to explain to me what the issue was about and I was horrified at what he told me. Apparently soya beans are used in some form or other in most processed food products. They are used in biscuits and chocolate, prepared foods of all kinds, even beer and baby foods. North America produces most of the world supply of soya beans and scientists there had changed the genetic make up of the plant by inserting genes from other organisms. This had been done to create a soya plant that was resistant to a weedkiller called 'Roundup'.

Monsanto, the giant American chemical company, developed the new soya bean. They called the seeds 'Roundup Ready'. Monsanto also made Roundup! The idea was that farmers could now plant Roundup Ready seeds. When the plants started to grow, weeds would also grow but, instead of weeding mechanically, they could now just spray the whole field with Roundup weedkiller and that would kill the weeds but not the soya plants. This seemed like a good way to sell more weedkiller as there was no other apparent benefit.

I wasn't sure at this point if genetically modifying soya beans was actually a problem but it sounded to me like interfering with nature and instinctively I didn't like it.

'If our customers don't like it, why don't we write and tell them we won't sell products made with genetically modified soya?' I asked Bill.

'That's a problem,' he replied. 'Only 20 per cent of the American crop is genetically modified but they are mixed with the 80 per cent of conventional beans and you can't buy them separately. You have to eat GM soya whether you like it or not!'

'That's outrageous,' I said. 'It can't be right that it should be happening.' I wrote to the customer who had asked what our stance was and said I agreed with her arguments and we would find out more about the problem.

Russell Ford was settling into his new role. At the next board meeting he made a presentation, which went down well. He simply put up two slides. One gave the 'traditional or conventional' view of what a Marketing Director's job was all about. It said, in effect: 'Bow ties, winning awards, artistic temperament, long-term results, building a brand.' The other gave the 'Russell' view of the job: 'Commercial, profit-motivated, realistic and recognition that adverts are to put cash in the till, not win awards.' We all thought we had made the right decision in appointing him.

I spent many hours in Russell's office talking to him about food. Our business was about walking a tightrope between what people will spend on food, either through choice or ignorance, and the absolute quality of the product. Did Russell know for instance about fish fingers? Originally they were made from fillets of cod cut into one-ounce fingers and then lightly breaded. It was a good quality product for children. Then somebody had the idea of using a cheaper white fish fillet. Then instead of using fillets, how about using offcuts of fish and mincing it? Then, what about making them 10 per cent smaller and why not put on a much thicker coating of breadcrumbs? Why sell expensive fish when you can sell breadcrumbs for the same price? The end result is a fish finger that is smaller, made from cheaper minced fish and is mainly breadcrumbs but it's still called a fish finger. If our competitors sell those for 99p and we're charging £1.50 for the real thing, do our customers know the difference? Do they care?

Ice cream used to be made from fresh cream, eggs and sugar. Then it was skimmed milk powder and cheap fat. Now, most ice cream has not one atom of dairy product in it. Something called 'milk replacer' has been invented but who cares if it's sweet and cold and 49p for a bucket full? The problem is the same with just about any food product you could mention. Technology has made it cheaper and inferior. 'Don't let your children eat cheap burgers or sausages,' I warned Russell. 'I know what goes into them.' 'Have you ever wondered why that white milky stuff oozes out of bacon when you fry it? It's because it's pumped up with water, that's why. Why sell bacon when you can sell water?' Our problem was that good value wasn't always at the lowest price. We had to compete but we also had to be ethical. Our customers were mainly on a low income but they had a right to a choice. Russell took all this on board with enthusiasm.

I then told him about my latest discovery on GM food. 'Customers have a right to a choice. If they choose to eat it that's fine by me, but everybody is eating it without knowing it. Who do you know who's ever even heard of GM food?' I asked Russell. I told him about a project we'd run a few years earlier when everybody was concerned about 'E numbers'. We took them out of many of our products and flashed the packaging with a logo proclaiming 'no E numbers, no artificial colourings, no artificial preservatives'. Sales rocketed. I called in Bill Wadsworth and asked him if it would be possible to reformulate our own-label products to exclude soya or else find a GM-free supply. He said it would be impossible but he would look into it! We warmed to the subject. 'Just think, first we run an awareness campaign and then we could flash our packaging with a logo saying 'Contains No Genetically Modified Ingredients.' It's like the opposite of putting a health warning on cigarettes, it will be brilliant for sales!'

Jill McWilliam had written a letter in my name to *The Times*, condemning GM soya. That prompted a journalist to ring me one day for a comment for an article he was writing. I said GM foods sounded like 'Food for Frankenstein'. I'd coined a phrase that became widely used.

We'd been supporting the Cancer Research Campaign (CRC) as one of our charities for some time. Professor Gordon McVie, the head of the organisation, had asked if they could help us to promote frozen vegetables. I thought this was a gift from God! The 'five portions a day' of fruit and vegetables that we should all eat to help prevent cancer included frozen vegetables. Since frozen veg were frozen within hours of harvesting there were actually more of the cancer-preventing ingredients in them than in 'fresh' veg which, unless you grow them yourself, would always be several days old. We had flashed all our vegetable packaging with the Cancer Research Campaign logo and I'd attended several press conferences with Gordon to try to publicise the message. It was no different from them endorsing Boots suntan cream.

At one such press conference, just before it started, Gordon was complaining that a high percentage of children never ate vegetables and asked why couldn't we flavour them like crisps. I asked if he was serious and he said he was. Anything to get kids to eat veg is OK. I announced at that very same press conference that we would do it. The result was staggering. The press gave it massive coverage and we had to develop the product and get it in the shops in just a few weeks. The chocolate-flavoured carrot was born! We also had baked bean-flavoured peas and pizza-flavoured sweetcorn. We'd never enjoyed such publicity. We sold enormous quantities of the products for a few weeks and then sales dropped to zero. It didn't matter. We'd raised awareness for the CRC and we'd raised the profile of Iceland.

While Iceland had been going through its difficult period over the last few years we'd kept a very low profile as far as the press was concerned. I was now beginning to appreciate the value of good publicity. Asda were brilliant at getting their name in the papers for the silliest stunts. Holding church services in their stores on a Sunday, employing people to walk your dog while you did your shopping, giving roses away on Valentine's day. We decided to crank up our own publicity machine.

One morning, while driving in to work, I heard a lady on the radio talking about her missing son. She had kept his room just as it was when he'd disappeared although that was six years earlier. She said there wasn't a day when she didn't think about him. It was very emotional listening. The point she made was that although she'd reported it to the police, they didn't have a national register. The police force just a few miles away, in the next county, might come across the child but be unaware he was reported as missing. Only a small obscure charity called 'The Missing People's Helpline' kept a national register and ran an awareness campaign. A few years earlier I'd heard about Safeway in America who'd run a very effective campaign by putting pictures of missing children on milk cartons. The milk carton is ideal for such a message as it stares at you every morning while you eat your cornflakes! I'd tried then to get our buyer to do it but there wasn't much enthusiasm. When I got in to the

The launch of Iceland home delivery.

home delivery

it's easy as...

1 shop ...& spend £25 in-store

2 pay at the till...

3 free home delivery

Putting Missing People on Iceland's milk bottles saved lives.

Andrew Gosden

missing people

Registered Charity No. 1020419

Age at disappearance: 14
Andrew has been missing from Doncaster since 14 September 2007. He was later seen in Kings Cross station in London on that day.

Andrew, please call the Runaway Helpline on Freefone 0808 800 7070 for confidential advice and support.

Seen Andrew?

Freefone
0500 700 700

Iceland

fresh pasteurised

Semi Skimmed Milk

℮ 2.272L

less than 2% fat (4 pints)

Use By:

Retailers in retreat on Frankenstein foods

Iceland is reaping rewards from its policy on GM food and its retailing rivals are following suit. Alex Jardine reports on how retailers have changed their minds

The major supermarket chains must have been kicking themselves last week as Iceland unveiled its annual results. In a tough climate where the other food retailers are fighting it out on price, the mass market frozen food retailer managed to turn in a strong set of figures, with food sales up by 12% and profits up 10% to £55m.

The reasons, according to Iceland, included the very public ethical stance it has taken against genetically modified food. By banning GM ingredients from its own-label products and launching products such as a 'green' range of fridges and freezers (called Kyoto after the Kyoto conference on climate change), Iceland has done wonders for its brand, drawing new customers into its stores and even winning praise from Friends of the Earth. But when it called a ban on GM ingredients last May, Iceland's stance was derided by other retailers; at a time when Monsanto was heavily advertising the benefits of GM, they dismissed it as a PR stunt. Nine months on, with GM foods rapidly replacing BSE as food's public enemy number one, Iceland's approach has definitely spurred the other supermarkets into action.

But the question of whether GM 'bans' are genuine investments or misleading PR still hangs in the air. Tesco – the grocery market leader – has refused so far to issue a GM ban, claiming it will only do so when it can truthfully claim to have eliminated all traces of GM ingredients. A

spokesman says: "We believe other supermarket chains are being extremely disingenuous to their customers. It is very difficult to source non-GM ingredients, and to eliminate them from products. We want to make sure that we can deliver our promises rather than offering customers false hopes."

So is Iceland being honest with consumers? Its chairman Malcolm Walker – the man who claims to have coined the phrase 'Frankenstein Foods' – was quick to condemn a recent critical article in *The Express*, which claimed that Iceland was incorrect in describing own-branc foods as non-genetically modified. He argues that because materials can be trans-

ferred at a molecular level, even in the air that we breathe, as a result the food industry has to work with tolerance levels. Walker said: "In a climate where tolerance levels have yet to be agreed for genetically modified food, we work with levels that are under 1%, when the accepted tolerance level for organic food is 5%. In recent tests at Iceland, of over 300 products, only one was found to have any trace of GM materials and this was at a level of one part in half a million. Anyone with a reasonable understanding of biology or chemistry will know that materials can be transferred at a molecular level, so it is impossible to say that no trace of GM can be present at a molecular level."

Walker also stresses that the anti-GM stance was not originally intended as a marketing initiative: "We were responding to letters from our customers and it seemed like the right thing to do. Don't forget that we had always taken an environmental stance, from banning mechanically recovered meat to refusing to buy prawns from Norway because of their whaling."

Walker insists the GM ban has not been easy. The company has gone to great lengths to persuade suppliers to buy non-GM ingredients, he says. "When we took the decision we faced quite a lot of hostility in the industry." But the power of the retailers means suppliers know they either comply or lose the business.

Sainsbury's points out that by working in a consortium it will become easier to eliminate GM ingredients. "By combining our buying power with other supermarket groups we are able to find farmers who are willing to grow non-GM crops," says a spokesman. Tesco now remains the sole major retailer which says it has no plans to eliminate GM ingredients from its own-label foods. Many observers feel it is only a matter of time before Tesco too adopts an anti-GM policy.

Campaigning: Iceland's chairman Malcolm Walker has led the way on anti-GM food policies, with rivals now following suit

SUPERMARKET POLICIES ON GM		
Supermarket	Own-brands with GM ingredients	Future Policy
Tesco	150 out of 20,000	No plans to eliminate GM ingredients
Sainsbury's	40-50 out of 1500	Own brands GM free by end of summer
Asda	39 out of 4000	GM free in next 3 months
Safeway	150 out of 9000	Gradually phasing out GM ingredients
Somerfield	150 out of 4000	Asking suppliers wherever possible to use non GM
Marks & Spencer	100 out of 3000	GM free in 3 months
Iceland	0 out of 900	GM free since May 1998

HOW FROZEN VEG CAN HELP PROTECT AGAINST CANCER

Inside -
Your questions
answered!

Why frozen veg
can be just as
good for you
as fresh!

Iceland links with the Cancer Research Campaign to promote frozen vegetable consumption.

ICELAND

Your Guide to Food You Can Trust

made with
NO
GM ingredients,
artificial colours
or flavours

Food You Can Trust.

Malcolm and Stuart Rose announce the Booker deal, August 2000.

Andy Pritchard, Iceland
FD, MD and co-founder of
Cooltrader.

Keith Hann, Iceland's
PR adviser.

Mail on Sunday

You have infuriated your investors, the City is outraged... so how did you enjoy the Maldives, Mr Walker?

From Teena Lyons
on Kuda Huraa in the Maldives

ARM-in-arm with wife Rhianydd, Malcolm Walker strolled along the soft, golden sand as the waves of the Indian Ocean lapped on the shore. It was a moment of quiet, playful encouragement as his childhood sweetheart and wife of more than 30 years struggled to get the hang of water-skiing.

Enjoying the luxury of the £250-a-night private island resort of Kuda Huraa in the Maldives – a resort so exclusive it even has its own time zone – Walker looked like a man without a care in the world.

And no wonder he seemed relaxed and happy last week. After all, little more than a month ago, Walker, chairman and co-founder of food retailer Iceland, had pocketed £13.5 million from selling almost half his stake in the company.

More than 3,400 miles away in London, Iceland investors were feeling less sunny. In mid-December, when Walker cashed in his shares, the price was riding high, comfortably above 329p, helped by an upbeat presentation to analysts given by Walker at Iceland's Deeside headquarters on the very day he started selling.

But now? A profits warning from the company last week sent the stock plunging and Iceland shares closed on Friday at only 204p. Walker's timing in selling his shares was exceptional: they were at their peak. The hapless investors who bought from him then have seen the value of those shares melt from £13.5 million to less than £8.5 million.

The presentation, now acknowledged last week, the day before a profits warning, Iceland shares closed out and were hurtling higher. I realised that at the time he needs to chat to his advisers.

I'm not the type to sit on the beach all day

Lap of luxury: The Walkers were paying £250 a night for their Maldives hotel

extraordinarily well-timed share sale, but enquiries were met with a firm 'no comment'.

But at last, this pint-sized Yorkshireman began to appreciate just how furious the City is with the way he has behaved. Walker spent last Thursday evening sitting in the hotel bar with his mobile phone clamped to his ear, engaged in agitated conversations with colleagues back in Britain.

By Friday morning, Walker and his wife had checked out and were heading home. I tracked Walker down. He feels he needs to chat to his advisers,' said an Iceland insider.

Walker's belated acknowledgement that he has some explaining to do might have been provoked by the watching Financial Services Authority. Its offshoot, the UK Listing Authority, has been in touch with Iceland's head office already. It routinely asks questions when a director deals in shares in the two months before the announcement of price-sensitive information.

Iceland, of course, insists that Walker did nothing wrong. His share sale was carried out with the approval of other board members. Walker, say his allies, had wanted to sell some of his Iceland shares earlier in the year, most of his personal wealth is tied up in the company, and he wanted to spread it around other investments.

But this was only a short time after Iceland's merger with cash-and-carry group Booker. Stuart Rose, Booker's chief executive, became head of the merged group. He asked Walker to hold back because having the chairman sell a huge chunk of his holding would hardly be seen as a ringing endorsement of the deal.

So Walker waited – until mid-December. Walker's shares were sold through broker Charterhouse between December 14 and 19.

Iceland doesn't pretend that it was not aware by mid-December that sales were flagging. Walker knew, and other directors knew. Indeed, the decline became more severe after the start of December over the month, sales fell by 5.5 per cent.

But still, when investment analysts were invited to the company's North Wales headquarters near Deeside, the picture painted to them was positive.

'The presentation wasn't quite as enthusiastic as we were used to,' said one, 'but Walker was very upbeat. I asked the finance director whether my forecasts were on track – because they were at the top end of the market. He said they were fine.'

One investor who had a one-to-one meeting with Walker claims he was given encouraging news. 'He said business had eased back a bit at number nine over Christmas, but I'm not alarmed because they had eased back on promotions, which with hindsight was a bad decision,' said the investor.

'But he said that now they had reinstated them, sales were reviving. With the benefit of hindsight, it is obvious he was, at best, economical with the truth.'

Iceland offers no public explanation for Walker's actions. Privately, insiders suggest that though sales were looking groggy, directors were confident they could hit the City's profits estimates.

The City is deeply sceptical about the explanation – and angry. 'Malcolm Walker should resign – immediately,' said one analyst. 'He can't be trusted.'

Will he ever be trusted by the City again?

'He is history,' fumed another. 'The City has previously admired the acumen of a solitary electrician who left school with only an O-level in woodwork. And Iceland has brilliantly ridden the wave of the public's burgeoning love of all things organic – an affair that, only now, appears to be cooling. Investors have been happy enough – even allowing directors the indulgence of a company jet. The registration number of Iceland's previous plane was the boastful VP-ICE.

But this is not the first time Walker has, to put it mildly, raised eyebrows with his self-enriching activities. In 1997, he and three others had the effects of a disastrous three-year run that had seen the share price slump. Their share options, giving them the right to buy at a price way above the level at which they could

Deeside
5,451 miles

INDIA

Sri Lanka

Maldive Islands   Kuda Huraa

Indian Ocean

be bought in the market, were worthless. These options were replaced by a new set at a much lower price, giving the directors the prospect of a profit if the market price rose above 79p.

Walker himself was given options over 1.29 million shares. Remarkably, the new options package coincided almost exactly with the nadir in Iceland's share price. Within a

It's not the first time he has raised eyebrows

year, with the price up, his options were worth almost £2 million.

All Iceland's investors benefited from the run, so there were no complaints. But this time round, there is no cause for celebration.

Additional reporting: Jenny Little and Ben Laurance.

Away from it all: Malcolm Walker and wife Rhianydd relax on holiday

A memorable holiday in the Maldives.

Iceland chief executive Bill Grimsey – "We're making good progress"

Bill Grimsey; with a turkey.

Daily Post

Supermarkets price war sees Iceland's profit melt

Bill Grimsey with Bill Hoskins, his Finance Director.

hursday Dec 28	Friday Dec 29	Saturday Dec 3
	(Holiday Japan · partial)	*(Holiday Japan · partial)*
	10.00 Watford Hilton Loveday Waymorth PWC Takeover project 0207 229 9650 12. P. Hollinger Regent Hotel	
	Lunch	

Bill Grimsey's diary entry, 29 December 2000: 'Takeover project'.

office, I rang the Missing People's helpline and we soon launched the idea in Britain with a new picture every month on all Iceland milk cartons. We generated massive publicity over the next few years with regular TV and press coverage and we found several children as a direct result of people seeing them on our milk cartons. I know we saved lives.

We held another managers' conference at the Birmingham ICC on 30 October 1997. It was just as successful as the first one but what a difference a year had made. Sales were improving, home delivery was being rolled out nationally and there seemed to be dozens of new initiatives every month. Morale was on a high. We had invited our suppliers to hear the same conference presentations on the previous day. Usually, retailers always try to extract money from suppliers at such meetings but we didn't. We just wanted to tell them what we were doing and give them confidence it was working. We felt we were 'on a roll' and our suppliers were beginning to share that belief.

One negative piece of unwelcome publicity occurred around that time when the financial section of *The Observer* included an article about the share options we had cancelled and reissued earlier in the year. Following the advice of Russell Edey, the board members, including me, had waited three months after the capital reconstruction for the share price to rise before we issued our new options. The price hadn't risen but had dropped back to 73p. Ben Laurance, the financial editor of *The Observer,* had found out about this months after it had happened and been publicly disclosed. He decided he didn't like it and wrote a very damning article about Iceland and called the company 'a corporate disaster area'! I was furious with what I thought was a very unjust article and rang him up to tell him so. It's the only time I've ever done that with a journalist but the call didn't go well and I ended up calling him 'a tosser'. That phone call came back to haunt me a few years later.

Another new initiative was prompted by a visit I had from John von Spreckelsen. John was the Chief Executive of Budgens and had done a really good job in developing a niche for his southern based supermarket chain, which gave him a credible defence against superstore competition. John was worried that David Simons of Somerfield was going to make a bid for Budgens and was looking for some kind of alliance with Iceland. We had several meetings and while I wasn't keen to merge with Budgens, we got on very well together. Eventually we decided to start working together on a trial basis and see where it led. Iceland took over the frozen food section of a Budgens store and they helped us convert an Iceland store into a convenience format. The experiment worked really well with sales massively up in both stores. Iceland had many stores, mainly in the south of England, where we felt a convenience format would work better than a freezer store. We did two more stores with John but the threat of a bid from Somerfield receded and we continued to develop the convenience format on our own. We called the stores 'Iceland eXtra' to differentiate the concept from a normal store.

The eXtra stores were a lot more complicated to run than a normal Iceland and overheads were much higher but we did achieve substantial sales increases and we felt that, as we refined the formula, profits would also increase. We started slowly rolling them out by converting selected Iceland stores.

Mark Hudson left the company on 17 November 1997 and I didn't attempt to replace him. He was a good management consultant and eventually went back into that field. Innovation and flair were finally moving the company forward. Two years of science and analysis had achieved nothing. I stopped any more development on 'supplier partnering'. After recording like-for-like sales only 1.1 per cent ahead for the first half of the year we were able to report an increase of 7.4 per cent for the second half.

Two years earlier, even though things looked grim in Iceland, I'd placed an order to build a 70-foot sailing boat. It was something I'd always wanted and I would dream of sailing around the world. It was perhaps due to some influence from the bad times at Iceland that I called the boat 'No Rehearsal'. (As in 'life is ...'). The boat was completed during the summer and my children Richard and Alexia had accompanied the crew in sailing it from Southampton to the Balearic islands in the Mediterranean. Ranny and I then enjoyed a two-week holiday on the boat but it was now waiting in Las Palmas to start in the 'ARC race' to St Lucia. On 19 November I flew out there with John Prestt and John Lawrence, a friend from YPO, to join the boat and start the race on the 23rd. It's not by any means a serious race and is designed for 'amateur cruisers' but we sailed across the Atlantic in twelve days and arrived second by only two hours out of a race of over 100 boats. For the first time in several years I was relaxed and happy to be away from the office, content in the knowledge that everything was going well.

In March 1998 our analysts' meeting was a pretty upbeat affair. Our share price was over £2 and still rising and our like-for-like sales were up a massive 16 per cent for the first eleven weeks of the year. We had recovered most of our credibility in the City and home delivery was finally being recognised as a winner. Andy Pritchard had been the Iceland Finance Director for several years, with Bernie Leigh having the title of Group Finance Director. Bernie now moved aside to give Andy the Group title and we promoted Tarsem Dhaliwal to Andy's old role of Iceland Finance Director. In May we had another analysts' meeting following our AGM but held it in Deeside. We gave them a tour of the office, visited stores and also the Woodward's operation in Rhyl. We entertained them to dinner at the Crabwall Manor Hotel where I made a speech and told a joke which somehow caused great hilarity and managed to seriously embarrass Frank Davidson (the analyst who had urged shareholders to vote against our capital reconstruction). Frank didn't turn up for the next day's tour and I never saw him again. We brought Alan Birchall along to sing and by one o'clock in the morning had all the analysts joining in, singing Alan's 'Iceland song'!

Mark Astaire from ABN Amro and Tony Allen from Rothschilds attended the event and I mentioned to Mark that I wanted to sell some of my Iceland shares. We had a long debate about this with him urging me not to because it 'wasn't a good time'. There was no reason why I couldn't but with Mark it was never a good time and he admitted that. I didn't sell.

Also in March we held a press conference to expose to the world the frightening infiltration into our food supply of the genetically modified soya bean. We also announced that all Iceland own-label foods would be free of GM ingredients from 1 May 1998. We invited Greenpeace to attend, and for the first time I met Peter Melchett, their Executive Director. I had joined Greenpeace myself years earlier but only so that when I wrote to Greenpeace members (who thought we were connected with Iceland the country and were accusing us of killing whales) I could start my letter with 'I too am a member of Greenpeace ... '. The press conference succeeded beyond my wildest dreams. We'd hit a nerve – and also a publicity jackpot! The press and television news gave it massive coverage. The media and the public were on our side and liked what we were doing.

We'd wrong-footed the supermarkets, who at first defended GM and were dismissive of our campaign, but then slowly started to follow our initiative. Too late for them, because we were now seen as the pioneers of consumer choice and safe food. My own motives for doing this were equally balanced between gaining a commercial advantage and my genuine concern that genetic modification on a commercial scale was wrong. No amount of pious claims from the biotechnology industry about 'feeding the world' cut any ice with me. They were just as much a profit-focused enterprise as we were and I believed much of the 'gold rush' that was starting into commercial genetic modification was frivolous, unnecessary and potentially dangerous.

Iceland was fast becoming an 'ethical retailer'. Our record of recycling ozone-depleting freezer gases, boycotting prawn supplies from whaling countries and our many charity initiatives were all things that I was proud of but I wasn't embarrassed to shout about them and try to turn them into a point of difference for Iceland. They were certainly good for sales and our constant high profile in the media brought in new customers and impressed the media and the

City. We had also by now completed the roll-out of our telephone shopping business. This was catalogue-based but we were already looking to develop an internet system which we eventually managed by October the following year. We were able to claim this and home delivery as environmental initiatives as they cut down on car journeys.

In October 1998 we launched yet another major 'green' initiative which Mark Bates, Russell's successor in the appliance division, had dreamt up. Iceland became the first company in the world to relaunch its entire range of own-label fridges and freezers using environmentally friendly hydrocarbon gases instead of the ozone-depleting CFCs. Greenpeace, who normally shy away from any kind of commercial involvement, felt this was such an important step they made it the first product in the world they ever commercially endorsed. We renamed our new appliances the 'Kyoto range' after the world environmental agreement reached in Kyoto, Japan. I thought that was a stroke of pure genius!

I got to know Peter Melchett and many of the staff at Greenpeace very well. I sympathised with most of their aims and objectives and in spite of their 'looney' image, I found them sincere and dedicated. I believe no sane person could actually object to the majority of things they try to achieve. They have been pioneers in uncovering and stopping so many environmental abuses. It's just that sometimes their methods are rather unconventional which suits me fine. At least they act on their beliefs. They are always ready to work with industry in a sensible way if industry just shows a willingness to improve its environmental standards. They are also commercially realistic and more than happy when companies profit from environmental initiatives.

My own publicity profile was increasing all the time and Iceland were never far from the public eye. I became the 'Mr Greenpeace' of the retail sector and it certainly helped sales and profits. We finished the year with a 29 per cent increase in our earnings per share and like-for-like sales up 12 per cent for the year as a whole.

In January 1999 I took Andy, David Brown and Russell Ford for a few days on my boat in the Caribbean. It was meant to be an off-site 'brainstorming and bonding' session but it didn't quite work! Russell was by now a main board director of Iceland and he had also taken responsibility for buying. His title was Trading Director but his demand for autonomy and his constant pushing for promotion was becoming a problem. I found him difficult to manage. He was talented in many ways but his style was becoming increasingly wacky and unorthodox. He had recruited a new advertising company called HHCL and I felt he was increasingly under their influence. The two slides he put up when he took on the marketing role were now ironic with Russell becoming more temperamental and further removed from our customer base by the day. There was a lot of friction on the trip and it didn't work as I'd hoped.

This was my 29th year in Iceland and I was increasingly feeling ready for a change. I felt we had successfully reinvented the company, our credibility and share price had been restored, and we were now on a sound footing but I was no nearer to finding a successor. I wasn't sure that Russell would ever be capable of taking over from me and, if he was, it wouldn't be for a very long time. I didn't want to risk the upset of looking for someone else and just kept hoping that Russell would mature and settle down. Bernie retired in June and at about the same time I decided to make Russell and Andy Joint Managing Directors. The two of them didn't get on but the move was designed to give Russell more opportunity to widen his experience and also to balance his wacky style with Andy's, which was much more conservative. They were to run the company between them with Andy combining his role as Group Finance Director with looking after logistics and support services, and Russell running trading.

Russell was well committed by now to our 'Food You Can Trust' campaign. He was desperate to make his own mark on UK retailing and wanted to launch his own idea on the scale of home delivery or the ban on GM food. He came to see me with his idea, which was to turn the whole of our frozen vegetable range organic. The organic bandwagon had just started to roll with sales increasing every week and the supermarkets increasing the space they gave to it. Organic food was very expensive and not for our customers. Waitrose and Sainsbury's could sell it but we hadn't a chance. I was keen on organic food myself but would never have considered it for Iceland. Russell reasoned that organic vegetables were only expensive because it was a cottage industry. If we went overseas to buy the product, because of the thousands of tons of frozen vegetables we would need, it would be possible to buy at only a small premium of around 10 per cent.

I was sceptical but Russell assured me his new vegetable buyer was researching the market and this was the case. If we could contract for next year and just increase our prices slightly, before we launched the organic range, we could claim we would offer organic vegetables at no extra cost. Even our customers would buy organic if it didn't cost any more. It would be a real point of difference, a major coup and would fit very well with our ban on GM foods and our green image. How much would sales increase by, 20 per cent? I agreed that if it really was only a 10 per cent premium, we should do it.

By this time I'd had another publicity success with eggs. At the annual Iceland charity golf match I was being harangued in the bar afterwards by one of our egg suppliers who'd had too much to drink. He was giving me grief for causing them problems by insisting their chickens were fed on GM-free soya. I told him to stop worrying, our next stage was to take artificial colourings out of food products and he should be thankful that wouldn't apply to him. After all, you don't put colouring in eggs, do you? 'Of course we do,' he replied. I was stunned.

The very next day I discovered that several chemical colouring ingredients were added to poultry food to make the egg yolks any shade of yellow you like. They even had a colour swatch, like a paint chart, to pick the colour. Is nothing sacred any more? If you stop feeding the colouring, it will have worked through the hen's system in only three weeks and the yolks will become paler and more natural. Genuinely free-range hens would eat beetles and insects which provide colour in the yolk. Very few hens are genuinely free-range and so most farmed eggs would have naturally pale yolks. We launched our own range of eggs free from artificial colouring, to the usual fanfare of publicity we had come to expect. The press loved the story and were particularly horrified when I waved the paint chart. I posed for publicity photographs holding one of my own hens that I keep at home. Free-range of course.

In July, Russell Ford received an anonymous phone call from an employee about David Brown and the way he ran store operations. The content of the call was convincing and worrying and Russell passed it on to me to deal with. The Stores Director in any retail company is in a powerful position but he needs to be tough and strong to control hundreds of branch managers and the fiddles and stealing that a few of them inevitably get into. However, it's very easy to develop a bullying style and become infected with the same type of arrogance one finds among some of the buyers. David usually delivered what he said he would deliver but his behaviour was causing me growing concern, as was the tight group of area and regional managers who were his friends.

One concern I had was how cleaning contractors were being used more and more in our stores at the expense of employing our own cleaners, who I thought were cheaper and did a better job. I had raised this issue on several occasions but was always assured that contractors were more cost-effective. I eventually spoke to the anonymous informant myself and then I called in Kroll, the private security company, to investigate. Over the next few weeks they uncovered a myriad of companies that several of our store operations people were involved in, and a whole series of scams they were running while creaming off commissions from contractors. Not only that but our London region was practically run as the personal fiefdom of several senior staff, who were fiddling expenses almost openly. Hundreds of thousands of pounds were involved. Over many weeks we built up a picture of what was happening and eventually brought in the police.

They planned a number of coordinated early morning raids on the houses of some of our staff, spread from London to Chester. A number of our employees, including David, were hauled off and prosecuted and eventually several of them were jailed. The discovery caused us a lot of problems. Not only had the goings-on been widely known about at a lower level but their behaviour had caused a lot of damage to staff morale and the credibility of the company in the eyes of many of our employees. It took us a long time to repair the damage and rebuild the confidence of some of our staff in the London stores. The press soon got wind of the police dawn raids and the very mention of any 'financial irregularities' sent our shares into a tailspin. Was this the tip of some massive fraud that would bring the company down? We managed to stabilise things and soon convinced worried investors that only 'petty cash' was involved, which of course in the scheme of things it was!

I was without a Stores Director now so I decided to do the job myself. I enjoyed getting involved at the 'coal face' again but it wasn't really practical. After six months, I promoted a regional manager, Mark Yeo, into the role.

Alan Smith was by now Chairman of Bhs. I still saw him occasionally and apart from him trying to convince me to buy Bhs from time to time, we agreed a deal, possibly as a precursor to further involvement, whereby Iceland would run an 'affordable M&S' at Bhs. We opened eight food halls within Bhs stores but they were not as successful as the ones in Littlewoods. Bhs and Littlewoods suffered from many of the same problems such as lack of direction and management indecision.

We were still performing well at Iceland, our home delivery operation was providing a real point of difference and our internet shopping operation was growing all the time although the vast majority of our orders came by telephone to our central call centre at Deeside. Some analysts were excited by the possibilities of the internet and this started to cause us a problem and create a cloud over our share price. The 'internet bubble' was well underway, but as a practical retailer I thought its limitations were obvious. It would never totally replace the high street but for a time some analysts genuinely thought it would. We were labelled the 'old economy' and many people who should have known better were looking ahead to what they thought was inevitable: a time when city centres would be nothing more than housing or entertainment centres and shops were obsolete. It was even rumoured that Walmart in America were now building all new stores with dual use so that they could be converted to housing when the internet revolution happened.

Our home shopping operation was carried out by picking the customers' orders in-store. The order would be received centrally and transmitted to the customer's local store for picking and delivery on the home delivery van. This was an obvious and low-cost way of doing it but most analysts believed in central picking centres. We tried to suggest that combining the old and the new, clicks and mortar, was the way forward but it was hard work. If some of the analysts had ever run a business they'd have had a much more realistic view of the world. Webvan in America was a 'start-up' internet grocery operation which was going to be warehouse-based, expand at lightning speed across America and make supermarkets redundant! It reached a stockmarket valuation of $5 billion before it opened its first branch. Of course it went bankrupt fairly quickly!

We finished 1999 with a 9 per cent increase in like-for-like sales and an 18 per cent increase in earnings, building on like-for-like sales growth of 12 per cent and a more than 30 per cent rise in earnings in 1998.

15

The New Millennium

I hate New Year. All the forced gaiety and kissing at midnight sends me into depression! I'm always amazed at the number of other people who admit to feeling the same way if it ever comes up in conversation. But 31 December 1999 was, of course, different. There had been so much hype during the previous two years that Ranny and I had fallen for it and booked 'The Samling', a luxury private hotel at a mega price in the Lake District, with a group of friends. After much uncertainty two of our three children, Alexia and Richard, joined us but Caroline was having her year off. She phoned us at what was midnight for her, from a beach in Fiji, as we drove to the hotel.

I'd borrowed a TV projector from Iceland and as we were finishing dinner at midnight all the celebrations from around the world were screened on the wall of the dining room. At least I thought it was from around the world but then I realised it was the best of everything 'British' from the multicultural Dome! The world didn't end, though, and after all the pain we'd been through with our computer department I was slightly disappointed that the lights didn't go out and Armageddon arrive. Some of our IT staff were working that night for wages which would provide a fortnight in Barbados, but I didn't ring them for an update. Somehow I knew the Millennium bug was a damp squib.

Driving into work on 3 January 2000 I couldn't help but reflect on events of the last few years. I'd been successful in 'reinventing' Iceland but after nearly 30 years I was sick of the business and beginning to hate going into work. I wanted a rest or at least a change. There was so much I wanted to do with the rest of my life but I was trapped. I had no successor and no real prospect of getting one. We would comfortably hit our profit figure for the last year but already that was history and now the whole cycle was about to start again. How could we keep growing by just doing more of the same? We already had 760 stores and at that time it felt like we were running out of towns for new ones. Organic growth wouldn't provide the excitement the City was looking for. We seemed to be reaching saturation and without another new initiative or serious diversification further growth would become impossible.

Andy and Russell were as awkward with each other as ever and barely spoke to one another. Andy despised Russell and I was seriously worried about him. I knew in my heart he would never be capable of running the business but I just hadn't the energy left to get rid of him and get stuck in myself. To develop a successor would take years. Keeping him was almost as much of a problem as he was difficult to control, and uncontrolled he had the potential to cause all kinds of problems.

However, sales were good and for January and February at least the Monday morning sales meetings were full of the usual razz and hype and self-congratulation. Andy wasn't impressed and kept warning that in spite of good sales we weren't making the profits we should be. We'd just built a new £35 million distribution centre in Enfield. This was still massively over-budget on running costs every week and just didn't seem to be getting any better. We also seemed to keep having any number of 'one-offs' hitting the profit line but I was less concerned about these problems as they would be fixed eventually and the underlying trading performance was good. Nevertheless, we did seem to be throwing away the benefits of this good sales period and I was worried about our apparently increasing inability to deal with the basics – and, in particular, for Russell even to recognise them.

Russell needed more experience outside buying and marketing and I was keen to get him involved in the reality of store operations rather than the 'make believe' world of marketing. Marketing ideas dreamed up in the office don't have quite the same appeal when you are trying to implement them in 760 stores that are all different in size, sales performance and management capability. Russell needed to experience this. I had enjoyed running store operations myself since David Brown left but the reality was I just didn't have time to do the job justice. Pulling Russell away from buying and marketing and getting him to take an interest in stores was difficult in itself. Steve, our Buying Director, would no doubt welcome Russell spending his time somewhere else but Russell seemed to have a real problem with Steve and wanted to keep personal control of buying. It was all a bit messy.

I was trying to strengthen our store operations team and recruit a new retail regional manager and was determined to interview all the candidates myself. The headhunters had put forward a man called Trevor Tutt and I spent a couple of hours with him in my office.

My usual technique in an interview was to get the candidate to tell me everything about themselves and their career history, chronologically, with me interrupting and asking questions as we went along. Then I'd tell them everything about Iceland and the job on offer.

Trevor had spent all his life in retailing but the last couple of years he'd spent at Booker, the wholesale cash and carry operator. The more he told me about the company the more fascinated I became. Booker sounded like a giant business that dominated its market but, from the stories Trevor told me, no one seemed interested in investing or driving the company forward. As a retailer, Trevor felt that most retail principles still applied to the company, even though it was a wholesale business, but these were not being followed. All he could see were missed opportunities.

Everyone knew Booker was in trouble but no one seemed to know much about the business or why it was in trouble. Retail companies are always in the news and the public are familiar with them but Booker was known as an 'agri-conglomerate' and considered to be in an 'unglamorous' sector of the stock market. Outside that industry no one followed its fortunes. I did know a little bit about the company and the broad spread of its activities. Booker used to own the Budgens supermarket group and when they sold the business we looked at buying it. They were into forestry and fish farming and as it turned out a hundred other businesses which eventually started to lose money. They ran up big debts and there was a real possibility the company might go bankrupt.

Alan Smith had been Chairman of Booker and was still a non-executive director. He'd suggested I should buy the business a couple of times but I wasn't interested in even discussing it with him. The company seemed to be in a real mess and he didn't know what to do. Eventually he brought in a guy called Stuart Rose as Chief Executive. Stuart had spent the last eighteen months selling everything off and just about all that remained was the cash and carry business which was the original unglamorous 'cash cow' that had funded everything else.

When Trevor had gone, I got hold of Andy and Russell and suggested we go and visit the local Booker in Chester. Something about my discussion with Trevor Tutt had inspired me. I knew where the store was, in a brilliant location at the end of the motorway, but you could no longer see it from the road as it was completely hidden by an overgrown hedge. As we arrived it looked a sad place. A massive building and car park but it obviously hadn't been painted for years and rubbish and litter were everywhere. Entry was strictly for trade only but, although I'd never been in, we had a card in the office for the staff canteen so we used that. Many people I knew had cash and carry cards. There was a certain kudos in being able to 'get in' to somewhere you weren't supposed to. You felt you were buying things 'wholesale' but the reality was it was just more convenient to buy some things in bulk by the case and store them in the garage.

Inside the building the first thing that struck me was how vast it was, but with an enormous amount of wasted space. It was quite gloomy and we realised that at least 50 per cent of the fluorescent light tubes weren't working. I counted them and over 200 were dead! As we wandered round we couldn't help spotting things that we wanted to buy for home, catering size rolls of cooking foil, large boxes of bin bags, a case of beer. We slowly stacked up our trolley and ended up spending over £300 between us on things that you either don't see in the supermarket or it was just convenient to buy while we were there, like the case of beer.

They sold everything a supermarket would sell and more, except by the case. They had a butchery section with a good range of meat; they sold stationery and garden furniture, those umbrella-shaped gas heaters for your patio. In fact it was really a hypermarket but a very tired one. There was a café section, which had closed down years ago but they hadn't even bothered to move the old equipment. Instead, it was just roped off. Their refrigeration equipment was twenty years out of date and their frozen food range was appalling. We could see opportunities to increase sales everywhere.

I've always had a theory that if you are going to be given the challenge of running a retail business, it shouldn't be Waitrose. How could you ever improve it? Better to be given the Co-op where there's lots of opportunity. This looked a better business opportunity than even the Co-op. Andy and Russell agreed. I thought about it a lot over the next few days and became very excited about the possibilities. I knew Booker was up for sale from talking to Alan Smith and Somerfield had already tried to buy it but the deal had fallen apart. There were bound to be buying synergies available by putting together their sales of £3½ billion and ours of £2 billion, and also cost savings, but the real opportunity was to grow sales in the business. Booker looked like a slumbering giant that had been neglected for years and was held in such low regard we could probably do a cheap deal.

I recognised even then that this wouldn't look like an obvious thing to do and people would be surprised if Iceland and Booker got together. Somerfield taking over Kwik Save had generated a lot of hype and excitement at the time. Even retail analysts who should have known better only saw two retail companies and the cost savings that would come from putting them together. I knew that deal would never work and said so at the time. How could you turn Kwik Save into Somerfield and run it as one business? It was always doomed to failure. They had different customer bases, products, pricing structures and cultures. I remember having a conversation with Andrew Fowler, one of the most respected retail analysts, and putting this to him. 'I don't give a shit,' he said. 'There's enough cost savings and synergies in the pipeline to underpin the share price for the next three years, that's all anyone's interested in.' I think it underpinned the price for about three months and the disaster that followed shook the City's confidence and would make it much more difficult for us to do a deal which people might perceive as being similar.

The Iceland/Bejam deal was of course something different and quite unique, simply two identical businesses getting together and just losing one set of overheads. Booker and Iceland were such totally different businesses it wouldn't be possible even to think about turning one into the other but you could have two entirely different front-end formulas with a shared 'engine room' behind. I felt that without any front-end integration it would be seen as low risk. Iceland was running out of growth opportunities and looked like it would become much more pedestrian in its performance. I was attracted by the idea of another leg to our business with real development potential.

There was something alien, to a retailer, about a cash and carry's entry policy. Customers coming into Iceland were welcomed with open arms. 'Please, please come in and spend your money' would be our attitude. We'd do anything to get them through the door. A cash and carry was more akin to a nightclub with a bouncer on the door, only letting in those privileged few who qualified. I thought lots of people would like to shop in Booker and wondered why they didn't relax their entry policy or even open to the public like Costco. Trevor Tutt felt the same when I asked him about it but said it would be difficult to change attitudes as the staff at Booker had known no other way and saw restricted entry as a cornerstone of their business. Booker's customers were small shopkeepers and caterers and it was felt they wouldn't want to meet their own customers in there. I wasn't so sure.

I decided to ring Stuart Rose and sound him out. We arranged to have dinner and we met at the Halkin Hotel, London. I recognised Stuart from his photograph that had recently appeared in *Retail Week*, alongside mine, as one of the retail personalities of the year! I'd never met him but knew him by reputation. He'd started his career at Marks & Spencer and one of his claims to fame was introducing wine into their food hall. He'd gone on to join Burton and worked for the legendary Ralph Halpern. When Gerald Hoerner took over and split the business into two, Debenhams and Arcadia, Stuart's mate Terry Green got Debenhams and Gerald ran Arcadia himself, leaving Stuart without a job. He was out of work for a short while but then when GUS (Great Universal Stores) bid for Argos, and the CEO of Argos fell ill with cancer halfway through the bid, Stuart was offered the job, largely because he was available immediately. It was a strange position where he couldn't really lose. His real job was to defend Argos in the bid and force GUS to increase their price for the company, which they did. Stuart was on a success fee (or a 'lose fee') of £500,000 for just a few months' work. I suppose he only had to be careful he didn't actually win the defence! He was deemed to have done a good job by the City and Argos shareholders did very well out of the exercise. He was out of work again when Alan Smith recruited him for Booker.

I wasn't sure what to make of him at first. We had a drink in the bar and to begin with it felt like I wasn't getting his whole attention and talking to him was quite difficult. When we went through for the meal, he seemed to relax and somehow we got straight into discussing the deal without much in the way of foreplay. It was apparent he enjoyed his food and wine and we got on well. Stuart told me the Booker story and how he had cleaned up the business and paid off a lot of the debt through sales of dozens of subsidiary companies. He agreed no one had ever invested a penny more than they'd had to in the cash and carry outlets themselves, although a few years ago a huge investment of £90 million had been made in a completely unnecessary distribution network called 'Project Heartland'. This was the biggest single factor in the group's difficulties. He said they were in the middle of selling off part of the depot network. Booker's recovery was such that they expected to make £45 million in profits in the current year. I asked him about the chances of relaxing the door policy at Booker and he said he felt it was an obvious thing to try but there would be terrific opposition from within the business.

He reeled off some figures which amazed me. There were about 100 Booker cash and carry branches with over 2 million square feet of floor space, of which 20 per cent was surplus to their current needs and therefore unused. Ninety per cent of the population of the UK were within a 25-minute drive of a Booker but the biggest surprise was that the average rent of their stores was only £4 per square foot as opposed to about £25 to £35 for a typical supermarket. OK, a big disadvantage was that many of the units had tight planning restrictions for wholesale only but what an opportunity and what a low-cost infrastructure to build from. Stuart was keen to do a deal with a retailer and felt size was important and that an infusion of new ideas would help Booker grow. He was also aware of the possible cost savings and synergy benefits that should come from such a deal and saw no downside. We discussed the possible stock market reaction to a deal. Cash and carry was seen as a declining market and therefore rated very lowly. Retailers were rated much higher and while we agreed the PE rating for a combined business wouldn't be as high as Iceland had currently, we felt it unlikely the group would fall to the Booker rating. A deal was likely to be earnings-enhancing from day one.

I said I was keen to take things a stage further and that this deal 'felt right'. I wasn't sure where Stuart stood with his personal ambitions so I decided to put his mind at rest. I said that in my experience deals often got done, or didn't get done, because of ego. I explained that I had no ego tied up in this deal and, while I wanted to do the right thing by Iceland, I also wanted to retire and release some of my cash from the business. I was happy to stay on as non-executive Chairman but I would want Stuart to run the business. We had a long discussion about this with Stuart asking me how I could let go of 'my baby' but I convinced him I genuinely wanted a break. I would be more than happy still to be involved with the business – and in fact I had a million ideas as to what we might do with Booker – but I just didn't want to run the company day-to-day any more. Stuart enjoyed a good reputation in the City, he was younger than me and it seemed an obvious choice for him to be the CEO. I thought it would solve my succession problem and go down very well in the City.

We discussed the rest of the management team. I suggested Andy should be Group Finance Director and Stuart agreed. I asked who would run Booker and Stuart told me about Charles Wilson, a younger guy he had worked with at Argos and Burton. He rated him very highly. Stuart asked who we had at Iceland and I explained the situation. I said Russell was in the obvious position to become Managing Director but it would be a high risk. I said he was 'either a wizard or a wanker' and, given a free rein, he would either turn Iceland into Microsoft or bankrupt it. After some discussion we agreed we would give him the job but keep a close eye on him. If he didn't work out we'd replace him. Stuart then told me it was not his original intention to stay at Booker but Iceland and Booker together was a different ball game and he saw it as exciting and he would love the challenge. Stuart had a habit throughout the meal of thrusting out his hand for me to shake whenever we reached any point of apparent agreement. It was a strange thing to do but somehow gave me the impression he could deliver what he was saying.

I couldn't believe how far we'd got over one meal. We agreed the next stage would be for us to meet again, this time with Charles

Wilson present, and exchange some numbers. Then we'd look at the possibility of using the famous Ernst & Young cost price comparison programme and see what the buying synergies looked like. I reported back to Andy and Russell and suggested we had a deal if we wanted one. They were both obviously desperate to meet Stuart as they would be working for him but Russell seemed more interested in what Stuart's management style was like than finding out whether the deal actually made sense. I guess he felt he wouldn't be much involved in the evaluation process anyway as it would largely be a numbers exercise. We agreed we would tell nobody else at this stage, as any leak would kill the deal before it started.

I met Stuart and Charles in a meeting room at a suitably remote hotel I can't even remember the name of. Stuart and Charles couldn't have presented a greater contrast. Stuart was smooth and well dressed and talked a great deal about big picture stuff but without much in the way of detail. Charles was much younger but looked older than you knew he must be. He was softly spoken, mild mannered and very polite. His collar was two sizes too big for him, which emphasised a large Adam's apple. The knot in his tie was enormous. I never saw him dressed any differently. He had an amazingly high forehead and his whole appearance was that of an academic. I liked him straight away and somehow you took whatever he said seriously. In spite of the contrast Stuart and Charles complemented each other very well.

Charles turned out to have an encyclopaedic grasp of the Booker business and we spent a couple of hours talking through our respective operations, our strengths and weaknesses, and exploring what benefits we could bring to each other through a merger. Provided the cost savings and buying benefits we hoped for were actually available, we could see no downside to the deal. Iceland and Booker as trading entities would be unaffected and the group would benefit from cost savings and shared expertise. We decided to set up an evaluation team which should consist of Charles and Mike Camp, the Booker Finance Director, and Andy Pritchard and Tarsem Dhaliwal from

Iceland. The deal was essentially a 'nil premium merger' but for practical reasons it was only possible for Iceland to take over Booker. In
any traditional takeover, price is an issue and a big premium would be
expected for the company that was being taken over. In this case both
sets of shareholders would benefit and we agreed the price Iceland
would pay for Booker would be based on our respective share prices
that day. I shook hands a few more times with Stuart during the
meeting and we left with a deal 'in principle' but subject of course
to a mass of conditions.

The team set to work and both companies gave their cost price
files to Ernst & Young who ran their programme. Price comparisons
are notoriously difficult to achieve because of the many variables. The
actual basic cost price of a product is just one element of price. There
could be discounts and over-riders for achieving volume targets,
advertising allowances and many other areas of supplier 'support'.
We had to attempt to build all these factors into the equation. The
computer program could only compare exactly the same products,
the same bar code in fact, so if Iceland stocked one brand and Booker
an identical product but under a different brand, it was discounted.
Different pack sizes were also excluded, along with supplier promotions, so the final number of products actually compared would only
be a small percentage of the range. Whatever number the computer
finally threw out, it would relate to a small proportion of sales but
it could then be grossed up to arrive at the true potential for buying
savings.

Our distribution systems were looked at for opportunities to share
transport and storage and our head office systems were evaluated for
areas of duplication. Although both Stuart and Charles hated their
head office at Wellingborough and would have been happy to close
it down we decided that would present too much risk. There should
be more than enough cost savings without anything so dramatic.
Booker also had a smart corporate headquarters in Buckingham Gate
in London where Stuart based himself. He explained they had sub-let
nearly all the space and it was handy for Stuart who lived round the

corner. He wanted to keep it as his base and it was useful for meeting suppliers and, because of the sub-lets, it cost us virtually nothing. We also tried to guesstimate what our areas of strength would do for sales in each other's business and the profit impact of that. If Iceland couldn't double Booker's frozen food sales we should all go home! Booker took nearly £1 billion a year in booze sales and Iceland took nothing by comparison. Surely their expertise could help us? Iceland and Booker together would become the largest sellers of Coca Cola in Europe! Surely that would give us some clout with the supplier?

About ten days after Ernst & Young took our cost price file, Andy called me into his office to tell me he had a buying number from Ernst and Young. There were £7½ million of savings to be had from simply buying existing products from whoever had the best cost price. We thought that was a high number. If you assumed similar relative buying strengths on products that weren't compared, if you added in benefits from one company changing suppliers for better terms in exchange for the extra volume, if you added in the extra discounts we could squeeze from suppliers simply because we were bigger, the number was enormous ... but hypothetical. By the time we finished adding everything realistic together we came up with big buying price savings for the remainder of the year 2000 and even bigger cost savings for the following year. We decided to play safe and cut the numbers by 25 per cent so we had plenty up our sleeve.

We all agreed the deal made sense and we should go ahead. It was time to tell the non-executive directors and bring in our advisers. Secrecy was paramount but now the net was widening, the chances of a leak increased dramatically. For that reason I decided one broker on our side was enough. ABN Amro were our 'corporate' brokers and it wasn't really necessary to tell Ossie, our joint broker from Charterhouse, at least until nearer the time. We put together a presentation and had a big meeting at ABN's offices in Broadgate with the advisers and non-executives present from both sides to test their reaction. Mark Astaire of ABN Amro was very bullish: he thought the deal was brilliant and our share price would go through the roof on announcement. He rated Stuart Rose as a star performer. He told me his Dad had made a lot of money out of Booker shares and he'd even had breakfast with Stuart to thank him. ABN were big supporters of Booker.

Meanwhile, problems at Iceland continued to get worse. Sales were slowing up a little, while Wincanton, the operators of the new Enfield depot, were just not getting either costs or their delivery performance under control and I was having to escalate our complaints and requests for compensation to the level of their Chairman. Profits just weren't coming through at the level sales dictated and we were forced to go to our suppliers for better deals to prop up the profit line. There was nothing unusual about that, but it was a shame that it was necessary in a good sales period.

Russell's behaviour was getting more bizarre than ever. The organic vegetable initiative was coming together but he seemed determined to extend it into other areas without waiting to see if vegetable sales were successful. It was as if he was on an organic mission. He was about to launch a range of organic ice cream that was produced by a local factory near where he lived. He told me about a deal he could do with surplus organic milk from Denmark that we could buy at the same price as ordinary milk and we could therefore turn all our milk to organic ... at no extra cost. The only problem he could see was the fact that it was Danish and English farmers might not like it. I was cautious but humoured him and suggested he should find out more before we discussed it again.

He was also pushing more than ever, and completely unreasonably, to be appointed sole Managing Director and to be given his big chance. He appeared not to have an atom of self-doubt and although I tried on many occasions to explain where his areas of inexperience were, it didn't shorten his timescale. I wanted him to run store operations, to get involved in distribution and shopfitting, and to understand how the office worked. I felt it might take a couple of years but he had to experience all areas of the business before he could run it. Of course the Booker deal would change all that and I'd already told him that if it came off he could have the job. Hopefully in the new structure it would be less important for him to understand 'the back office' and we could replace him anyway after the deal was done if he didn't perform.

Russell somehow didn't seem convinced the deal would happen. One day I'd arranged to take him out on store visits but we only got as far as the local Little Chef. After two hours and five cups of tea he basically gave me an ultimatum. He could see no future at Iceland for a man of his talent unless I agreed to make him the MD regardless of what happened with Booker. I was totally confident the deal would happen but the last thing I needed was any upset in the management team which might jeopardise or delay the deal. He was blackmailing me but in the end I thought 'sod it, he can have the job'. If the Booker deal didn't happen why not give him a go, he might make it work and I'd decided I was just going to retire anyway. He was my only option for a successor without going through a lot of disruption and spending a year or two finding a replacement. If I did replace him there was no guarantee the new guy would work out anyway. A lot of people would be horrified at the idea of Russell running the business but he did have a following. Anyway, it wasn't going to happen, the Booker deal would come off and he'd be a less important part of a bigger business with more management support.

16
The Deal

It was a beautiful spring morning, the sun was shining and thousands of rhododendrons in my garden were in full bloom. It was the kind of day when you realise there is more to life than going into the office every day. Stuart and I walked slowly round the garden, conversation alternating between garden talk and the price of our respective shares. The Booker share price had risen since we had agreed the price of the deal and Stuart obviously had problems with his non-execs who felt they should now get a better price. I kept reminding Stuart we'd shaken hands on the deal price but he was trying to say we hadn't actually agreed anything and anyway it was his Chairman who was causing the problems. We were both pretending we would walk away from the deal if the other didn't agree.

Andy Pritchard kept running the numbers but the reality was it didn't make much difference anyway. It all boiled down to what percentage of the enlarged company the Booker shareholders or the Iceland shareholders would own. The benefits from the deal to both Iceland and Booker shareholders were huge and we were only arguing about pennies. Some compromise was called for, as saving face often becomes a bigger issue than the dispute itself. My strategy was to offer a tiny increase and with a lot of anguish and pained expressions say there was no more and I would have to walk away.

I planned to hold out probably longer than he expected and let him fly back to London without a final agreement and wait for him to come back to me.

We stood on the lawn in front of my house and it really was a beautiful day. 'I'll tell you what,' said Stuart, 'When this is all over, I'd like to come back here with my wife and drink a glass of champagne in your garden.' I hoped he would. We were getting to like each other. I drove Stuart to the airport and saw him onto our plane and let him go without an agreement. His Chairman was John Napier and several people had warned me that he was a pretty awkward character. Stuart explained that he was feeling excluded from the deal and might block it. He suggested I should meet him for dinner and stroke his ego. The deal wouldn't happen unless I did. I left it with Stuart to organise.

Booker still had borrowings of £273 million and their principal bank was Barclays. I imagined they'd been through some pretty tough times with the banks and were paying some penal rates of interest because of their low rating. We enjoyed a good relationship with Barclays and they knew we were keen for another deal. They'd made a lot of money out of us over the past 30 years and only the year before I'd been invited to lunch with Martin Taylor, their Chief Executive at the time, as a sort of thank you for the 'buyback' success. If a deal was done the total borrowings of Iceland and Booker would still be the same. We weren't looking for any extra money, but it would all be under the Iceland umbrella and Iceland was highly regarded. Andy and I saw no problem with the banking facilities and arranged to see Barclays' credit committee. We talked them through the deal and they promised to come back with a decision in ten days' time. They asked if we'd been to see anyone else. On previous deals we usually ran two horses. Royal Bank of Scotland was always keen to work with us but Barclays always came up with the goods in the end. On this occasion we said they had the deal to themselves but it had to be a fast decision. They left us with a warm feeling and we decided the only argument would be about interest rates.

Assuming the deal was going to happen we'd drafted a timetable and we felt it was important to announce the deal at the same time as the Booker half-year results, which would be good. The deal would then go final just before our half-year. We had often talked about changing the Iceland year-end from December, which is a bad time for a retailer with important Christmas sales to digest, to the more usual company year-end of March. Booker's year-end was already March and this seemed like the appropriate time to make the change. This would mean the enlarged company would have, for one accounting period, a fifteen-month 'year'. Suddenly things looked tight and we had to go into overdrive to meet the deadlines. We had to get the banking facilities in place and each company would have their auditors carry out due diligence on the other. We had to organise the mechanics of the deal through our respective merchant bankers and stockbrokers and we had a prospectus to publish. Not least we had to agree the final price and I had to stroke Napier.

Napier insisted we meet at the Savoy Grill which was about as public a place as possible if you wanted to be seen by other business people or financial journalists. Stuart gave me a few pointers about how to humour him and said he would come along to make the introduction and then disappear and leave us to it. He would rejoin us for coffee at the end. Napier had a growling voice you had to strain to hear, and it was rather like meeting a fierce headmaster. I was lectured for two hours about his business successes and in particular his current miracle working at Kelda, the Yorkshire water utility, where he was CEO. He put me straight about the minimum price that would be acceptable for Booker and we eventually agreed a small increase on the original deal. I don't think I've ever disliked anyone so much at the first meeting. He seemed to have the most incredible chip on his shoulder about people who had more money than he did. He'd bought a lot of Booker shares when he took the job as Chairman and stood to make about £1 million profit on the deal.

We'd only got a few days left before the planned announcement of the deal and incredibly there had still been no hint of a leak. Then Barclays came back with a bombshell. They couldn't do the financing; the deal was too big for them. I was stunned. If that was the case, why didn't they tell us at the outset rather than leaving it to the deadline? I rang several people I knew at Barclays including Derek Arden, a senior director. 'What do you mean too big?' I asked. 'It's £600 million and you're already lending it to us between Booker and Iceland. You've just got to combine the two.' The truth was probably that the syndicate of banks that made up the Booker loan had been through the worst and were now enjoying a high rate of return and why would they want to unscramble everything and then re-lend the same money to us at a lower rate? Barclays would have to take on the initial debt and then sell it down to other banks and they were worried that some of the banks would not want to come back into the syndicate even under the Iceland umbrella. The deal still involved Booker and their name and reputation was about as low as you could get. The banks weren't interested and didn't want to know about Booker's recovery. They just remembered the bad times. Booker's reputation with the banks was very much worse than we had realised.

There was an advert running at the time and I'd seen it several times at the cinema. Anthony Hopkins played a big shot, talking about big deals and big companies and big everything. Big being used in every sentence including how you need a big bank ... Barclays. I replayed this to Derek and he cringed on the telephone. I don't think it was the first time that advert had come to haunt him. 'OK,' he said, 'We're a little bank.' I rang John Maguire at RBS. I liked John. He was a senior director at RBS and played the guitar in a rock 'n' roll band. I'd seen him perform at a club in Preston, a restaurant where you dance on the tables at the end of the meal. 'Have I got a deal for you!' I said, and he was in my office the next day.

In the end, Barclays and RBS agreed to do the deal between them but would only lend £500 million. Andy reran the cash flow and decided it would be enough as we had another £50 million offer from Rabobank. We were now only a few days from our planned announcement and the terms of the loan still had to be agreed.

Barclays had already quoted the rate of interest they were going to charge us at an obscene percentage over base. I appealed to John at the joint lenders RBS and, after reconsidering, they decided not to reduce the rate, but to increase it! I was furious but felt we were in a corner. It was as if Barclays had deliberately delayed things to take us so close to the deadline that we had no alternative but to agree to their demands. The real blow came when they said they also wanted an 'arrangement fee' of £6 million. This was grossly excessive in my view and seemed like blackmail at such short notice. I complained that our past relationship appeared to count for nothing but it was clearly take it or leave it.

We had to publish a prospectus, which would be sent to both sets of shareholders that would explain every detail of the deal and the rationale behind it. Several drafts would normally be prepared before the final document would be printed, overnight, the day before the deal was announced. As issues came up, and were discussed and agreed, the document was continually revised. One such issue was share options. Some Iceland staff, including me, had options that were issued three years previously and had just matured and were ready to be cashed. Normal practice is for staff in most companies to cash share options as soon as they mature. They are seen as part of salary and a new kitchen or car has probably been planned with the proceeds. The fact that a deal was in the making meant these options had to be put on hold.

Booker staff on the other hand had massive share options that had still a couple of years to run before they matured. Very often one of the rules with options is that if the company is taken over this triggers the options and they can be cashed immediately. Because Iceland was technically taking over Booker it meant their staff had the right to cash their options early and Stuart Rose would pick up £3 million on the deal. This was actually fair and no one in Iceland had a problem with it. It was their reward for turning round Booker, paid a bit early! Of course they could have elected to roll over their options into the Iceland option scheme but the cash was attractive to everybody and it went into the prospectus that staff would cash their options.

Stuart also presented me with two other issues he wanted in the document, which caught me by surprise. One was that he wanted the option to change the name of the new enlarged group. No one had thought of a new name at that stage but I didn't have a problem with this and could quite see the logic behind it. Booker people wouldn't want to feel they had been swallowed up by Iceland but would be happy to belong to an independently named holding group which included Iceland, Woodward's and Booker.

Stuart also wanted me to put a date on my retirement. I was desperate to go non-executive but had been vague about the timing. I wanted a little flexibility to go when I felt the time was right, probably sooner rather than later. I had been so high-profile in the press that I was worried my retirement might not go down too well and I didn't want the announcement of my retirement to deflect from the Booker deal. Stuart came on very strong about this and insisted I put a date in the prospectus. At first my natural inclination was to resist and certainly Iceland's advisers and my fellow directors felt it would not be well received by the City. But I could see Stuart's point of view. Nobody really believed I would let go and I could understand Stuart being worried that I would hang on or change my mind and he wouldn't get a clear run at the job. I took it as a good sign that he wanted a definite date from me, as it meant that he was obviously keen to be in charge. I saw my job after the merger as handing over to Stuart and supporting him and teaching him all about Iceland. There can only be one boss and it was going to be Stuart. I would probably have gone in November 2000 if I had had the flexibility, but under duress I agreed on March 2001, which gave me a little more time. I don't know why I wanted it.

The deal was to be announced on Thursday, 25 May. The night before all the Iceland and Booker directors were in their respective lawyers' offices along with the entourage of other advisers. Andy and John Berry were still closeted with the banks finalising the terms of the banking covenants. Next morning at 7am the announcement of the deal was to be made and then we would hold an analysts' meeting at 9.30am followed by a series of presentations to shareholders which was likely to go on all week. Amazingly there had been no hint of a leak and Mark Astaire was still confident our share price would rise sharply on announcement.

I was really worried about Charterhouse still being kept in the dark. Ossie had been a good friend for years but there was always friction between him and ABN, especially over sharing fees. Mark always felt ABN did all the work on a deal and Ossie, as joint broker, used to pick up half the fees for doing nothing! I always used Mark for corporate advice but, while Charterhouse didn't really have a corporate department worth talking about, Ossie had a far better understanding of the market and he did the majority of business in Iceland shares. I knew Ossie would be seriously put out that he hadn't been brought into this deal but I had expected that I would have been able to see him before now and explain everything.

The banking details should have been sorted out by now and were holding everything up. I had expected the whole deal to be signed and put to bed by mid-afternoon. I wanted to practise our presentation to the City with Stuart and we still had to bring in the ABN and Charterhouse analysts, after the market had closed, so they could be fully briefed for the next day. I thought we all might even have dinner together and an early night. The lawyers were organising the mountain of papers that had to be signed by all the directors but nothing could be done until the banking covenants were agreed. Barclays and Royal Bank of Scotland each had a team of people at their lawyers' offices, Simmons & Simmons, and were ploughing through the agreement with Andy and John Berry at a leisurely pace as if they had all the time in the world. I was getting increasingly frustrated and panicky and had already rung John Maguire to try to get him to hurry things up but he said it was out of his hands.

Tim Steadman, our lawyer from Herbert Smith, decided at about 7pm that 99 per cent of the detail was really agreed and it would be

OK for the Iceland directors to sign up and then John McLachlan and Russell could leave. Iain Sharp and Tom Knowlton gave their approval by telephone. I kept speaking to Stuart but there was no chance Napier would allow the Booker directors to sign up until 100 per cent of everything was agreed and the document typed. At 10pm I rang a friend who gave me the home phone number of the Chief Executive of Barclays. I rang him but he wasn't in. I spoke to Andy several times but he couldn't tell me how long it was all going to take. All the meat of the agreement was settled. They were just finessing the detail. It was as if they were being deliberately awkward.

At 1am Stuart rang to say the Booker directors were going out for something to eat and would I join them? We drove around in a convoy of cars and tried a few places which were all closed before settling on The Groucho Club where Stuart was a member. We all had their luxury beef burger and chips with some good red wine that Stuart selected. After the meal I went round to Simmons & Simmons' offices and into the banking meeting at 3am. There were at least twenty bankers and lawyers around the table and I blew a fuse. I accused them of ineptitude and blackmail and hypocrisy. Barclays had deliberately delayed until we had lost all our negotiating power. I asked them what the point of the meeting was. How could we negotiate anything when we were announcing the deal in four hours and they held all the cards? Why didn't they just go and write out everything they wanted and we'd sign it? They all looked stunned at my outburst. The bankers all stood up and left the room without a word. I felt a lot better. John Berry and Andy Pritchard thought it was all highly amusing and couldn't possibly have made anything worse.

We hung around for a couple of hours and read the morning papers while negotiations resumed and finally everything was agreed and typed up. Booker then held a full treatment formal board meeting, where they went through everything in great detail. Napier was enjoying his last moment of power. I thought it was quite sad that all the board seemed to be so scared of him. He asked everyone in turn if they understood and agreed with the terms of the deal. I thought

The cold war

Shops slash prices as Walker opens new store in North Wales

By Steve Bagnall Daily Post Staff

MILLIONAIRE Malcolm Walker sparked a frozen food price war in North Wales yesterday.

The former Iceland chairman launched his new first frozen food store, Cooltrader, in Wrexham and immediately undercut his old firm's prices.

But this morning Iceland was expected to hit back by reducing their prices in retaliation.

It is an intriguing battle which will save money for North Wales shoppers.

The official launch of Cooltrader on Island Green had been a closely guarded secret, but the doors were finally opened yesterday.

A little way across town, staff at Iceland said they would be reviewing their prices in response and added yesterday's prices would be different to today's prices.

But Mr Walker revealed he had no designs on setting up a rival chain on the scale of Iceland.

He said: "We will see how it goes. I have no plans to build an empire. I want to keep things small.

"I wanted to have time off. This is an opportunity to set up another company in the frozen food business.

"It is unique, very different to Iceland, and the suppliers have been very supportive of us. There are very little overheads."

Mr Walker laughed off suggestions he had tried to poach staff from Iceland.

" I advertised for jobs in the local paper, and when the word got round that I was setting up a frozen food store, I started getting calls from senior staff at Iceland who were interested in coming over," he said.

"I didn't need to poach because it was coming the other way. These rumours are not true – I have not taken any staff from Iceland."

His former company had threatened to take legal action against Mr Walker claiming a clause in his contract prevents him from opening a rival firm for two years.

Yesterday, Mr Walker dismissed the threat.

He said: "I don't have a valid contract with Iceland and there is nothing in the world to stop me opening this shop."

An Iceland spokesman refused to say whether they would take legal action.

He added: "Malcolm Walker has reneged on an agreement and Iceland will deal with the competition the same way it deals with all its competition. I cannot comment on the matter of legal action."

The company refused to comment on whether prices would

□ PLAYING IT COOL: Malcolm Walker at the opening of his new Wrexham store, and, right, unveiling Iceland's new image last year

be cut, but one senior staff member at Iceland's Wrexham store said prices were under review and there would be surprises today.

Inside Cooltrader, shoppers were busy getting to grips with the offers, including 50p Christmas puddings.

Mr Walker yesterday promised to deliver food and groceries at rock bottom prices against rival firms. But he insists Cooltrader will be different to Iceland.

The shelves will be packed with a constant turn-over of available bargain stock, snapped up from suppliers and on the shelves in less than 48 hours.

Mr Walker left Iceland controversially after selling £13.6m worth of shares last December.

Weeks later, a series of profit warnings was issued by the company and Iceland shares then dropped from a high 346p to 141p. An investigation is under way into alleged insider trading, but Mr Walker is confident he will be vindicated.

"My shares sell had nothing whatsoever to do with the share price drop," he said. "I would expect an inquiry, but I am 1,000pc confident that I have done nothing wrong.

"I enjoy being in business, and it was never my intention to retire. We have streamlined the structure here, there is no advertising, no buy one get one free deals, basically the money goes into the low price."

steve.bagnall@dailypost.co.uk

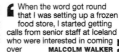

❝ When the word got round that I was setting up a frozen food store, I started getting calls from senior staff at Iceland who were interested in coming over ❞

MALCOLM WALKER

Mumph

I'M NOT STEPPING ASIDE, YOU STEP ASIDE

The launch of Cooltrader.

Nigel Woodward,
friend and
Iceland's first
supplier.

Steven Walker, friend and
business partner.

Jon Asgeir Johannesson of Baugur.

The Viking raiders – L to R: Palmi Haraldsson, Jon Asgeir Johannesson, Gunnar Sigurdsson.

Baugur circles BFG as profits continue to fall

By Teena Lyons

ICELANDIC corporate raider **Baugur** is waiting on this week's results from **Big Food Group** before making a decision on whether to bid for the company.

Baugur already owns 23 per cent of BFG, which runs the struggling Iceland frozen food chain, along with wholesaler Bookers and a logistics operation, but has previously said it had no immediate plans to bid for the conglomerate.

Under City takeover rules, Baugur has been barred from making a move for BFG for the past six months after its statement last October that it would not be making a bid. It has been free of that restriction since last month and is now understood to be waiting for this week's results before making a decision.

The Takeover Panel-imposed ban has expired and conveniently coincides with the publication of BFG's final results on Wednesday, when the company is expected to announce a slump in pre-tax profits from £42.9 million in 2002 to about £31.5 million this year.

According to sources, Baugur will be 'watching with interest' the latest figures from BFG and, along with the fall in headline profits, the news is not expected to be positive.

The company's last quarter's trading statement issued last month showed sales declining at an increasing rate of 3.6 per cent

Gamble: Bill Grimsey in banking on the new Iceland stores

against 2.9 per cent in the previous quarter, and some analysts are even predicting the company's pre-tax profits could come in at about the £28 million mark.

Along with overall figures, Baugur will also be watching to see how the next generation of Iceland stores, on which chief executive Bill Grimsey has staked the future of the brand, will be performing.

Baugur chief executive Jon Asgeir Johannesson has been scathing about the new stores and the drive to take the chain upmar-

ket. Much of his company's attention will be focused on how well the refurbished businesses are trading by comparison with the rest of the retailer's estate.

The Reykjavik-based group has built up holdings in a number of undervalued British retailers recently, including stakes in House of Fraser, Somerfield, Mothercare and Selfridges.

The current wave of merger and acquisition activity in the sector appears to have reignited its interest in BFG.

Mail on Sunday

Larus Welding of Landsbanki and, later, Glitnir.

Man who went into the cold

In 2001, he was frozen out of the food business he founded. Now Malcolm Walker and Iceland have been reunited reports **Sarah Ryle**

Fruits of his labours? Walker left Iceland as a plc, at a time when the stock price was starting to dip. Now it's private again, but shares are trading even lower.   Photograph by Dave Chancellor/PA

Profile

Name Malcolm Conrad Walker

Age 59

Born Huddersfield, west Yorkshire

Family Married for 35 years to Rhianydd; one son and two daughters

Education Mirfield Grammar, Huddersfield. Four O-levels and a 'degree in common sense'

Career Trainee manager, Woolworths, 1964–71; founded and ran Iceland 1970–January 2001; founded Cooltrader 2001

Interests skiing, shooting, business, sailing, home and family

ON FRIDAY, four years and 11 days after he was so rudely interrupted, Malcolm Walker once more strode through the doors of Iceland's Deeside headquarters.

His telephone had not stopped ringing all week, and this was not surprising: corporate stories rarely come more colourful than this one and Walker has a personality easily big enough to bear the weight of events. The very fact that he has returned to the company he founded with £30 in 1970 and ran until he was drummed out on 31 January 2001 is remarkable. But he has denied this is a sentimental journey. 'When Baugur contacted me, it seemed a good idea to get back in,' he has said.

It is typical of Walker's career that there is an additional bit of colour: Friday was his 59th birthday. He is one of those businessmen who makes headline writers' jobs easy, intentionally or otherwise.

Was he nervous the night before? Not really, lay that in case to him. He laid back from a winter break in the Maldives only a few days beforehand. That was an interesting choice for a holiday, given that he was visiting those paradise islands four years ago when his empire was wrested from him.

By last Thursday he was raring to go, a keenness sharpened because he was apparently unable to visit the headquarters before that moment. He could not do anything about that, despite having secured the company's 750 or so shops

been wondering about their new job boss: Walker sold half his shareholding back in December 2000 for £13.5 million a matter of weeks before a profit warning that wiped almost half the value off the stock. But he was looking forward to finding some familiar faces, shaking a few hands and perhaps opening a few dusty cupboards and filing cabinets. He cannot wait to find out what has gone on

Wellingborough, Northamptonshire.

Walker and Grimsey have had a difficult relationship. They were kept in different meeting rooms during Baugur's protracted negotiations leading up to the acquisition of BFG. Walker had hired Grimsey to replace Stuart Rose, now M&S chief executive, who left unexpectedly to take a job at Arcadia in November 2000. Grimsey came with a

started officially in January 2001, had a good look at Christmas trading. The BFG board decided on a profits warning, delivering a second soon after. Walker had to go. This was not the exit he had planned.

The Serious Fraud Office investigated Walker's December share trade. He found out via a second-class letter to his lawyers last October that the investiga-

believes that the future lies in convenience stores. 'Iceland's strength is in frozen food, but if you walked in there you would not be sure what it stood for at the moment,' he has said.

Baugur's youthful boss, Jon Asgeir Johannesson, started his retail career with deep-discount shops in his native Iceland and he thinks there is a gap in the UK market. Last week his approach to Somerfield was announced.

Walker does not buy into the rationale behind Baugur's 190p-per-share interest in Somerfield, as it is explained by City retail analysts. Rhys Williams of Seymour Pierce thinks a deal would 'create a significant food retail operation that offers substantial cost efficiencies' while Anthony Platts of Wise Speke says the City has ignored Somerfield because of its disappointing sales and pension deficit, but that combining it with Iceland makes 'perfect sense'.

Walker, however, believes that he is in the driving seat and will lead the new interest in taking on Tesco, Sainsbury or Asda on their own battlefields. The only attraction he sees in discounters Netto or Aldi is that they, as private companies, have a low profile to be envied and emulated.

No – frozen food is Walker's game. He started Iceland with a colleague from Woolworths, which sacked them both when bosses worked out they were moonlighting by buying frozen food in bulk and then splitting it up into shopper-friendly portions.

Malcolm goes back to Iceland in 2005.

Iceland head office at Deeside.

The original Roxy American diner.

The refurbished Roxy staff restaurant.

Kerry Katona and round pound pricing.

malcolm walker

ICELAND'S COMEBACK KID

Malcolm Walker has made a spectacular return at Iceland Foods and tells Liz Hamson frozen food is back

Iceland's comeback kid.

Retail Week

Breaking news and top jobs at **retail-week.com**

February 6, 2009 £4.95

THE EXTENT OF THE FALLOUT
- The reaction on the high street
- Uncertainty over Baugur's quoted company interests
- Baugur-backed retailers defend their businesses

Pages 2-

BAUGUR TEETERS ON THE BRINK AS IT IS FORCED TO FILE FOR PROTECTION FROM CREDITORS

Baugur in meltdown

By Amy Shields

Baugur's tangled web of retail investments will move closer to unravelling today as the investor begins a moratorium process likely to lead to administration.

Baugur was forced to file for protection from its creditors under the Icelandic equivalent of Chapter 11 bankruptcy – as exclusively revealed by *RW Online* on Wednesday – after negotiations with failed Icelandic bank Landsbanki over debt restructuring failed.

It followed a move by Landsbanki, one of Baugur's funders, to file a petition to place a Baugur subsidiary, which owns stakes in House of Fraser, Hamleys, Aurum and Iceland, into administration.

Landsbanki appointed PricewaterhouseCoopers on Wednesday to take control of key Baugur subsidiary BG Holdings. It is understood that the administration hearing will take place in the High Court in London today.

Landsbanki said discussions with Baugur "did not produce any acceptable proposals so we have taken steps to protect these valuable assets". Baugur will enter the moratorium process, enabling independent accountants and lawyers to evaluate the group's assets over a three-week period.

The period can be extended if required but it will almost certainly end in the demise of one of the most prolific retail investors of recent years.

"It is inevitable that Baugur will go into administration," said one source close to the investor.

Pali analyst Nick Bubb said: "People always knew that Baugur was a house of cards that would collapse."

Sources told *Retail Week* that the decision formalises the situation that has been ongoing since administrators were appointed to Icelandic banks including Kaupthing, Glitnir and Landsbanki in October.

Baugur-backed retail chiefs acted quickly to distance themselves from Baugur and insist it was business as usual.

House of Fraser chairman and Baugur shareholder Don McCarthy told *Retail Week* that the development would not affect the department store chain. "It crystallises the situation and it is now about bringing clarity to the situation for the individual companies going forward," he said.

It is understood that the management of House of Fraser, which between them control about 17 per cent of the retailer, could buy back Baugur's stake in the business.

Mosaic was similarly quick to distance itself from Baugur, emphasising that the investor, which has a 49 per cent in Mosaic, is a minority stakeholder.

Kaupthing, which holds the debt in Mosaic, is understood to be keen to back Mosaic as a viable fashion business and realise assets at a later date.

However, developments this week could open doors to potential changes of ownership with equity up for play as well as debt.

One Baugur-backed retail chief said: "The dam has broken. This situation has been in play for months." However, he stressed that Baugur's latest difficulties meant little more than a change in shareholding and control of the retail assets.

Baugur also has stakes in retailers including Jane Norman and Whistles, as well as public holdings in Debenhams and French Connection.

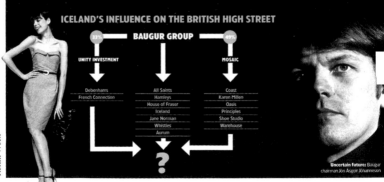

ICELAND'S INFLUENCE ON THE BRITISH HIGH STREET

BAUGUR GROUP

33% → UNITY INVESTMENT

49% → MOSAIC

UNITY INVESTMENT	BAUGUR	MOSAIC
Debenhams	All Saints	Coast
French Connection	Hamleys	Karen Millen
	House of Fraser	Oasis
	Iceland	Principles
	Jane Norman	Shoe Studio
	Whistles	Warehouse
	Aurum	

?

Uncertain future: Baugur chairman Jón Ásgeir Jóhannesson

Retail Week

Baugur goes bust, February 2009.

Iceland's 40th anniversary party, 18 November 2010.

Malcolm and Rhianydd, 18 November 2010.

Malcolm
and Peter
Hinchcliffe
reunited,
18 November
2010.

Malcolm and the new Iceland
mum Dame Edna Everage,
18 November 2010.

Malcolm standing at the North Pole, 2010.

In training for Everest: Richard and Malcolm Walker at the summit of Kilimanjaro, 2011.

it was a bit pointless to be asking those kinds of questions at this late stage. Finally, they signed up and I got back to my hotel at 6am. I just had time to shower and change and then I was on my way to ABN Amro to explain the deal to their salesmen at their morning meeting.

17
A Bad Start

I can't say I was feeling prepared for what was about to happen. During the negotiations, Booker had used their own advisers and we'd used ours. The presentation which we were about to make to the City analysts had been designed by a committee and it turned out to be the proverbial camel! Charles Wilson had written most of it but I'd been involved and so had Andy. Keith Hann of Hudson Sandler had also been involved and so had Booker's PR people, Brunswick. With all the fuss with the banks over the last few days nobody had given the presentation much attention. I wasn't confident.

It was decided to hold the meeting at Brunswick's offices because they had a bigger meeting room and their offices were also much smarter than Hudson Sandler's. This put Hudson Sandler at a psychological disadvantage as Tom Kyte and Sophie Fitton of Brunswick were already acting as if they had our account. The new enlarged company would only need one firm of PR advisers so one would have to go. Brunswick had gone to town and provided platters of fruit and bacon sandwiches for breakfast. They had also taken over running the agenda for the day and scheduling our meetings and photo opportunities. Michael Sandler was looking decidedly put out. Keith was his usual droll and fatalistic self and looked as though he'd thrown in the towel already.

I suddenly remembered I'd not rung Ossie. This was going to be embarrassing and I was not looking forward to making the call. He was livid. He told me I'd made a fool of him. His clients had already been on the phone and he knew nothing about the deal. His colleagues in the office felt he should resign the account. I tried to explain that it hadn't been necessary to include him early on but I had intended to brief him yesterday, then things had gone wrong and we'd been up all night. I apologised as best I could. The market had just opened and Ossie told me with some satisfaction that our share price was dropping. He said the whole thing had been badly handled and only he was capable of salvaging the situation so we needed to talk fees! I got the clear impression of a threat – pay up or your share price will suffer but I couldn't say I blamed him.

I put away my mobile and looked at Mark Astaire. Mark was still adamant we shouldn't have brought in Charterhouse any earlier and he reminded me there'd been no leak! I said: 'Mark, you're my adviser but much as you don't like sharing fees, politically this was a bad thing to have done and we should have brought him in at some point long before now. If he wants to, he can do us enormous damage by not supporting the deal. You're going to have to share your fee with him.' That went down like a lead balloon but our share price was going much the same way and in the opposite direction to the one Mark had forecast.

We comforted ourselves by deciding that the news had come as a shock to the market. No one had ever anticipated the deal and no one understood it either. Things would surely improve after the meeting. I then got a call at 9.20am from Ossie to say the Clerical and Medical pension fund had dumped 6 million shares onto the market, forcing the price down to £2.20. They hadn't even made a phone call to ask for an explanation of the deal. I knew they'd paid £3.00 for those shares and this was the second time they'd done that in four years. Were they mad? In any event they had trashed our share price to a new level and done us enormous harm. Ossie then rang back a few minutes later to say he'd placed a large chunk of the

Clerical shares with Jupiter. If he'd not done that the damage would have been worse.

We started the meeting. The room was packed but it just didn't have a good feel about it. You could sense the bewilderment among everyone there. I introduced the presentation and then Stuart, Charles and Andy all took their turns in delivering part of the message. It just didn't seem to flow properly and we all lacked the necessary energy and enthusiasm. Questions came next and it soon became apparent that the announcement had taken everyone by total surprise and was a complete bolt from the blue. No one had even considered the possibility of a deal like this and, to make it worse, no one in the room knew anything about Booker. Booker was listed in the Financial Times share index under 'food manufacturers', which was a hangover from its days as an agri-conglomerate. Iceland as a retailer was followed by a completely different set of analysts. Questions mainly centred round why I was retiring and what was a clean, quality, niche business like Iceland doing getting mixed up with a mess like Booker. I didn't realise I was so popular and I think Stuart and Charles were surprised that our reservations about announcing a date for my retirement had been so valid. Also, while neither of them had any great affection for the Booker business, I think they were hurt by the harsh comments about the company and the unfavourable comparison with Iceland.

Then someone asked Stuart what was in it for him and what was his motivation for taking on the role of CEO. His reply was glib: 'I've got a bigger train set to play with!' Stuart looked as if he had given up on the deal already but his answer was decidedly not helpful and of course was widely quoted in the press the next day. A lot of questions were directed at Stuart as to whether he would really stay with the business or move on to a fashion company, which was where everyone thought his heart was. He said all the right things about having confidence in Iceland but I did notice he never, actually, categorically denied he would leave. He left that open by saying things like, 'You can never tell what the future might hold.'

Andy teamed up with Stuart and I teamed up with Charles and we set about visiting all the fund managers we could to explain the deal. My first port of call after lunch was Jupiter who were very supportive having just bought a chunk of the Clerical and Medical shares, but strangely one of the fund managers who was most interested in the deal was their ethical fund manager who was already a big holder and worried about our status now we were talking over a business selling cigarettes. We debated this and then left it open for another day. At 4pm I had to go and see Charterhouse and grovel. Ossie had all his salesmen in the meeting and I did an A1 job of eating humble pie and telling them how I'd made a big mistake and now I needed them. Would they please support me? Ossie seemed pacified by my performance and then told me he wanted half of ABN's fee. He didn't know what we were paying them but asked for half a million. I said that wasn't a 'fee' but a 'fine' and I would wait and see how our share price performed over the next few weeks.

A war council was convened at the offices of Cazenove who were acting for Booker. There was a cast of thousands and it was complete chaos. Everyone's mobiles going off all the time and no one really in charge. There were Rothschilds, ABN Amro, Charterhouse and Hudson Sandler for Iceland; Cazenove, Warburgs, Merrill Lynch, Lazards and Brunswick for Booker. The day hadn't gone well and we had to plan our strategy to recover the situation. Everyone agreed that without Clerical and Medical dumping their shares the day could have had a different outcome. Stuart's mobile went and it was Kate Rankine of the *Daily Telegraph* who was going to do an article saying the deal would be rejected by shareholders. She had no basis for saying that but, once written, these things can gather their own momentum. We rang her back on a speakerphone and Stuart, who knew her well, went into overdrive to talk her out of it. Stuart bet her a lunch, anywhere in Europe, that the deal would go through! It seemed to work and the subsequent article wasn't nearly as damaging as it might have been. She decided on a different tack. She knew Iceland had a company plane and spent the rest of the conversation asking questions like 'What colour is it?' I countered, 'What does it matter?' Then she asked how many seats it had and how much it cost. All interesting stuff for the readers next morning.

That night I had a long-standing dinner engagement I felt I just couldn't get out of. Months ago Peter Melchett, the Executive Director of Greenpeace, had asked me to host a dinner for the Trade Minister Stephen Byers and half a dozen business people with environmental interests, to discuss how it was possible to be an environmentalist and a successful business person at the same time. Charles Dunstone of The Carphone Warehouse was one of my guests and also Renée Elliott of Planet Organic. I apologised to everybody in advance in case I fell asleep at the table! It was a good dinner and I liked Stephen Byers. He promised to take our message to Tony (Blair)! I got to bed at midnight after probably the most exhausting 48 hours of my life without sleep. I didn't sleep that night in the hotel, either. I lay awake with everything churning round in my mind wondering what on earth I'd done. I decided this deal was a big mistake.

I had another day in London that was much the same as the one before, then flew home for the weekend. Kevin Threlfall of T&S Stores rang on Saturday morning from his holiday home in Portugal. He was mortified. He'd just heard about the deal and wanted to tell me he had only just dictated a letter to me which gave a full outline of his proposal for a merger between Iceland and T&S. I couldn't believe it. We'd met several times over the past year to discuss a merger between Iceland and T&S Stores but he'd felt it was too early for him. He'd played too 'hard to get' and now he'd missed his chance. However, in all honesty, I did think by now that that might have been a much better deal.

The next three weeks were a blur with five or six presentations a day to analysts and fund managers to explain the deal. At first we had two teams – Andy with Stuart and Charles with me – but, after the first week, we decided someone had better run the business so Stuart and I carried on with the presentations while Andy and Charles went back to work. We did 54 presentations in three weeks. Gradually the share price recovered and the deal went through without a problem. Most of the fund managers asked why I was stepping down and I always replied, 'There can only be one boss and that will be Stuart but I will still be around as non-executive Chairman and I hope to contribute a lot to the company and especially to Booker.' Most asked Stuart if he intended to stay for the long term and his answer was always reassuring, but I noticed never binding. We had three solid weeks talking about the synergies of the deal and during that time I could see it evolve even more in Stuart's mind that we could integrate a lot more of the 'back office' than we had previously thought. We discussed at length the possibility of relaxing the door policy at Booker and also segmenting the Booker stores with the twenty biggest being turned into a Costco type operation. By the end of all this, I was becoming increasingly confident the deal would be a big success.

Iceland was slowly getting its house in order. The Enfield depot running costs were gradually coming under control and the organic vegetable launch, planned for October, was looking like it might succeed. The marketing department had arranged a sponsorship deal with The National Trust, which we felt would lend 'credibility' to our organic initiative. It was decided to 'announce' our organic vegetable launch in June. This is a common marketing trick to get two bites of the publicity cherry. One when you 'announce' and the next when you actually go live. The announcement worked well with massive press coverage, all of which was positive. Journalists, as a breed, are mainly of the 'organic mind set' and were enthusiastic about our plans. Sales in store increased dramatically for a couple of weeks and lots of new customers came in looking for the low price, organic frozen vegetables ... which wouldn't be on sale until October!

As soon as the deal went through, Stuart organised an 'away day' for both the management boards to get to know each other. We went to Stapleford Park for an afternoon of presentations where every director introduced themselves and their departments. We had a grand dinner and an overnight stay. Stuart spent £3,000 of his own money on some impressive wine to go with the meal. The main priority was to set up cross-company teams responsible for delivering the cost savings and synergies, buying being by far the most important area to concentrate on. Steve Archdeacon had been through this before with the Kwik Save/Somerfield merger. He told us they had delivered far more than their original estimates of profit benefit and explained how they went about it.

A plan was put together where each supplier had to attend a series of three meetings, each one escalating in seniority, with the idea of clinching a final deal on the third meeting. Suppliers were categorised according to how easily we thought they might concede to our demands. Some smaller suppliers were expected to give in easily because they hadn't the 'muscle' to resist. Larger suppliers like Coca Cola or Walkers Crisps would be a lot more difficult, as they had the strength. It was expected that the final meeting, for the more difficult cases, would be taken by Stuart. No one really knew how much we would be able to extract in total but we all believed we would comfortably exceed our target. To be safe, nothing was budgeted from the top fifteen suppliers as, from the likes of Coca Cola, we might get £2 or £3 million or we might get nothing.

Stuart's induction to Iceland never really happened. He flew up with Charles for two days at Deeside but spent most of it closeted in a small meeting room on his mobile phone. He did try to meet most of the directors for a 'one-to-one' but their meeting would inevitably be delayed or cancelled or, if it took place at all, he would infuriate the director he was supposed to be winning over by asking questions and then not listening to the answers. Stuart had a pager, which seemed to go off every five minutes. It was silent but would vibrate and he would get it out of his pocket and fiddle with it and look at it, all the time. The result was that everyone accused him of obvious boredom, he made no friends in the business and everyone found him arrogant and uninterested. Women, in particular, found him sexist and patronising. He would call them 'm'dear' and after asking Kathy, my PA, to do something would usually follow it up with 'There's a good girl', which would drive her insane! He often referred to even senior staff as 'boys and girls'. Russell hated him with a vengeance. I spent most of the first few weeks after the merger speaking up for him and trying to persuade everyone he was a good guy really and just had an unfortunate manner. He did have an arrogant façade, which I know wasn't intended on his part. I just don't think he found it easy to relate to people.

Andy, Russell and I paid a flag-waving visit to Booker's headquarters in Wellingborough, which for me turned out to be the only time I visited the building during the next six months. Charles ran the operation with great attention to detail and anyway my role was to bow out over the next six months, not get more involved in the day-to-day running of another business. I was, however, looking forward to visiting Booker branches and coming up with sales ideas.

We soon fell into a routine. Stuart and Charles would fly up to Deeside on Wednesday morning for the 'integration meeting', when we would discuss progress on synergy and review the latest sales figures. Stuart always intended to stay overnight but never did because he always had a meeting or a dinner he couldn't get out of, so they would usually fly back the same evening. There was a lot of initial enthusiasm for radical changes and the accelerated integration of the two businesses. Stuart and Charles even talked about closing Wellingborough altogether and moving everything up to Deeside. We even agreed to buy a four-acre site to build a new office extension. Soon, though, these ideas evaporated and it seemed as if their only interest was the short-term delivery of the buying synergies and as many cost savings as possible.

The Iceland half-year results were announced in September. I expected Stuart as the new CEO to lead the analysts' meeting but he didn't want to. Stuart's argument was that I should take the meeting because they were Iceland figures we were announcing. However, nobody was going to be interested in the trading figures, which were pretty much as expected. This was the first meeting since the deal and everyone would be looking for a progress report. I introduced the meeting by saying this was the 32nd set of figures I'd announced as a public company over the last sixteen years. Thirty one of those announcements had been an increase in profit. I said this would be my last analysts' meeting. It was 30 years since I'd founded the company and I had now handed over to Stuart. Russell, Charles and Andy all presented parts of the meeting but then Stuart did wind up at the end.

The day before the meeting we had a practice run-through at the Booker office in Buckingham Gate. Keith Hann as usual was there but also Jenny Nibbs, who was Booker's adviser on investor relations. Jenny was very good at her job and far more knowledgeable than Keith about investors and their attitudes. Keith tended to deal only with brokers' analysts. Andy was very keen to keep her on alongside Keith. However, it didn't help again to have two people giving their different ideas for the presentation.

After the practice, I asked Stuart in front of everyone for permission to sell some of my shares in the business. I said I didn't know how many I wanted to sell but perhaps half my holding, it depended on demand. I wanted to sell before the calendar year-end, as we would then effectively move into a six-month closed period, with the exception of a few days in March (because of our fifteen-month accounting period) when I would be prohibited from dealing. I had been prohibited from dealing anyway for the last five months, as first we were in discussions with Booker on the merger, so dealing was not allowed, and then as soon as the deal went final we were into the statutory closed period before our results announcement. This would be lifted the day after the half-year announcement. I thought this was the perfect time to sell.

Keith agreed but Stuart disagreed. Stuart said he felt quite strongly that I should not sell any shares, as it would be seen as a vote of no confidence in him or the business. Jenny said she felt it was too soon after the deal to sell but if I left it until November or December, when things had settled down, it would be OK. Keith disagreed and said if I was going to sell I should sell now, straight after the results. Stuart said he would not be happy if I sold. I argued my case. I pointed out that Stuart had just cashed in £3 million worth of options when he could have rolled them over into the Iceland scheme and, after all, I was retiring and I had already told him I wanted to sell when we first met. However, Stuart was adamant so I reluctantly agreed not to sell. I then explained that I would have to sell about 27,000 shares as I had made an investment in 'As Nature Intended', an organic supermarket set up by my daughter Caroline, almost exactly one year ago and, unless I made a capital gain before the end of the month, I would lose rollover tax relief. Stuart said, 'I still don't think you should sell any shares.'

I couldn't believe what he was saying. He knew I wanted to realise some of my investment in Iceland, we'd talked about that before we did the deal, but to object to me claiming rollover relief was unreal. I said 'Stuart, you are asking me to throw away over half a million if I don't sell those shares, you wouldn't do that! I've agreed not to make a big sale but you are asking me to throw away money. There's no way you'd do that.' He wouldn't budge so I told him I intended to sell anyway and I would ask the permission of the board at dinner that night. He agreed that if they agreed, he'd agree, but he wasn't happy. We went to Harry's Bar for dinner and I got the necessary permission from the non-executive directors.

I was really looking forward to my retirement and had started to make plans. The idea was that I would keep my office and PA as part of my salary package but nothing had been agreed about how many days a year I would work. I actually wasn't sure about keeping my office. I would need an office somewhere to run my personal affairs but I could imagine it would be impossible to go into Iceland and not get sucked into the day-to-day problems of the business. I wondered how long it would be before I could resign as non-executive Chairman and cut my ties with Iceland altogether. I used to daydream about having a year off and travelling and all the hundreds of things I had planned to do.

Rhianydd and I were invited to stay with a friend in Mallorca for a long weekend. We had a small house in Marbella but had often thought about buying a bigger house abroad, somewhere we could spend time and large enough to have people out to stay with us. The problem was, where? We expected a lot of research would be necessary to find the right place and even the right country. We decided to spend a couple of days touring the island and look at a few houses while we were there. Just as when we drove up the drive in Broxton on our first visit, before we even went into the house, we knew it was the right one, so in Mallorca we found the perfect house for us almost too easily. We couldn't think of any reason not to buy it. Mallorca itself wouldn't have been an obvious choice for us but it's accessible, it has sunshine and the island is well suited to boating. The house was in a perfect location at the foot of the mountains, in rustic style and with a large garden and four acres of orange trees. We'd found our first retirement project!

18

The Booker Prize for Fiction

I had to admit to a growing unease about Stuart. He just seemed to be making no effort to get to grips with the business. Charles was as busy as ever running Booker but seemed to be developing an increasingly hostile attitude towards Iceland and to me. Stuart was relaxed and genial and I enjoyed his company but it felt like no one was running the business. Stuart certainly wasn't, in my view. I had no involvement in Booker and Charles seemed to want to block any 'interference' from me on integration. All we seemed to talk about at our weekly meeting was last week's sales shortfall at Iceland and the progress on buying synergies and short term cost saving. Integration seemed to be off the agenda.

Charles had an amazing attitude towards running Booker. Everything was about saving more and more money, closing distribution depots and cutting staff. No one ever thought of investing one penny in the business to drive it forward. I thought Russell meanwhile was completely out of control. All he seemed to be interested in was organics. The vegetable launch was getting close but sales in Iceland were dropping off and this was not the time to 'invest' in more organic ideas. A leaf out of Charles's management stylebook would have been more appropriate in the Iceland business. Russell was desperate to do his 'organic milk deal' and we were beginning to realise he'd taken buyers off their day-to-day product development programmes to look for organic ideas. I thought he was mad. I was the Greenpeace member and Mr Green in the press but, much as I was personally keen on organics, I knew it was not for our customers. Vegetables were different. There was to be no noticeable price premium and the whole thing was really a marketing stunt but to extend the range further, especially when we hadn't even tested vegetable sales, was madness. With sales the way they were, we couldn't afford any diversion into costly experimentation. Russell was told to scrap the milk idea and put all organic development on hold.

Sales in Iceland were becoming more and more dependent on 'Buy One Get One Free' or BOGOF. Tom Knowlton had voiced his increasing concern at our board meetings that we were on a 'drug' and we had to get off it. He had seen the whole thing before in North America and kept telling us that in the end no one made money out of BOGOF. We knew he was right but it had worked very well for us so far, although we now wondered if Iceland had so many promotions in store that it was becoming difficult to buy anything that wasn't on promotion! We had always declared our store sales 'gross' including the value of the 'giveaway' item. The giveaway element now amounted to almost 15 per cent of sales, so you could argue our sales were technically overstated. This didn't really matter as showing gross sales had the effect of lowering the percentage profit margin; whereas if we showed 'net' sales and excluded the giveaway item it would show a higher percentage profit margin. The actual cash profit was the same either way and we had internal reasons for everyone focusing on gross sales. The product, free or not, had to be handled and transported through the business and we monitored overheads as a percentage of the gross figure. Besides, we had done it that way for years, it was just that BOGOF had got bigger every year and risen by 1 or 2 per cent of sales each year to the level it was at now. Our auditors were still happy with the way we accounted for BOGOF but we all agreed it was now too big and we would have to show sales net from the following year.

Tom's warnings finally persuaded us to pull back from BOGOF for the October/November promotional period. We knew this would have the effect of reducing gross sales but our profit percentage would increase and hopefully so would our net sales. Every week sales were now below budget in Iceland but it was obvious to me where we were going wrong. I didn't like our advertising, the buying department had lost focus and our product range and pricing was lacking structure. In short, I felt most of our problems were self-inflicted but the good news with that is that it could be put right. I finally had to recognise that Russell was causing serious damage to the business and, however inconvenient it might be in the short term, we had to replace him. Stuart had told me something which explained a lot about Russell's behaviour earlier in the year. Apparently Russell had been headhunted in January as Chief Executive of a syndicate put together by the Carlyle Group who were planning to take over Kwik Save. He in turn had recruited two of our senior people, Sara Jamison and Karl Martin, and the three of them had spent weeks planning the project and writing the business plan. They had approached Booker to provide the warehousing and distribution for the company and had several meetings with Charles before their bid finally failed. I saw that as the ultimate treachery. Before the merger Stuart had promised Russell he wouldn't tell me about it but now he felt I needed to know.

By this time Russell had no decent relationship with anybody on our operating board. Even Karl and Sara had abandoned him. One minute he was an evangelist for organics, the next it seemed obvious from his attitude that he intended to leave the business. He hated his job and was confused about his future. He'd worked out, though, that if he left before our results announcement in March we might consider the news damaging to our City image. He wrote me a long rambling letter complaining that he was underpaid and demanding a bonus if he stayed until March. I should have fired him on the spot. The company would be better off if he wasn't there but it was Stuart who had to make the decision.

Although we were struggling for sales, our profits were still achievable and we had, in theory at least, a lot going for the business for next year. The synergy benefits would be massive, I thought we would comfortably exceed our expected buying benefits and we had many sales initiatives, from consolidating Woodward's and the Booker catering departments to rolling out home shopping from Booker cash and carry depots. This year was looking tighter than it should have done but, provided we got our house in order at Iceland, next year should be good. When we put together our profit target at the time of the deal, we obviously put down a figure we were comfortable with and had a 'margin of safety'. Every week that went by, our sales were below budget but our profits were still intact although the margin of safety was getting smaller every week.

One of my pet projects was the 'mobile shop'. Just as my early home delivery experiments in Iceland had attracted ridicule, so did the mobile shop! I was undeterred and convinced that here was an innovative and massive future business stream for Booker. A couple of years earlier I'd been to Holland to visit Vendex, a food retailer with several different fascias, a cash and carry operation and a fleet of 500 mobile shops. Mobile shops in Britain seemed to die out in the late 1950s. I remembered them as scruffy, overpriced operations in old vans serving rural areas. In Holland they are a national institution and have definitely reached the 21st century. Vendex offered a franchise operation, which was run from their cash and carry depots.

The 'vans' themselves were brightly painted articulated lorries, which contained a modern supermarket on wheels. They were brightly lit, clean, well stocked and seemed to sell everything. They had a checkout with scanning, chilled and frozen foods. They were run by owner-drivers who docked at the Vendex cash and carry every night to replenish their stock. Vendex designed the vehicles, arranged the financing and provided all the support needed for the would-be self-employed shopkeeper-driver. Charles decided it couldn't do much harm to Booker and I was 'allowed' to go and play with the idea. I bought a brand new left-hand drive vehicle from Holland. I recruited a driver and when I found out Charles was making Trevor

Tutt (the guy who gave me the Booker idea in the first place) redundant, I rescued him and made him manager of the mobile shop project.

Trevor planned the routes and got the project up and running and sales grew every week. Here was just one more idea to grow the Booker business. If we could only put some aggression and enthusiasm behind this project, I believed we could have almost 1,000 vans on the road with all the drivers replenishing at Booker. We had managed to roll out over 1,000 home delivery vans in only eighteen months at Iceland so why not?

I became so concerned at Stuart's apparent lack of interest in the business that I went down to see him at the Buckingham Gate office for an ultimatum. Stuart and Charles were in a meeting with Procter & Gamble and called me in to introduce me. There must have been a dozen people from P&G in the meeting, plus the Booker buyers, and the topic for discussion was their sales plans for next year and also cost price reductions for the new enlarged buying operation. After they'd gone Charles told me the benefits were not as great as he'd hoped as the Iceland spend with P&G was very little. He quoted a figure and I realised he'd massively understated the Iceland spend. I was even more concerned then that things weren't under control either in Iceland or with the Booker team on buying synergies. The meeting ended in a row and me telling Stuart he had to 'get a grip'. Charles would not accept any criticism and was all too ready to blame all problems on the Iceland staff. I told them both I would be gone in a few weeks and the problems would be theirs alone so they had better accept what I was saying. Stuart said he did accept my criticisms and he promised he would spend more time in Deeside. He then suggested the two of us go to Harry's Bar for lunch!

By mid-October I decided I had to bring things to a head. I went to Chester to look for flats and made a shortlist I was going to present to Stuart. Flats to buy, flats to rent, I didn't care. We found a nice one overlooking the racecourse I thought he'd like. I even found him a part-time housekeeper. I got him to stay up in Chester for three days and two nights. We visited stores and we looked at flats. I drove him myself and spent hours in the car telling him where I thought we were going wrong and how he had to get rid of Russell. Ranny was away, so he stayed at my house and I cooked a steak dinner and we drank two bottles of good wine. Kate Rankine rang him on his mobile in the middle of this for a gossip about M&S. We went to a wine bar the next night with Andy and, over more good wine, we got him to promise he would take one of the flats in Chester, spend a minimum of two nights every week there, and he also agreed to fire Russell. I felt we had a breakthrough.

Russell was on holiday that week and when he returned on Monday morning I went to see him for a chat. It was the usual 'how was the holiday?' sort of conversation and as usual Russell didn't waste any time in telling me how unhappy he was and how he really ought to resign. He walked right into it. He resigned probably without realising he was going to and was relying on me to talk him out of it. This time I let him! I was over the moon that at last we had started to get to grips with our problems. I rang Stuart and told him the good news that I had saved him a job and the company a compensation payment.

Somehow I could feel the tension down the telephone line and then Stuart's voice, almost in a choking tone, saying 'I'll be up tomorrow.'

I knew something was wrong and in my heart I could guess what was about to happen but I refused to admit it, even to myself. On Tuesday morning Stuart flew up with Charles and he walked into my office with a strained look on his face. His first words were, 'I've been thinking, you are the one who ought to be running this business.' I suddenly felt numb and said 'Stuart, don't even think about it, we have a deal. You run the business, I retire.' 'No,' he said, 'You understand the business far better than I ever will, you should run it. You can't spend the rest of your life fishing!'

I asked Stuart if he was about to resign but he said he wasn't, he just felt he didn't understand the business and he couldn't run it. I told him not to worry about Russell going, I would run Iceland myself in the short term and we would get a replacement by March. We carried on the conversation in this vein for most of the day. I suggested if he really wanted to go, he owed me a year. He had to let me retire first, in March. That was our deal. I asked him if he had another job and he said he hadn't but he'd had offers. I asked him to join me for dinner that night and we could talk further but he said he didn't want to. He wanted to be on his own, he had some thinking to do. I said I couldn't carry on with all the uncertainty and asked him for a firm and binding decision next morning. He was either going to stay and get on with the job or tell me he was leaving. He promised he would make a decision.

I knew what the answer would be and, sure enough, next morning his first words were, 'I'm leaving.' I have to say, he looked as if they were the hardest words he had ever spoken in his life. 'You fucking bastard!' was my instinctive response, followed by a tirade of abuse, which included most of the four letter words I'd ever heard. Stuart sat there and took it all, shamefaced. I asked him where he was going and he said he couldn't tell me, he hadn't had a formal offer letter yet but it would be a fashion business. He'd told me, probably a week before he was ready, because of Russell. Suddenly, I had a horrible thought, 'Are you taking Charles with you?' I asked. 'Er, I haven't offered him anything, how can I when I don't have a job myself yet? You'll have to ask Charles if he's going.' 'Stuart, don't mess me around, is Charles leaving?' Stuart admitted he was.

'That's bloody great,' I said. 'My Chief Executive is leaving, he's taking the Managing Director of Booker with him and the Managing Director of Iceland has just resigned. That leaves just me, who's supposed to be retiring in three months. Thank you, Stuart.' I accused Stuart of dishonesty, I said he'd never intended to stay and everything now started to fall into place. I thought Stuart had objected to my share sale in September only to keep me tied in to the company financially. I also felt his insistence at the time of the deal on putting a date on when I would retire was not because he thought I might hang on but quite the opposite, he wanted to know how long he'd got. Naturally he denied all this but in fact Stuart gave an interview about six months later to *Management Today* which was repeated in the *Evening Standard*. I was surprised to read his admission that he had had the job offer from Arcadia at the time of the Booker deal. He said he told them he wasn't available but he would be later in the year. I felt like I'd been conned!

The trouble was everyone seemed to know he wouldn't stay except me. Many analysts, fund managers and several financial journalists had all commented that he would leave. There had also been much speculation in the press that he would be offered the M&S CEO job. I am sure Stuart encouraged that and certainly spent a lot of time talking to Kate Rankine and other journalists, feeding them gossip about M&S. I had believed Stuart would stay at Iceland for two reasons. First, he told me he would and, second, the business about my retirement date in the document convinced me, but for the wrong reason.

In the middle of our argument, Tony Pearce, the Managing Director of Birds Eye, arrived for a meeting with Stuart. This was to be the first of the final 'buying synergy' meetings with the big suppliers and Stuart had to negotiate a better deal for next year, plus a cash payment for this year. All the suppliers had been told at the time of the merger that improved terms, whenever they were agreed, would have to be backdated to the time of the deal. Birds Eye was part of Unilever and Tony was negotiating with Iceland on behalf of all the Unilever businesses. Stuart broke off and went to see Tony. I went to see Russell.

Russell knew nothing of my conversation with Stuart but he'd obviously had time to reflect on his resignation the day before and decided he'd been hasty. It was almost amusing watching him backpedal, claiming he was enthusiastic about the business really and hadn't intended to resign. Unfortunately, I had no choice but to let him stay. Losing Stuart and Charles would be bad enough both for the City and for company morale but if Russell went as well, damaging as

I thought he was for the business, we would lose all credibility. Stuart returned from his meeting with Tony Pearce and told me he had got £2 million for the current year. That was brilliant news as nothing was budgeted. If we could get similar amounts from the other 'big fifteen' suppliers, it would really help our profits this year.

There was nothing more to say to Stuart. He asked me not to tell anyone, as he hadn't had the formal job offer yet. I didn't particularly feel like doing him any favours but it wasn't in my interests to announce his departure at this stage. I had to plan it. All my own plans were shattered, I didn't see how I could possibly retire now but I desperately wanted to. My mind was racing. I rang my friend and lawyer Peter Bullivant and, as always, he offered to talk things through with me. We met within thirty minutes in the garden of a local hotel. I'd had an idea, I would resign myself immediately, before Stuart announced he was going. That would spoil his plans and force him to stay unless he really wanted to damage his reputation with the City by leaving a ship in trouble! It would also trash our share price but I couldn't have cared less about any subsequent share sale I might make, I just wanted to go. Peter, of course, counselled me not to and apart from daydreaming, there's no way I could have done it. I would have damaged my own reputation and, more importantly, let our staff down. I rang Keith Hann and asked to see him in London that night. 'When's he leaving, then?' was his response!

I travelled down on the plane with Stuart and Charles and apart from telling Charles he had a contract and I wouldn't release him, nobody had much to say. I felt I needed Charles for a few months. I didn't get on with him but I knew nothing about Booker and I would have to get up to speed with that business. I met Keith in the Dolphin Square restaurant, which for some reason was almost empty. I relied on Keith for advice and trusted his instinct. He didn't think the news of Stuart's departure would be much of a shock to anyone and joked our share price might even go up on the news! He agreed it was a problem for me, though, and couldn't see any other alternative than for me to get stuck in for another year or two. It could take that long to find a successor. I told him I felt we'd been in 'drift' for nine months and nobody had been running the business and it had suffered. I said we would still make our profit number but it was 'tight'. We speculated on where Stuart was going and decided it was Arcadia. I suggested the Arcadia shareholders were probably the same people as the Iceland shareholders and how could they be happy with Stuart when he'd let them down at Iceland? Keith suggested they probably wouldn't care.

We talked about who was out there as a possible replacement Chief Executive and Keith asked me if I'd thought about Bill Grimsey. I asked who he was, I'd never heard of him. Keith explained he was available immediately as he'd just left Wickes, the DIY company, after a takeover. He told me Grimsey had a great reputation and had spent most of his life in food. He was a client of Hudson Sandler when he was at Wickes. I told Keith I was seeing Whitehead Mann, the headhunters, in the morning and would ask them to put him on the list.

Stuart didn't visit Deeside again but we spoke on the phone and agreed we would postpone any announcement until after the Booker Prize ceremony on 7 November.

The Booker Prize was one of the most wasted PR opportunities in the history of corporate sponsorship. Every year a glittering dinner would be held at the Guildhall, attended by a galaxy of business, media and literary superstars. The event would be televised and written about in the press before and after the event but nobody seemed to know it had any connection with a grubby cash and carry business that originally founded the award and continued to pay for it. The cost of the event was about £350,000 paid for directly by Booker.

I fully understood that the Booker Prize had become a national institution and the prestige and independence of the award could be seriously damaged by too much commercialisation. However, there was massive scope both to enhance the publicity for Booker and now Iceland and also to get other people to pay for it by way of 'sub-sponsorship'. That was one thing Charles and I agreed on! I'd had a little fun over the previous weeks in suggesting to the press we might change the name to the 'Iceland Prize'. I didn't mean it, of course, but it had worried some of the old buffers connected with the event and also brought us more publicity for the company than the event had generated for years.

Stuart as the ultimate social animal was in his element hosting the Booker Prize. He'd invited lots of his mates and contacts and we'd both been through the list of company friends and advisors and invited them. No one turned down an invitation to the Booker Prize. Over the previous week I'd got used to the fact that I was back running the business for a year or two and much as I felt Stuart had stabbed me in the back, I found him a difficult bloke to dislike. I believed he genuinely hated himself for what he had done. Ranny however had no such benign thoughts. I was a bit worried as to what she might do or say to him and, sure enough, when I arrived early at the Guildhall, with Andy and Peter Bullivant and our wives, Ranny made a beeline for Stuart. An enduring memory I shall always have is of Ranny berating Stuart like a schoolmistress. She gave him both barrels! Stuart stood there, shamefaced like a schoolboy, and took it all. Everyone kept a respectful distance and tried to stifle their laughter. It made Ranny feel a lot better and I think Stuart felt he had been cleansed!

It was a brilliant evening and we all really enjoyed it. Stuart insisted I stand with him at the entrance and welcome our guests and shake everyone's hand as they arrived. It was like a wedding reception except the divorce was already arranged! It was all a blur of smiles and handshakes to me but Stuart seemed to know everyone. I had to make a welcome speech but I put a coded message in it that Stuart wouldn't be there the following year. It must have been too subtle because no one picked up on it except for Keith Hann, but he was in the know anyway. I didn't realise at the time I wouldn't be there the following year either!

Stuart was on a twelve-month contract and I suppose I could have made him sit at home on 'gardening leave' but I would have had to pay his salary and we couldn't afford the indulgence. He left, to his own timetable, on 13 November. I didn't think of it until it was too late but I made a half-hearted attempt, without success, to get Adam Broadbent, the Chairman of Arcadia, to pay for his early release. Stuart was paranoid that there should be no press leak, as the board of Arcadia hadn't yet agreed the pay-off of Gerald Hoerner, his predecessor. When the date was fixed for the announcement that he was to replace Hoerner on the Monday, I was convinced Stuart would leak it to the press for the Sunday. I decided to beat him to it and made my own press leak for coverage on the Saturday. The idea was not just to wrong-foot Stuart but, in giving the story ourselves, we could ensure a more positive spin and also it would give the City the weekend to get used to the idea.

The idea worked. Our share price didn't even move and the way the story was written it looked like the leak had come from Stuart. We of course denied any involvement on our part and made all the necessary accusations against Stuart but the best impact was on Kate Rankine. She was convinced Stuart had done the dirty on her and not given her the story first! She was furious with him and not a fan of his for a long time after that. She gave him some pretty unfavourable press.

19
I've Got My Job Back

At least I was back in charge and could do things my own way. Stuart was gone, Charles was going and Russell would be out just as soon as I could find a replacement. In a way it was quite liberating. Our investors, understandably, wanted to see me for an update but for once I had to say 'no', I just couldn't, I had a lot of work to do. I made a few speeches to Iceland staff to 'rally the troops'; I made light of Stuart's departure and had to pretend I never wanted to retire anyway. I also had to have a crash course in Booker.

Charles always maintained Booker ran itself. It had a good and capable management team who for years had been neglected and given no resources. They were used to carrying on regardless as the group directors played musical chairs with the company. Ken Bootyman, who had been there for years and knew the business inside out, ran store operations to an incredibly high standard. Operations Directors have to be a tough breed to survive and it probably helped that Ken looked like Reggie Kray! Booker was a very stable, very boring business. Sales never varied much week to week. In a good week sales might be up half a per cent, in a bad week down half a per cent. Booker was a supertanker that would not easily be knocked off course but equally it was almost impossible to accelerate without radical work to the engine room. Iceland by contrast had always been an incredibly volatile business. I used to describe it as a Ferrari. Take your foot off the gas pedal for a second and it slows, but equally sales could accelerate dramatically with the right input.

I attended a couple of Booker management board meetings with Charles in the chair and was stupefied at the amount of detail they went into. Their management accounts were so detailed that they were meaningless to me. I made several presentations to Booker management and head office staff. I told them costs had been cut for so many years there was nothing left to cut. It was time to invest. I think they liked what I said and they liked my informality.

Charles had agreed to stay until the end of January but everyone knew he was going and the jockeying for position among the Booker directors started immediately for who was going to be his replacement. Simon Bartholomew at Whitehead Mann was looking for two Managing Directors and a Chief Executive. I asked them to include three of the Booker directors on their short list. I spent as much time as I could in Wellingborough, trying to understand the business, and I also started a round of store visits. I visited the Booker corporate office in Buckingham Gate. It was really 'Stuart's pad' and there was no need to keep it now. We decided to close it down. I found it sad that there was so little memorabilia left of the old company. Booker was started as a trading company based in Liverpool by the Booker brothers and for most of its 200-year history was involved in shipping and trading to the West Indies. Their business included sugar cane farming and the production of rum in Guyana. There were a few old company seals left and three oil paintings of sugar plantations. They were originally part of a set of twelve but Stuart told me the others had been 'borrowed' by former directors. We sent everything to Wellingborough for safekeeping.

I was more convinced than ever that we could evolve the top cash and carry depots into a Costco type operation. That was a long-term project but massive short-term gains could come from better buying. Shaun Birrell, the Buying Director, was a gentleman and also very capable but I thought the whole buying department was weak and unchallenged. I had several meetings with Whitehead Mann and among the shortlist we had one of the top guys from Costco. He came to two interviews and really wanted the Booker MD's job but I planned to recruit him in addition to a new MD to develop the Costco concept.

A couple of analysts rang me and suggested that if I was going to replace Stuart – many people thought I might recruit a Chairman and take on the CEO's job myself – I might like to consider Bill Grimsey. Our non-executive director Alan Smith also rang me with the same suggestion. Apparently Grimsey had worked for Alan, briefly, when he was at Kingfisher. I asked Whitehead Mann to contact Grimsey and get him in for an interview. He seemed to be very highly rated and above all, available. They rang me back and said they'd spoken to Grimsey but he definitely wasn't interested and he wouldn't even come to an interview. 'What's the problem?' I asked. 'Right industry, right company, wrong location, he lives in Radlett and won't move,' was the reply. 'Oh Christ, not another Stuart Rose,' I replied. 'Someone else who won't move north.' I thought for a minute and then said, 'Look, I've had an idea, ring him back and tell him Booker's office is in Wellingborough, which isn't too far from Radlett, and while the Iceland office is in Chester (it always sounds better than Deeside) we have a private jet so commuting will be no problem.' Simon did not think this was a good idea. I think he felt the suggestion was flash and vulgar! I insisted, however, and it wasn't long before he rang me back and said, 'I'm amazed, it worked. The interview's fixed up for 6pm on Thursday.'

The interview rooms at Whitehead Mann's offices for the top people they recruit are furnished with sofas, deep armchairs and coffee tables. The drill was they would bring in the candidate, make the introduction and then leave us alone for as long as it took. I'd budgeted an hour. Two-and-a-half hours later we were still there. I couldn't believe my luck. Grimsey was perfect for the job in every respect. He gave me his life story from starting as a Saturday boy at Bishop's Stores, which was taken over by Budgens (then part of

Booker). From there he moved on to Tesco, where he had roles in new store development and training. He then went to Park 'n' Shop in Hong Kong for five years and after an unsuccessful few months at Kingfisher (he called it his big career mistake) he went to Wickes DIY. Grimsey was running their South African operation when Wickes had their famous accounting scandal and their share price crashed. He persuaded the Chairman to make him the CEO and over the next couple of years restored their fortunes and share price and became a hero in the City.

Wickes was then taken over by Focus Do It All and Grimsey was out of a job. He was still being paid by Wickes and there was a big argument going on over his pay-off. Bill Archer, the boss of Focus, was refusing to give Grimsey any pay-off for some reason but Grimsey reckoned he was owed a year's salary of £300,000. In reality he would get a lot less than that and if he got another job he'd get nothing anyway as he'd suffered no loss. The solution seemed to be to keep paying him, so he'd just had a few months paid holiday and was now ready to get back into retail, preferably food.

I told him everything about Iceland. I'd made my mind up he was the man for the job so I invested a lot of time telling him the story, warts and all. I told him I wanted to retire and cash in some of my shares. I told him how I felt I had been conned by Stuart. I told him about Russell and all the mistakes we'd made in the last year and I told him I had to deliver £130 million in profit that year and we would, just, but we'd have to throw in the kitchen sink to get there. I also told him about all the opportunities in Iceland, my plans for Booker and Woodward's, and how I wanted to stay on as non-executive Chairman and be part of the future.

Grimsey was impressive. He sat on the edge of his chair through-out the interview. He was eager, he came over as hungry and he wanted the authority and the challenge – in fact he was the complete opposite to Stuart. He laid it on a bit about his principles and beliefs and how he developed his staff and how the training budget would always be the last one he would ever cut. He felt it necessary to tell me he was a man of considerable honesty and integrity and his only concern in running a business was to protect the interests of the shareholders. He told me he was really interested in the job and would like to take it further. I told him the package on offer would be exactly the same as Stuart's. He would get a basic salary of £500,000 plus bonus and options. It was a big pay increase for him and he made it clear that if the job was right he'd take it and forget about his dispute with Bill Archer.

I suggested that the best way to progress things would be for him to visit Deeside. I'd show him round the office and introduce him to some of our people. We could visit Iceland stores, a Booker cash and carry and Woodward's, and he would then get a feel for the business. I suggested he should do a trial run on the jet. Harnish, our London chauffeur, would pick him up from home, drive him to Luton and then he would fly to Chester airport to arrive for 8.30am. He could see how the timings worked and how easy it all was. I also suggested the best way for us to get to know each other would be for him to bring his wife and stay the night at our house. I said I would also invite Andy and Debbie Pritchard round for dinner. Grimsey thought this was a great idea and we agreed they would come up the following Monday.

I had another name on the short list, Paul Mason, the Managing Director of Asda. Following the Walmart takeover of Asda, many people were leaving now the initial honeymoon was over and it was open season for the headhunters. I had already met another Asda director I was considering as a replacement for Russell. I met Paul for dinner at the Moss Nook restaurant near Manchester airport. The big problem, as with almost any other candidate, was that he'd have to give at least six months' notice. Grimsey was available next week and it gave him a clear advantage. I liked Paul, who was a solid retailer and could undoubtedly do the job, but I decided to push ahead with Grimsey and keep Paul on the back burner for another week or two as insurance. Paul eventually went to Matalan to replace Angus Monro.

Roger, our local chauffeur, arrived at my house with Bill Grimsey and Bill's wife Jan at 8.30am on 4 December. They loved the jet and had found the whole journey very easy. We had a coffee and Danish pastry and then Bill and I set off for the office and Jan stayed behind to prepare for a day in Chester sightseeing and shopping with Ranny. We agreed to meet for lunch. I drove Bill to the office in my Aston Martin and explained the plan for the day.

We had a coffee in my office and then I took him in to see our Personnel Director Janet Marsden. I had taken her into my confidence and she knew why Bill was there. Bill and Janet hit it off straight away when he explained to her that he was big into staff development and, however bad things were in a business, the last budget he would ever cut would be the training budget. Music to the ears of a Personnel Director.

We joined the ladies for lunch at The Brasserie in Chester. We went on to visit a couple of Iceland stores and the local Booker and I even showed him the mobile shop. I was able to illustrate in stores the mistakes we had made but also point out the opportunities. We got back home at about 7pm and Andy and Debbie arrived for dinner about 8pm.

It was a friendly and chatty dinner but I'm not quite sure who was trying to impress whom! I was desperate for him to join us. Andy and Debbie were probably a little wary, wondering what he would be like as a boss. Bill was very keen to make an impression and Jan, his wife, had plenty to say and clearly wore the trousers. Bill told us about his collection of Triumph motorbikes and Jan told us about their old lifestyle in Hong Kong. She also told us about how when they went out motor biking in England, they would stop at the pub with other bikers dressed in their leathers, and 'no one would ever guess she was a millionairess!' Bill would also apologise every twenty minutes for being so fat and tell us that he had put on too much weight over the last few months of his holiday. We stayed up late and drank a lot of wine and I felt that, whatever the personal idiosyncrasies, here was an energetic guy who I could work with and who could do the job.

Next morning after breakfast, Roger had arrived to take them to the airport and I took Bill on one side and asked him if he wanted the job. He said he would love the job, it was everything he was looking for but there was just one condition. He wanted to see the company books first and he also wanted a medical. He felt it was a reasonable request for him to see the state of the finances of any company he was about to get involved with. I agreed and suggested he come up to Deeside the following Monday. I couldn't see why he wanted a medical, though, and was anxious not to delay things. He said it was the proper thing to do and asked me to organise it. I went into the office later that morning and told Andy that we had him on board but he wanted to see the books. Andy made some crack that he might change his mind if he did, but it wasn't a problem.

I told the non-executives and our advisers where we were up to and I also rang Ossie at Charterhouse to tell him. Everyone thought it was great news. I had several conversations with Alan Smith and he was very anxious that I should 'land him'. We had an analysts' visit to Deeside arranged for Thursday, 14 December. This was a crazy time for us to hold such an event, so close to Christmas, but Stuart had arranged it months before and I felt we shouldn't cancel it. The reason for the trip was to introduce all the food retail analysts to Booker and to make presentations about our future plans for Booker and how we were going to integrate and develop Woodward's Foodservice into the Booker catering division. I hoped that if Bill confirmed he was joining us on Monday, we could announce it on the Wednesday. He could then attend the analysts' meeting on Thursday and the dinner we had planned for them on the Wednesday night. I felt that would be a good way to introduce him. I couldn't help but think how my world had changed in just six weeks, from retirement, to back on the job for two years, to retiring again. I was over the moon.

20
The Share Sale

Back to Plan A!

I realised that once we'd announced that Bill was joining us, and that I was again planning to step down to a non-executive position, there was nothing to stop me selling my shares in the business. However, I wanted to get the analysts' meeting out the way first. After that there were just two weeks left of the 'open period' when I would be allowed to sell. After Christmas we would effectively move into a six months 'closed' period when I would be prohibited from selling shares.

After everything that had happened during the last year, I could at last carry out the original plan I'd agreed with Stuart Rose and retire from my full-time job and sell my shares. There is never a right time to sell shares, especially if you are high-profile and the founder of the company. Directors' share sales have to be reported immediately and are usually picked up by the press. If a director is selling, then it's assumed he must know something is wrong and often the share price will drop as a result of the sale. But it didn't seem unreasonable for me to be selling as I was retiring after 30 years and a share sale would surely be expected.

Over the years, whenever I sold shares in Iceland, I would judge the success of that sale by how little it affected the share price. I would always try to sell into a strong market. I told Ossie that, if everything went to plan over the next week, I might want to sell some shares and I asked him if he thought there was a demand in the market. If there wasn't, it would be more difficult to sell as it would trash the price. I hadn't decided how many shares I should sell but I thought maybe 4 million, depending on demand, which would be half of my total holding including options. I would leave the other half as an investment in Bill Grimsey! Ossie said there was a strong market but of course it could all change in a day.

Tax laws had changed in recent years to encourage 'entrepreneurs'. A dotcom founder could own a business for two years and then sell out having created nothing but smoke and mirrors and pay only 10 per cent capital gains tax. I'd held my shares for 30 years but they didn't qualify for tax relief. In the past I'd paid 60 per cent tax on share sales and this time I would be paying 40 per cent. Iain Sharp, one of our non-executive directors, had sold his company for £70 million a couple of years previously and gone to live in Jersey without paying a penny in tax. I had spoken to Ernst & Young, our company auditors and my personal tax advisers, several times over the past year about any possible way of reducing my tax bill in the event of a share sale. They said there wasn't one unless I went to live abroad.

I rang them again and Sue Sinagola, one of the partners, brought over a partner from their Leeds office called Keith Harbage to explain how I could save millions if I invested in one of their 'film schemes'. The Government had given tax breaks to encourage investment in British films. Accountants will always approach companies and wealthy individuals with complex ideas to minimise tax and charge big fees for the idea. At first the film scheme seemed very attractive but over the next few weeks I realised I wouldn't be avoiding tax but only postponing the payment. The way they tried to sell the idea without coming entirely clean about how it worked was worthy of any double glazing salesman! I came to the conclusion the whole idea was a bit dodgy and really bending the rules too far. The only people who were certain to make money out of the wheeze were Ernst &

Young in the fees they charged. I abandoned the idea and decided I'd simply have to pay the tax.

Bill Grimsey arrived at 8.30am on Monday, 11 December, having flown up in the jet. We had a cup of coffee in my office and I explained that I had Andy Pritchard as Group Finance Director and Tarsem Dhaliwal as the Iceland divisional Finance Director waiting in the board room to go through the figures. I said, 'Bill, if you don't mind, I won't join you as I can't even read a set of accounts.' Bill replied, 'Oh, I can. I can hold my own with any accountant.' I showed him into the room and left them to it.

I went in to join them at about 12.30pm and asked, 'Is everything OK, are you happy with everything, Bill?' to which he replied, 'Everything's fine, I'm happy.' I'd arranged a medical for Bill that afternoon with a very attractive female doctor who was also a sex therapist! He was quite disappointed when her male partner saw him but at least he was pronounced fit! When Bill had gone I asked Andy if he'd shown him everything, at which he looked at me as if I was stupid and said, 'Of course I did, he's going to be my boss in two weeks.' Andy and Tarsem had been through all the figures with Bill and explained how tight the budget was if we were to hit the analysts' expectations but they'd explained all the adjustments and provision releases and explained about the unbudgeted buying synergies. We were comfortable we would hit the number. There was also a lot of good news around. The future looked very good as a result of the merger and big cost and buying savings were expected to come through the following year.

While Bill was having his medical, Tarsem asked if he could see me along with Andy, Steve Archdeacon and Russell Ford. Something had cropped up he thought I should know about and he wanted Mark Filby, our internal auditor, to explain the results of a review he had undertaken on organic vegetables. I knew that Mark was doing this review as there had been an objection from Russell that the audit department shouldn't interfere in his area. This was all that was necessary for Tarsem and me to ensure that Mark *did* carry out his planned review. Mark was going to check prices and quantity commitments and confirm whether we had too many or too few vegetables for our needs and whether the buyer had done a good job.

Every year we committed to buy thousands of tons of vegetables from farmers and merchants on nothing more than a handshake. Nothing was binding but each year we managed to secure supplies and keep a good relationship with the suppliers. Going organic meant dealing with a whole new range of suppliers from all over the world but we had to keep flexibility and the option to revert back to conventional vegetables if the project didn't work. Mark felt it worthy of investigation and I agreed – particularly as Russell had objected.

Mark was stony faced and explained he'd uncovered nothing short of a real mess. He felt we were massively overcommitted and the prices were not as competitive as we'd been led to believe. He said this could cost us millions. Any assessment of over-commitment obviously depended on expected sales levels. These were currently disappointing but we'd had supply problems, we'd not had a proper launch and we all expected sales would improve considerably. If there was overcommitment then we were not legally bound in the majority of contracts and we could always revert back to conventional vegetables and sell on the excess. This was not good news but Steve assured me it wasn't as bad as Mark had made out. However, it did illustrate the total lack of control that Russell had exercised. Russell just didn't know where we were. I was furious with him. Steve and Mark were told to go away and come back with a proper evaluation and action plan. Steve's best estimate was that this could cost us £2 million but the real cost was the embarrassment at our own ineptitude.

I couldn't bring myself even to speak to Russell, who was due to go on holiday to Lapland the following week to see Santa Claus. How could the MD of a retail business go on holiday at Christmas? It didn't matter, though, we were better off without him and Lapland was where I thought he belonged! I think we both knew he wouldn't survive much after Christmas. I believed he had caused the company so much damage over the past year but I fully accepted it was my fault. I had allowed it to happen and I shouldn't have been so short-term in my thinking. I should have got rid of him twelve months ago.

When Bill returned from his medical I asked if he was going to accept the job and he said he would be delighted to. There was just one problem. We could announce his appointment on Wednesday of that week but he wouldn't be able to join us at the analysts' meeting. He had promised he would take his wife shopping in New York and in fact he wouldn't be able to join us at all until 2 January. I said I was disappointed but it wasn't the end of the world. The only consequence of that was we wouldn't be able to issue his share options until mid-March because we would be into the closed period. He said he wasn't bothered but he wanted to discuss his pension and his contract.

I'd agreed his salary and bonus but pensions were something I didn't understand and I said he should talk to John Berry. His request, though, was quite simple. He didn't want to join the Iceland scheme but he wanted the company to pay 25 per cent of his salary into his own pension pot. This was non-negotiable as his pension was very important to him.

His contract was also something for John to agree in detail but the bottom line was that he wanted his contract to be paid out in full if he had to leave the company for any reason. This was very unusual. Someone may have a one- or two-year contract but if the company breaks it, surprisingly the company doesn't automatically have to pay out the full contract. It all depends on your chances of getting another job. The individual has a duty to 'mitigate' and the company may take the view that, even with a two-year contract, the employee may get another job within, say, six months and therefore the company only has to pay out six months' salary in compensation. If the employee was much older and stood little chance of getting an equivalent job then the company might have to pay out in full. In practice this always leads to a negotiation on termination and it usually depends on whether or not the individual is leaving in 'good standing' as to how much he gets.

Bill's dispute with Bill Archer had become a matter of principle. He claimed he'd earned a pay-off and was ready to go to court but he couldn't possibly have won as he'd suffered no loss. Bill agreed he would drop the whole thing on joining Iceland, which he'd have to do anyway when he took another job, especially at a much higher salary. He said he didn't want this to happen again and therefore he wanted a two-year contract and a guaranteed pay-out in full if he left. I wasn't expecting him to be leaving so I agreed. Bill went see David Price who rubber-stamped his appointment and we signed him up.

I was over the moon. I was now only weeks away from retiring from my full-time job and I really believed that Bill was hungry and together we'd make a great team and have sales flying the following year. I still had another two weeks to make a share sale but I felt it was prudent to get the analysts' meeting out of the way first, just in case anything happened. The meeting after all was a potential source for market reaction. I discussed it with Keith Hann and he agreed I should wait and sell after the meeting. I rang Ossie and put him on notice that I wanted to sell. I didn't know how many shares to sell, it all depended on demand on the day, but if everything went well then maybe half, which would be 4 million shares.

I rang Bill and formally told him what I was going to do and he said he didn't have a problem. I rang all the non-execs and asked their permission and none of them had a problem either. David Price even commented that shares weren't 'family heirlooms' and I shouldn't worry about selling. He then went on to discuss the forthcoming analysts' meeting and asked if I would use it as an opportunity to 'dampen sales expectations'. I told him not to worry, I definitely wouldn't be bullish.

I then rang Mark Astaire to let him know I was planning a sale. I knew what his reaction would be and he didn't disappoint. Mark's standard response is always 'It's never a good time'. Over the previous ten years his attitude was always the same. He'd put me off selling shares in the past saying I should wait until after the next set of results. I'd wait and then there'd be another reason not to sell. On this occasion he joked with me that I knew what his answer would be but he said, 'If you're going to do it, I won't stand in your way.' I also cleared it with Andy and John Berry. No one had a problem.

Sales had not been good at Iceland. Booker was on plan and Woodward's was doing well but the decision to cut back on BOGOF had cost Iceland top-line sales. We had reinstated BOGOF in November but over Christmas it wouldn't make much difference, as people aren't as bothered about that kind of promotion. I believed the City was now expecting profits of about £130 million and we still expected to come in at about that figure in spite of the latest organic surprise. It was tight and such a shame that we had thrown away so much in sales and profits by mismanagement (or even no management for six months) but we were expecting a good Christmas and we still had three months to go before our new financial year-end. Our recent sales drop was easily explainable because we had cut back on BOGOF but we had a super promotional package ready for January. I expected additional buying synergies to more than make up for any profit shortfall. Of course, none of this stopped us putting pressure on the management and they all knew we had a big job in front of us to recover our sales momentum.

Many years ago we had started accepting High Street Vouchers at Christmas. This was a scheme run by Park Foods of Liverpool, the hamper company, and was nothing more than a glorified Christmas savings club. They had thousands of agents all over Britain collecting weekly contributions from savers who would then receive vouchers to spend at Christmas. They could be redeemed in many high street stores but Iceland was the only food retailer. Our voucher sales grew every year and we were expecting around £10 million in vouchers this Christmas. Normally, sales throughout the year are fairly predictable on a weekly basis and follow the pattern of the previous year but all that changes in the run up to Christmas. Because Christmas Eve falls a day later each year it affects the spending pattern of the final couple of weeks and often retailers complain Christmas is 'late'. The rate of redemption of High Street Vouchers is always a good indicator of the sales levels still to come. This year High Street Vouchers were running at a redemption level of 25 per cent below last year and so were redemptions of our own in-house savings stamps. This was good news. We knew how many vouchers had gone out from Park Foods and it was slightly up on the previous year so we were expecting a bumper last week with big sales still to come.

I felt quite confident about making a share sale and on balance felt the good news about the company outweighed the bad. Keith Hann suggested we should put out some kind of Stock Exchange announcement to let people know we were having an analysts' meeting as that in itself was information that should be communicated. It was difficult to know what we could say so close to Christmas but in the event we confined our comments to just saying we were hosting a visit for analysts and we remained positive on the Group's future prospects. We also said we were confident that all the expected benefits of the merger with Booker were real and achievable. Keith drafted the words and I was happy with them. We also had to make a separate announcement that Bill Grimsey was joining us and I was once more stepping down to a non-executive position. This went down really well and I had lots of phone calls including a message passed on by an analyst from Nicola Horlick's fund who said, 'We think Bill is the dog's bollocks!'

Our last analysts' meeting at Deeside had been a riot sparked off by my joke about Frank Davidson and then the late night revelry with the 'singing butcher'. Expectations were definitely high this time, particularly with it being so close to Christmas. I decided to bring in 'Renfield' the spoof butler and, since Stuart should have been at the meeting, a life-size cardboard cut-out of him was put next to me. I made a speech and took the Mickey out of Stuart and some of the analysts. I said how delighted I was that Bill was joining us and then Renfield took over and started insulting everybody and ended the evening as a disc jockey. We had everyone including myself dancing and playing the fool.

It was a really good evening and next day we had arranged a

series of presentations about the Booker business, Woodward's and home shopping. Woodward's was important in the Booker plan as we were going to exploit the catering opportunities the combined group would present. Home shopping would be revolutionised by transferring the picking operation to Booker outlets where we could offer a bigger product range. We then went to visit the local cash and carry in Chester and I think most of the analysts were truly amazed. Many had never been into a Booker before. We had transformed the Chester Booker branch over the past few months and the opportunities and excitement were there for all to see.

Naturally analysts always try to get you in a corner by themselves at these events and extract a little bit of extra information, especially about current sales levels. They were left in no doubt that current sales were poor but they knew about the BOGOF experiment and nobody was really bothered. Sales had been down for the last few weeks but would still be level for the half-year as a whole. Provided we hit our profit number (there or thereabouts) and even if we didn't because synergies were late coming through, nobody would be too bothered provided they came through in the end. I think most of the analysts were convinced about the Booker story.

Keith Hann missed the meeting but he started to send the feedback reports through over the next few days. His summary was as follows, 'I have never encountered such universal, unprompted and unstinted praise for an evening's entertainment as I got for the dinner at Crabwall Manor. The presentations were also well received, they definitely appreciated the background on Booker and were impressed with their visit there.'

He then went on to say 'The message that forecasts may need revision seems to have got through (except perhaps to ABN Amro) but few have actually done anything about it. In my view this reflects a mixture of seasonal indolence and the fact that they customarily revise forecasts across the sector in mid-January, following the Christmas trading statements of those who believe in such things'.

Certainly the individual comments attributed to the analysts left no doubt that they understood sales were under pressure.

One said, 'Reading between the lines, trade has dropped off a cliff and forecasts look vulnerable.' (He was on £139m.)

Another said, 'Trading is crap at the minute. I have brought my forecast back by £3m.' (He was on £134m.)

A third said, 'I'm cutting my forecast by £4m.' (He was on £136m.)

A fourth commented, 'It was a fruitful trip and very encouraging but if you pinned Andy Pritchard in a corner and asked about trading it is clearly not that good and perhaps you should take £1–2m off your forecasts if you can be bothered, which I can't.' (His forecast was £133m.)

Another concluded '... I could have added the core business is falling apart, but that seemed a bit mean.'

I was delighted with the results of the meeting. The analysts were impressed with Booker and the opportunities for the future but were also clearly under no illusion about current trading. As one commented, there was a mix of positives and negatives.

I rang Ossie and asked how the market was in Iceland shares. He said it was strong so I told him to go ahead and try to sell up to 4 million. He soon sold 2.25 million shares at 345.25p but said he would have to wait until the next day to sell more. I thought you only got one shot at this and had to report the sale within 24 hours so I thought that was all I would be able to sell. Ossie then said that as far as he knew I had five days in which to report the sale and I could also report the price as the average price of all sales made, which gave me a bit more flexibility. Over the years, all sales made by a director in Iceland had been reported the next day. I thought that was the rule. I asked John Berry to check in the 'Yellow Book', the Stock Exchange bible, and Ossie was right. I'd been misinformed all these years! I would have been quite happy with what he had sold already but this was good news in that I'd now got until Tuesday, provided the demand held up, to sell more.

On Friday morning driving into work I rang Ossie and his first words were, 'The wheels have fallen off.' 'What do you mean?' I asked. Ossie explained the market had dried up and he wouldn't be able to sell any more unless he lowered the price by maybe 20p. That was one thing I didn't want to do, not because I wouldn't accept a lower price but because I didn't want to drive the market price down and make it look like I was 'unloading'. Ossie did sell another 750,000 shares in the late afternoon on Friday, but none on Monday and none on Tuesday. I'd sold three million shares at a good average price without being seen to be 'dumping' and I was happy. Then, just as the market closed on Tuesday, Ossie told me he'd sold another million. That made 4 million shares sold and I was able to report an average price of 335p, which I thought was very respectable. The sale was reported to the Stock Exchange and didn't cause a ripple in the market. I felt we'd handled it well. Kate Rankine picked up on it in Saturday's *Daily Telegraph* and wrote a story but she was the only one and no institution or analyst even mentioned it.

Bill Grimsey went to New York for a couple of days but even though he wasn't officially starting until 2 January, he found time to work in an Iceland store and a Booker cash and carry during Christmas week. (I couldn't imagine Stuart Rose doing that!) He also arranged for his own photographer to be there and organised a press release. He achieved quite a lot of personal coverage including a couple of interviews. In one of the interviews he was asked what his greatest luxury was and he replied, his own 'personal guru'!

21
Breaking and Entering

Christmas was a disaster! Sales didn't come in the final ten days as expected. High Street Vouchers remained well behind budget (customers must have redeemed them somewhere else). It was the worst Christmas we'd had and many staff blamed the Christmas TV advert. It was a sombre 30-second affair featuring kids that looked like they belonged at Dr Barnardo's. Another masterpiece from HHCL!

Unfortunately lost sales at Christmas impact more on profits as they result in higher wastage of chilled and seasonal lines. Overstaffing also becomes a problem as you gear up staff hours to the sales budget and it's then too late to change. We had a computer breakdown immediately after Christmas, which cost us lost orders from the stores and wasted hours in the warehouse. It looked like anything that could go wrong did go wrong.

I knew then it was going to be very difficult to hit our profit number, as we'd absolutely no more in reserve. I didn't know by how much we'd miss it but it wouldn't be a complete disaster. A poor Christmas couldn't cost us that much. Sales were 5 per cent down over the Christmas two weeks but, taking the half-year as a whole, we'd still be able to report sales that were flat at worst or even slightly positive on the previous year. We'd still got three months to go before the year-end and we were geared up for a really strong promotional package and the resurrection of BOGOF. I was expecting sales to be positive again by the time we reported our profit figures. A lot of work also needed to be done with the top suppliers to earn profit contributions for the current year which had not been budgeted for.

On New Year's Day I was able to reflect how much had happened during one year. Vodafone don't have a signal at Broxton so it wasn't until I checked later for messages that I heard Stuart Rose's voice. 'Hello Malcolm, Stuart here. Just ringing to wish you a happy new year. You've found your new Chief Executive and sold your shares so I hope there are no hard feelings. Give me a ring and I'll buy you dinner sometime.' It was over a year before I took him up on the offer.

Bill Grimsey arrived at the office at 8.30am on 2 January. I was actually quite excited and looking forward to it. I'd arranged a whole series of meetings for him with our senior management over the next couple of weeks. His office was all ready and we'd even installed a laptop in his home that was networked to the office. He didn't know how to use email, but he was willing to learn. I felt at last we would now be able to get things moving. We had a coffee in my office and I joked about his press coverage and asked him about his personal guru. He explained he was a great believer in personal development and so he employed a mentor. He said he spent some time with this guy every week or so and found it invaluable. Bill then said he wanted to tell me his ambition for the company. He felt he should have a goal to work towards and he intended to turn Iceland into the biggest and most profitable food retailer in Britain within the next five years! If anybody else had said that you'd have wanted to laugh but he wasn't joking.

Bill had been in my office maybe an hour when he said, 'I've had an idea. You know you want to get rid of Russell, well, let's get rid of him tomorrow and make Andy Pritchard the Managing Director of Iceland.' I was stunned, not only by his decisive action (there was going to be no messing about here) but at the idea of replacing Russell with Andy. 'You can't,' I said, 'Andy's an accountant, I'm not sure he can run the business: it needs a salesman.' But Bill had made up his mind. He suggested that Andy would be a safe option, after all he'd been at Iceland eighteen years, he knew the business inside out and, with Bill working alongside him, he was sure it would work.

Whitehead Mann were trying to poach a couple of guys from Asda but I knew that would take months. This was a quick solution. I wondered how Andy would respond. 'Let's run the idea past Janet,' I said. It would be interesting to get her reaction. Janet agreed with me and was not keen on the idea but it was going to be very difficult for me to object. Bill was in charge now and I could hardly veto his very first decision. 'We're not going to be any better off,' I said, 'We'll be looking for a Group Finance Director to replace him.'

'Ah,' said Bill, 'My mate Bill Hoskins, who was with me at Wickes, is out of a job but he has had another job offer. Providing we ring him within the next couple of hours, he'll turn down the other job and come to us. What do you think?' I suggested we talk to Andy and said I should see him first and pave the way. Bill said he'd ring Hoskins anyway as he was sure Andy would accept. I spoke to Andy and to my surprise he was quite keen on the idea. He saw it as an opportunity and said he didn't want to be a Finance Director all his life. I asked him if he was worried about somebody else coming in to take over from him and he said, 'No, he's seen the numbers. What's the problem?'

Andy obviously wanted to talk it over with his wife Debbie before finally committing but Hoskins had been given the job anyway. I asked what Bill wanted to pay him and he said 'The same as Andy' which was £250,000 per year plus bonus. I asked how much he'd been offered for the other job and he explained it was only £80,000 but it was a virtual 'start-up' based in Southampton and he was expecting to get some equity. I thought Hoskins wouldn't need too much persuading to join us.

Andy formally accepted the job and Bill fired Russell the next day. Bill then started his round of interviews with senior staff and over the next few days I made a couple of changes to his agenda to fit in with different people's workload. Bill did not appreciate this and made it clear nobody would change his agenda without consulting him!

I spent time talking Bill through the list of directors and senior managers in the company. I gave him my views, good and bad, on everyone. I explained that I had persuaded Charles Wilson to stay and run Booker until at least the end of January. Bill said he didn't want him around and he should go immediately. He got rid of him the very next day. I mentioned that Deborah Baker, the Booker Personnel Director, was leaving to go to Burberry. She was very good at her job but we didn't need both her and Janet so it was a good solution. Bill met Deborah the next day and took her out to dinner to persuade her to stay. He failed to work his charm so Janet kept her job!

Bill saw all the senior management one-to-one but organised a couple of presentations in the conference room for middle management. This was so he could introduce himself and explain his management style and his way of working. I said a few words of welcome but did feel obliged to confess I had introduced Stuart Rose in similar circumstances although, this time, I knew we had got it right. I said I was 100 per cent confident in Bill and that he would make a success of the company. Bill was a good presenter. The presentation lasted at least an hour and was all about himself. Who he was, what he believed in and the fact that he supported Chelsea and collected Triumph motorbikes. He went through his career history and explained how he was demanding but fair and that his only interest was in protecting the owners of the business, the shareholders. He had lots of slides and it was obvious he'd made this presentation many times before.

I was impressed and later I went round to canvass reaction, which I suppose was inevitably going to be guarded and suspicious. One senior manager commented that if he'd heard Grimsey say he was a control freak once during the presentation he'd said it twenty times. I realised he was right.

Hoskins turned up later in the week to introduce himself and I have to say I was shocked. If he'd not been so highly recommended by Bill and come with such a good reputation developed at Wickes, I think I would have got rid of him on some excuse, without even an interview. He was the scruffiest, oddest looking character I've ever seen. He wore a Mickey Mouse tie and braces, a baggy suit and was the spitting image of Coco the Clown. We chatted as I reflected on how appearances were deceptive and how I'd never have considered this guy as a serious candidate for our Finance Director if Bill hadn't brought him in. He was introduced to a couple of the other directors and Anne, the tea lady, was fussing round him when he started to tell us that his big obsession in life was The Spice Girls and how he had some amazing pictures of them he would want to put in his office. Everybody thought he was joking but he wasn't. He was seriously weird but no fool. Andy got the measure of him and said he looked like he knew his job.

One evening I was chatting with Bill Grimsey, who seemed to be worried about all the things that were wrong in the business and how everything seemed to be going against us profit-wise. He'd been quite distant from me since the day he started and didn't seem to want to spend much time with me. I told him I realised our interests weren't compatible. I wanted to show as high a profit number as possible and get somewhere near the £130 million the City was expecting, but I recognised that wouldn't be in his interests for the future. He didn't want to talk about it and changed the subject.

I decided to explain about how we had caused so many of the problems in Iceland ourselves and how easily we could put them right. I took him into the 'test store' next door to the office and just walked him along the cabinets, pointing out product confusion, bad packaging and pricing chaos. It was so obvious when it was pointed out and Bill seemed to appreciate the scope of what we would be able to do to improve things. Retailing isn't rocket science and if everyone is on the same team and pointed in the right direction it's easy. We were suffering a legacy from Russell. I explained that the first thing we should do was to organise a full range review. Buyer by buyer, product by product. We should personally sit there for maybe a week and we could revolutionise the product range. Bill looked at me and said, 'I don't work that way. I employ buyers to do that job and if they don't perform I get rid of them.' He was right, of course, but sometimes you have to be hands-on and I thought this was one of those times. Our buying department was in complete disarray after the events of the last year and this job would take forever to get done with our existing team. We needed some hands-on action for immediate results and I was surprised Bill was against it.

We talked about Booker and again I gave him my view on the future. I'd already gone through the Costco idea and how we could change the format of the Booker business but I admitted this was a three- or four-year project. However, I did tell him there was a shortcut to increased profits that would put at least 1 per cent on the profit margin within the next nine months. Get rid of 50 per cent of the buying department and replace them with high flyers. I told him that if you were a food buyer, you wanted to work for Tesco. Failing that Asda or Sainsbury's and maybe even Iceland but last of all you went into the cash and carry business and very last of all you worked for Booker in Wellingborough. The Booker buyers were, in the main, overpaid (they had to be to attract them there) and generally most of them were only cruising. We needed some enthusiastic new blood.

Carl Hamill had had two days out with me visiting Booker branches. Carl ran a small division of Iceland called ITEX, which specialised in exporting Iceland products to several countries but was also importing 'grey market' products into the UK for Iceland. Many manufacturers support different pricing structures in different countries. Coca Cola, for example, is only a fraction of the price in Spain that it is in the UK. The only problem is it has Spanish on the can! (Carl would bring it in from South Africa where it was labelled in English!) A clever entrepreneur, wheeler-dealer type person can make a fortune for the company by exploiting these pricing differences. Carl made £2.8 million net profit for Iceland in 2000. His big problem was that the buyers resented him. They hated it when he

Iceland

supports the Iceland
EVEREST
EXPEDITION

Raising
money for:

Alzheimer's
Research UK
Defeating Dementia

For more information and how to
make a donation, visit our website:
www.icelandeverest.org.uk

The Iceland Everest Expedition, 2011.

Climbing Everest.

Malcolm mucking about in a Yeti costume at Everest Advanced Base Camp.

Malcolm and Richard Walker at the North Col, 3 May 2011.

The Descent
of The Shard,
3 September
2012.

Lord Kirkham and
Malcolm before
The Descent of
The Shard.

The Iceland Antarctic Expedition team meets HRH The Prince of Wales.

The team in the Antarctic.

Malcolm on the Antarctic plateau.

Iceland says private equity cash not needed

Iceland founder and chief executive Malcolm Walker said he does not need funding from a private equity backer to take full control of the frozen food retailer, which is being circled by rivals.

Walker told *Retail Week*: "Our first choice is to gain full control of the business. We don't need the backing of another private equity firm, we have the funding in place from the banks, but obviously it depends on the price."

Walker, who has just returned from climbing Mount Everest to raise money for Alzheimer's Research UK, said he will do all he can to keep Iceland "an independent, autonomous business under the current management".

The winding-up committee of

Walker wants full control of Iceland

failed Icelandic bank Landsbanki has put its 67% Iceland stake up for sale and appointed Merrill Lynch and UBS as advisers. Walker and Iceland's management own a 23% stake and the remaining 10% is controlled by the resolution committee

of Glitnir, another bust Icelandic bank. Walker, who last year tabled a £1bn offer to buy the whole company, has the right to match any offer for Iceland.

Earlier this week it emerged Morrisons was eyeing Iceland. Morrisons finance director Richard Pennycook and strategy director Gordon Mowat have met potential advisers but their interest is at a preliminary stage.

A bid for Iceland would propel Morrisons' market share close to both Asda and Sainsbury's. It would also give the grocer a swathe of high street convenience stores and more shops in the south of England – two of the key growth areas identified by chief executive Dalton Philips.

Nomura analyst Nick Coulter

said: "Although we think Morrisons, alongside Asda, would see a reasonable demographic fit with the Iceland store catchments, the success of any deal would be contingent on the delivery of the sales uplifts from overlaying a Morrisons' offer on the Iceland stores."

It is understood that other grocers such as Sainsbury's could be interested in some Iceland stores if the chain is broken up.

➤ Morrisons has bought two more former Netto stores from Asda. The latest acquisitions are in Worsley, Manchester and Dunstable, Bedfordshire. The acquisitions add to the 16 former Netto stores that Morrisons bought from Asda in January, the first of which began trading as Morrisons earlier this month.

The auction for Iceland gets under way.

Kathy Wight, Malcolm's long-suffering Personal Assistant.

Tarsem Dhaliwal, Iceland's Chief Financial Officer.

Nick Canning, Iceland's Director for Customers and People.

Nigel Broadhurst, Iceland's Buying Director.

Iceland: Britain's Best Big Company To Work For, 2012.

ICELAND OPERATING PROFIT BY YEAR (£'m)

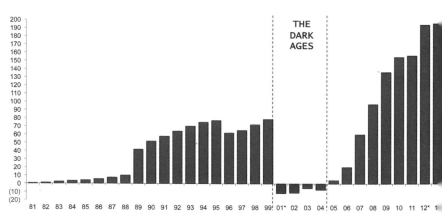

THE
DARK
AGES

01* : 15 month period to March (previous financial years to Dec.).   Post 2001, March year end
12* : 53 week period.   For comparability, graph shows the equivalent 52 week performance

Iceland's profit record.

disrupted a cosy relationship with a supplier and bought products cheaper than they could.

Most of the big retailers buy heavily on the grey market and we weren't doing enough of it. We were losing out. I explained to Bill that Carl had a big opportunity to make money for both Iceland and Booker and we should encourage him. He was not welcomed in Booker but now Charles had gone we should insist the Booker buyers work with him. The problem for Bill with all this was that Carl was an independent spirit and I admitted he was a 'bit of a maverick'.

Bill understood what I was saying and he wrote everything down in his notebook as he always did during a conversation. I told him I already had a specialist headhunter looking for at least ten new buyers and I had an interview lined up for a senior cash and carry buyer the very next night. Bill said he wanted to do the interview himself. I explained I had arranged to meet the buyer at my house in case she was recognised in the office. He invited himself along. I also explained that Iceland was in much the same position as Booker and needed new and more experienced buyers. I mentioned a guy called Andy Errington who had worked for Iceland previously and recommended we should see him. He wrote down his name.

The next night we drove to my house and I again mentioned my worry that our interests on profits for the current year were incompatible. I was now quite worried about Bill's remoteness and his apparent unwillingness to get too friendly. I suggested if he felt £130 million was pushing it a bit we should talk about it. He didn't respond.

We met the buyer and then I invited Bill to stay for supper. After a moment's hesitation he agreed. Conversation was pleasant enough but he was uneasy and obviously on edge and didn't eat much. He kept complaining he was too fat. There was one moment when he was discussing a personal matter when he seemed almost to lose control of his temper. His eyes bulged and he coloured up. I really was starting to see a scary side to him. He left as soon as he'd eaten.

We had a group board meeting arranged for Thursday, 11 January.

Bill Hoskins hadn't started yet but he attended the meeting anyway in order to get up to speed and meet everybody. It was the first time Tom Knowlton and Iain Sharp had met Bill Grimsey and he spent a few minutes introducing himself and then once again outlined his vision of making Iceland the biggest and most profitable food retailer in the UK. I was slightly embarrassed at this and Tom made some remark about the scale of his ambition and asked whether he was being realistic. Bill explained he was deadly serious.

Andy, Tarsem and Mike Camp, the Booker FD, presented a review of Christmas and the latest trading figures. They also ran through the latest forecast for the outcome of the year ending March and explained that the figure we were now looking at achieving was £121.9 million. We discussed whether we were in profit warning territory and if we needed to make any kind of announcement. We concluded that since it wasn't more than 10 per cent adrift from expectations, we didn't. I suggested that while we had never made a Christmas trading statement before, maybe we should this year in order to start to lower expectations.

I had booked a holiday when Stuart left as I'd not been away for a year and thought I was stuck back in the business. This had now come round and I was leaving the following Wednesday. We agreed that Bill Grimsey would consult with our advisers after Hoskins had started on the following Monday and he had checked and was happy with the forecast number. If a statement then had to be made while I was away, Bill would fax it to me and agree it with me before release. The mood of the meeting was quite jovial and bullish. The figures were disappointing but everyone seemed full of confidence for the future. Andy was full of plans for how he was going to sort out Iceland now Russell was out of the way. At the end of the meeting we played a copy of the Christmas TV advert and contrasted it with the one from the year before. The difference was astonishing and it seemed so obvious now why Christmas sales had been so bad.

I had made a request to the Remuneration Committee for their consideration before the board meeting. Over the years I felt my salary had been quite modest. As a large shareholder I'd never bothered pushing for a big salary and indeed for the first twelve years as a public company I'd issued options to everybody else but never to myself. Now I was retiring I was keen to maximise my final salary in order to improve my pension and I'd had a big pay increase on the Booker takeover. Even on profits of £121 million I'd earned a bonus of £500,000 but unfortunately this wouldn't be paid out until after the final accounts were published in July. This therefore wouldn't count towards my pension as I retired in March. I wanted to know if the Remuneration Committee would consider paying my bonus early and I suggested that if there were any reduction in the final profit figure for the year I would pay it back. They discussed this while I was out of the room and in the end agreed to pay the bonus early; and in the event that we didn't hit the profit number, then it was decided I could keep the bonus anyway as a 'lifetime achievement' award for building up the company.

The next few days passed without me seeing much of Bill. Hoskins had started but I didn't see much of him either and neither did Andy. One thing I still had to do, however, was see all the large suppliers for the final 'synergy meeting' and nail down the improved buying terms for next year plus the backdated cash contribution for this year which would of course help profits. Stuart had been going to do this before and had all the meetings in his diary but when he left they had to be rearranged so I could see them. I had rung Tony Pearce of Unilever after Stuart left to confirm he had offered £2 million. Of course he denied it but I had arranged to see him that day for the final negotiation. I explained all this to Bill and suggested he might want to sit in on the meetings. 'No,' he said. 'I'll take the meetings, you don't need to be there.' 'OK,' I thought, 'another job less for me.' I wasn't at all surprised by Bill's response as he wanted to be in control.

Bill saw Tony Pearce and afterwards I asked him how it went. 'Fine,' he said. 'We're looking at some good opportunities for next year but I didn't get anything for this year.' 'What?' I said, with some alarm. 'Stuart had already got £2 million out of him, it just needed confirming.' 'Well I couldn't get anything, they've closed their books on last year, it's too late. I got nothing.' 'Bill,' I said with rising panic, 'we wrote to all the suppliers immediately after the takeover and told them all the new terms would be backdated to the date of the takeover so he was expecting it.' I knew what was going on. Bill could have no interest at all in getting money for this year. It would be much better for him to push it forward. I was worried but there wasn't a lot I could do.

I was looking forward to my holiday and to retiring. I was starting to plan what I would do. I hoped to agree a decent package as non-executive Chairman and spend time developing As Nature Intended, my daughter's organic supermarket in London which I helped to run as a hobby. The day before I left, I had a word with Bill and asked him what he wanted me to do when I got back from holiday. 'What do you mean?' he asked. 'Well, I'm redundant.' I replied. 'I'm not complaining but you won't let me do anything or get involved in the business, I feel spare.' 'I'll tell you what,' said Bill. 'When you come back, why don't you go non-executive straight away? Don't wait till March.'

I was delighted. Bill went on to explain that my value to him would be in a chat once a week to pick my brains and get ideas. He said he should see me formally every week as Chairman to report to me. I thought that was a bit excessive and I know it was a daft question I asked next but I was already planning my week so I asked him which day of the week he would want to see me. We were sitting in my office at a meeting table and he looked over at my desk and nodded and said, 'Oh, I only want you here when I'm here. If you come in this building when I'm not here that fucking chair will explode!'

That night I told Ranny what he had said. She was livid and asked who he thought he was and why wasn't I furious with him. I said I was shocked and it was a bit rich when I'd run the company for 30 years but I said I wasn't bothered. I'd rather him be like that than like Stuart Rose.

We set off to the Maldives and arrived on Friday, 19 January. I felt as happy and relaxed as I'd done for a long time. I'd watched a film on the aeroplane on the way out called *The Shawshank Redemption*. Anybody who has seen it will know why I identified with the prisoner who finally gained his freedom!

The holiday was booked immediately after Stuart resigned and was meant to fortify me for another two years of hard graft, running the business. It was a long time since we'd had a beach holiday and I'd rarely had more than a week at one time. I intended to do absolutely nothing. We'd booked in at an exclusive island resort run by the Four Seasons. It was a tiny island in paradise with a collection of individual thatched villas dotted around. You had to take a fast boat ride for an hour from Malé, the main island with the airport, to get to the resort island. I'd taken my mobile phone with me but I didn't expect it to work there. I was quite surprised when it did although I didn't switch it on for a couple of days.

It rang on Monday, 22 January. 'It's a takeover!' Andy said. 'As soon as you'd gone they were into every department and they are trashing the profits.' 'What do you mean?' I asked. 'They have the same list you'd have on a takeover. They're into the property department, looking at dilapidations and asking Tim if we've any over-rented properties, they're into the buying department looking at deals with suppliers and knocking out lumps of cash. At this rate we'll be lucky to make £100 million.' 'Christ,' I said, 'If they knock it down to that level I'll have a problem.' 'You already have,' Andy said. 'There's been a newspaper article saying our Christmas sales were diabolical, the share price has crashed and there's been a lot written about your share sale. It looks like you're in trouble and your name's mud.' 'Oh bloody hell, where did that sales story come from?' I asked. Andy said the AGB figures (independent retail sales estimates) had been mentioned but he didn't believe that. He thought the story had been deliberately leaked.

I rang Bill to ask him what was going on and he said we had to put out a trading statement immediately and he would fax it to me. For the next few hours I had a knot in my stomach and rang both Keith

Hann and Kathy but nobody could give me any comfort. The press was apparently really bad but thank God I'd been blissfully unaware of it over the weekend. This had come on so suddenly and I felt helpless. The fax arrived and I was horrified. It wasn't a trading statement but in effect a profit warning. It quoted Christmas sales as being 5½ per cent negative over the last four weeks. He could have quoted six weeks as most other retailers did but four gave the worst number. It mentioned a problem with organic sales, which was bound to ensure maximum consumer press as well as financial coverage, and finally it said that Hoskins and Grimsey, who had been there only one week and three weeks respectively, were making a thorough evaluation of the integration process following the merger with Booker and would report back by the end of January. In other words, here's a black hole, just wait for the really bad news to come! The statement was going out and there was nothing I could do to change anything so I didn't even try. I asked Andy more about what was going on but he pointed out he was now the MD not the Finance Director and they weren't involving him in anything.

I was desperately worried and spoke to Grimsey for an explanation but he just said Hoskins was checking the forecast numbers and he would let me know when he had confirmed the final number. He said our advisers had recommended he should make a further announcement at the end of January but, until he'd verified Andy's number, he didn't want to get into a discussion. He had a further meeting planned with our advisers on Wednesday at 10am and would hopefully fax me the number tomorrow, Tuesday.

It was a bizarre situation. This should have been the holiday of a lifetime. I'd had a wonderful 30-year career building a national company. I was respected throughout the industry but now it was all running away from me and I had completely lost control of events. At the same time, here I was on a romantic holiday island and there was nothing I could do but wait. I rang the travel agent to enquire about flights home but decided to stay where I was for the moment until the Grimsey number had been faxed through.

I tried to put things out of my mind and enjoy the sun but it was impossible. We went game fishing for a morning to take our minds off things but didn't catch much. I envied the boat captain who appeared relaxed and carefree. 'What a life,' I thought as he moved round the boat, barefoot and weather-beaten. I couldn't sleep at night and kept churning things over in my mind. Because of the time difference I spent most evenings on the phone, trying to find out what was going on. Most journalists had my mobile number but I just had to switch it off and use Ranny's phone. I didn't want to talk to the press because I didn't know what to say. If ever I switched it back on, twenty journalists would have left messages wanting to speak to me. The organic part of the story got massive coverage but why was it all such big news?

The fax didn't arrive on Tuesday or Wednesday morning my time. Kathy told me both Bills and most of the accounts department had been working through the weekend and virtually through most nights in the office but she didn't know what was going on. She was eventually given a paper late on Tuesday night but told not to send it to me as 'I'd be asleep'. Eventually, on Wednesday at about 3pm in the Maldives, or 9am in Deeside, Kathy sent the fax through. I nearly had a heart attack!

I was expecting that Grimsey would have been very conservative with his accounting and forecasting and you would expect any newcomer to 'clear the decks'. There are always items in the accounts that are 'grey' and my philosophy has always been that if the auditors accept something, then I'm happy. Over the years there had been times when we had been conservative and 'tucked a bit away'. There had been other years when we had struggled and chucked everything in. This year was tight. I'd already admitted to Grimsey we were pushing it to the limit and I could quite understand how he would have been able to knock the number down to even as low as £100 million if he'd been ruthless. I was not expecting what I saw on the fax. I couldn't in my wildest dreams imagine how he'd got the number down to £62 million. Then there seemed to be another

£34 million of 'exceptional' costs to come off that. I thought maybe I was reading it wrong.

I rang him on his mobile straight away. It was 9.45am UK time and he was in London. 'I can't speak,' said Grimsey, 'I'm just going into a meeting but I'll ring you in an hour from the meeting and we can go through it.' He didn't ring.

I tried to get hold of Andy but he was in the meeting with the Bills, meeting the advisers. I rang Tarsem at Deeside and he talked me through the numbers. He explained there was a pension adjustment in there of £3.4 million. The Booker pension scheme was massively overfunded and had a surplus of over £150 million. Booker had enjoyed a contributions holiday for years. Apparently the actuaries had just informed us the Iceland fund had a shortfall. If that were the case then in normal times we'd have made it up over, say, three years. In this case however the two schemes were being amalgamated in just eight weeks' time so there would be a combined surplus. There was no need for the £3.4 million adjustment. The whole area of pensions, after an acquisition, is a minefield. Another £4 million had just been charged to profits in respect of the Booker scheme which Andy had been advised was incorrect.

They had made a provision for a VAT liability of £4 million. This was on top of £4 million always kept as a standard reserve. This was without foundation and the chance of ever being asked to pay any of the £8 million was virtually nil. A query had just been received from the VAT man, which we viewed as totally routine but it was enough of an excuse to raise a provision.

Buying synergy benefits had been reduced by £8 million because they weren't yet signed off but they were never intended to be at this stage. The final meetings still had to take place but I suppose why would they want the money this year when they could have it next?

A view had been taken on sales for the rest of the year and £7 million knocked off profits to reflect lower than expected sales. Not surprisingly sales were suffering, it was the last thing anybody was bothering about.

Tarsem went through a whole list of items they had knocked off the profits. Some you could argue had some element of justification but equally, you could argue the other way and the auditors would have accepted it. Some items were just an outrageous scam like the VAT.

Exceptional items are still deducted from profits but are considered 'one-offs' and 'below the line'. Companies often put things as exceptional if they can get away with it. They tend not to be viewed in the same way as a normal profit reduction but, once written off, the effect can be to enhance profits in future years. Over £34 million had been put to exceptionals including a write-off of the organic stock and property related items. It was clear what was happening. The Bills had seriously cleared the decks and lowered the bar for themselves next year but at my expense. Some of the changes they were making were for profit reductions and some were accounting changes. It was a takeover.

I rang the travel agent and booked the first flight home, which was the following night. I was marooned on a desert island for the next 36 hours.

22
Everything Hits the Fan!

Ranny's phone rang. It was 11pm and we were sitting at a table right on the edge of the sea with the magnificent canopy of stars that you get in the tropics for lighting. We were trying to enjoy the food but I was more interested in the wine. It was Grimsey calling.

I stood up and walked down a jetty. Grimsey was obviously on a speakerphone. 'Oh Malcolm, I'm so sorry I'm only just getting back to you but you'll appreciate we've had a long day and only just finished.' It was about 5pm UK time. He could have an almost breathless, soothing quality to his voice sometimes. 'Bill, these numbers aren't right,' I said. 'What do you mean, not right?' His voice sharpened up. 'I've been going through it with Tarsem and ...' 'Oh you've been checking up on me have you, why have you been talking to other people about this?' I couldn't believe his reaction. 'Of course I've been talking to Tarsem, I couldn't get hold of you, I had to know how the numbers were made up. Bill, I've spoken to Tarsem and you've knocked money out of supplier contributions.' He interrupted me. 'We can't find the money,' he said. 'What do you mean can't find the money?' I asked. 'We can't find it, we've looked in all the drawers and it's not there.' 'Bill,' I said, 'these numbers aren't right.'

Suddenly he exploded. 'I didn't come here to run this bag of shit,' he shouted, 'I resign!' There was a lot of banging and shouting and swearing in the background and then I heard a plaintive voice. 'Malcolm, Malcolm, calm Bill down, he's leaving.' It was David Price. Apart from David there were some of our advisers in the room, probably from Herbert Smith, Rothschilds and ABN Amro. Eventually Bill calmed down and even apologised. 'I'm sorry, but you have to understand we've had a very stressful day here but I'm telling you, if *anybody* questions these numbers, I resign.' 'OK Bill,' I said, 'I'm on my way back. I'll talk to you when I see you.' I rang Andy but he couldn't talk. He was on his way north with Hoskins.

I went back to finish my wine. 'Grimsey's just resigned,' I said, 'but then he changed his mind.' 'You shouldn't have let him,' Ranny said. 'You can't let him get away with this.' 'Ranny, think about the situation. If I argue with his numbers and he goes, Hoskins will go with him and how will that look, they've only been here two minutes? People will wonder what on earth they've found. We've had all this bad press, the share price has crashed and the City is expecting a profit warning. The damage is all done, plus I'd have to go back and run the company, which I'm not going to do. Mind you, when they announce expected profits of only £62 million, I can't imagine what will happen then but there's bound to be an investigation into my share sale.'

We discussed this for a while and then I switched on my mobile to check for messages. Instantly it rang and it was Alistair Osborne from the *Daily Telegraph*. 'Oh Christ,' I thought, 'What do I do now? I can't ring off.' I couldn't get into a discussion with him but when he asked if I knew sales were down when I sold my shares all I could say was, 'I believed we would make our profit number when I sold but of course now I wish I'd never sold them,' which was true. 'You don't know the half of it,' I thought, wondering what his reaction would be if he knew the latest profit number that was about to be disclosed.

Thursday was our last day on the island. We had to leave around midnight for an early morning flight. To keep ourselves occupied Ranny decided she wanted to learn to water ski and then we booked to go to the next island to see a working fishing village. We were back for lunch and spent the rest of the afternoon packing and tried to sleep. I rang Andy that evening and finally he could talk but he sounded totally defeated and all the fight had gone out of him. 'What did you say at the meeting when Hoskins was going through the numbers?' 'Nothing,' he replied. 'I just let them get on with it. I've had no involvement in putting the numbers together.' 'Why didn't you defend yourself?' 'There's no point. They're not going to change anything and he's in charge of my pay-off. He's already told me I won't be here after the weekend.' 'Haven't you said anything to Grimsey?' I asked. 'Yes, I told him no matter how you try, you can't get that number to less than a hundred but he just said, "That might be the case but if it is I won't be here."'

Andy told me there was a full board meeting planned for next Tuesday and they were going to make a Stock Exchange announcement on Wednesday. 'Andy,' I said, 'You have to defend yourself. How's it going to look if you don't? You have to give some kind of explanation as to how the difference has arisen. Even if you let them win every point you have to explain what's happened.' I wound Andy up to start putting information together and to find out as much as he could about how they'd arrived at the figures. Tarsem was in an awkward position. He was providing all the information for Hoskins and was scared to talk to Andy. Everyone was worried about their own jobs and confused about their loyalties.

We had a late dinner and then lingered at the table in the restaurant, killing time until the hotel launch left for the airport on the mainland. There were only one or two other couples about and we eventually decided to go back to our villa. As we were walking down the pathway a young woman ran up behind me and called my name. I turned. 'I'm sorry to interrupt, I know you're not going to like this Mr Walker but I'm Teena Lyons from the *Mail on Sunday*. There's been a lot of bad press at home and we thought you would you like to give your side of the story about your share sale.' 'Christ, I don't believe it!' I said and hurried away. She didn't follow.

We got back to the villa and I rang the hotel manager and asked him to come to my room. It was actually the assistant manager and it turned out he used to work at the Four Seasons in London. He knew me and he even knew the name of Harnish, our London chauffeur! I explained what had happened and he knew immediately who I was talking about. 'They checked in last night and claimed they were on a six-month world tour.' He even knew their villa number. 'They? They? You mean there's two of them? Oh Christ,' I said, 'One's got to be a photographer!' The manager was distraught and couldn't apologise enough for what had happened but of course he couldn't have avoided it. I couldn't believe the *Mail on Sunday* would send two people halfway round the world on the off-chance they might get a comment from me. 'I bet they're enjoying this assignment in the sunshine but I hope Teena Lyons likes sleeping in the same room as the photographer,' I said. The hotel only has doubles. Then I started to imagine what the photographer had been doing all day. Now I remembered that just before Ranny started water skiing, I briefly had a strange feeling about a couple next to me. 'How did they find us?' I wondered. Ranny remembered the phone ringing in the villa a couple of days ago and when she answered someone hung up. I suppose they found out we were in the Maldives and then rang all the posh hotels until they found us.

I rang Keith Hann and told him what had happened. 'You know who the editor of the *Financial Mail on Sunda*y is?' 'No,' I replied, 'Who?' 'Ben Laurance,' he said. 'Oh shit!' Ben Laurance, formerly of *The Observer*. The man I'd called a 'tosser'. He'd waited four years for his revenge! Keith claimed Ben Laurance was his best friend. He said he'd ring him to find out what was going on.

I realised that Teena Lyons wouldn't know we were leaving. The jetty for the launch to the airport was by the restaurant and the manager said they were both still in the bar. A few people had gathered already to leave on the boat. He decided to take us to the back of the Island to the staff quarters and he provided a separate launch for our James Bond style 'getaway'. It gave me some comfort to imagine them spying on our villa in the morning, not realising we'd left until late morning when the maids came to change the room over.

Keith Hann rang me on Friday morning. 'Where are you?' he asked. 'I'm just driving home from Manchester airport.' 'There isn't a motorbike alongside you with a photographer on the pillion, is there?'

'Very funny,' I replied.

'Ben Laurance is furious, he can't understand how you left.'

I spoke to Kathy next and she told me there'd been all sorts of funny phone calls to Chester airport asking about our plane and where it was. 'Oh, does Ben Laurance seriously imagine I could have flown home on it? That would make his day for a story. Does he think our little plane would do that distance? We'd need a 747!' I then asked Kathy to get the plane lined up for later, I would be going straight to London as soon as I got home and got changed.

I rang Tim Steadman at Herbert Smith and said I needed some advice. He suggested that maybe Edward Walker-Arnott could come in and talk to me. Edward was a legend in the legal world and probably the best corporate lawyer ever. He was previously the senior partner at Herbert Smith but had now retired. I was flattered that he'd come and give me advice. Edward had helped to float Iceland in 1984 and I'd consulted him personally on various issues over the years. He'd invited me to his retirement dinner a couple of years ago. Tim said Edward had always had a great affection for Iceland. I didn't get to their offices until about 7pm. I told him the whole story and he then talked for an hour about every eventuality. He said there was bound to be an investigation by the Financial Services Authority to see if the company had broken any Stock Exchange rules. This would relate both to the way I got permission from other directors for my share sale and to the question of whether I'd followed all the correct procedures. Also whether we had made any misleading Stock Exchange announcements or failed to make announcements in relation to anything that would affect the share price. He also explained that, if I was unlucky, there could be an investigation by the

Department of Trade and Industry to check on any insider dealing aspects of my share sale but this was always kept very confidential.

I knew I'd done nothing wrong but I was anxious that Herbert Smith would represent me if there were any problems, even though they were the company lawyers. Edward could see no conflict in this and said that from what I'd told him, there could be no problem in respect of any insider dealing allegations if the DTI did look at things. The FSA had no sanction anyway, even if it was found we had broken any rules, other than a censure. This was apart from what he described as their 'nuclear option', which was the delisting of a public company, something they were not going to do. He explained that a censure was just a letter saying we had broken the rules but it could be issued privately or publicly. He felt the worst outcome was bad press and said under no circumstances should I resign. He felt that would look as if I'd done something wrong. I said there was no way I could carry on working with Grimsey but he said I had to, for at least three months.

I left to go home but it was snowing and the plane was grounded. Grimsey was using Harnish somewhere so I used Peter, the Booker chauffeur from Wellingborough, who didn't really know his way around London. I stayed in London that night with my daughter Alexia, who worked as a stockbroker and loved her job. I was worried what impact any of this might have on her, as many of her colleagues and clients knew who her Dad was. Some of her clients would undoubtedly lose money on Iceland shares. In fact nothing that happened had any effect whatsoever. All her colleagues and clients were brilliant. They were totally supportive and sympathetic to her and to me.

I wanted to see David Price on Saturday afternoon but he lived in Lincolnshire and said it wasn't convenient for him. We talked on the phone. 'If we question their number do you think the Bills will walk?' I asked him. 'I do,' he said. 'They are not tied in, they don't have any share options. I really think they would leave.' 'Then we only have two choices,' I said. 'I can argue for a higher profit number and they both go. The damage is already done but that would make things look worse, plus I will have to run the company, or we can let them have their number and I have to suffer the consequences.' David suggested that if they did go and I did have to come back it would only be for a short time, say six months, but I told him I wasn't prepared to do it. Then he said, 'Anyway, it isn't their number or yours that we will allow but what the auditors decide.' 'Oh come on, David,' was all I could say.

I met Andy in the office on Sunday. I took in all the Sunday papers. The coverage had been non-stop all week and the Sunday papers were full of it. The *Financial Mail on Sunday* had really gone to town. There was Ranny learning to water ski. I told her at least she'd managed to get up and her picture was on page three! There was a double page spread devoted to the story with pictures of the hotel. They'd worked out it would take 103 million fish fingers laid end to end to reach the Maldives! They even reported conversations I'd had with other hotel guests. These were totally invented, as we'd never actually spoken to another guest the whole time we were there. The whole theme, of course, was that I was a rogue and had fleeced our shareholders by selling ahead of a profit warning.

Andy had been working hard and identified all the areas in dispute. He had collected quite a dossier of papers, letters and written professional opinions from accountants, lawyers and actuaries to support his numbers in most of the areas of dispute. Of course, some issues were merely a matter of opinion where you could decide either way and some were numbers that frankly we were 'chucking in', but which the auditors would have allowed. Andy's dossier showed, even after deducting £11 million profit for reduced sales going forward and a £4 million reduction in synergy benefits, a profit of £96.6 million compared to Hoskins' £62.6 million.

Eamonn McGrath, the Ernst & Young partner, came in to the office at my request. Andy had tried to get him in but failed. We had known him many years and I believed we had a very good relationship. He was a different man, like a frightened rabbit, and it was pitiful to watch him. He obviously had no choice but to support the new management and he was clearly worried in case he was going to be accused of anything. Andy discussed several of the numbers in dispute but he was suddenly black and white on everything and it was clear he was going to support the Bills every step of the way. He couldn't wait to get away from us.

I was in the office early on Monday morning and had a good walk around the place to let everybody see me. I was back and still alive. I was sitting at the round table in my office when Grimsey arrived. He came straight in and sat next to me. 'Oh, how are you, you must be very upset at what's happened?' He softly oozed the words in his breathless voice. 'Bill,' I said, 'I have no desire to stay in this company and work with you one second longer but I've been to see my lawyers and I've been told I shouldn't resign, so I don't intend to.' He hesitated a moment and then left. He came back a few hours later, presumably after consulting his guru or some other adviser, and told me he thought I should resign.

The Bills flew down to London and then the plane came back for Andy and me. Kathy and Claire, Andy's PA, had been busy collating and preparing nineteen sets of binders that we were going to hand out at the meeting. These gave Andy's version of the figures with supporting documentation. I was desperate to see our non-executives before the meeting next morning but none of them was arriving in time. Iain was flying in from Jersey on his own plane, Tom was flying in from Canada and Alan Smith and David Price were with the Bills anyway. We did manage to have an hour that evening with Mark Astaire, Tony Allen from Rothschilds and Ossie, to explain everything and go through the numbers. They were as bewildered as we were.

We all assembled in a meeting room at Herbert Smith's offices on Tuesday morning. There was the full board present although Iain at first wasn't even going to come. He'd had to postpone a skiing holiday and his wife apparently wasn't impressed. There were two people each from ABN Amro, Rothschilds and Charterhouse, three from

Ernst & Young and also Tim Steadman from Herbert Smith. It looked a formidable number of people around a long boardroom style table. Everyone was slightly embarrassed and uneasy and no one really knew what to say. I had to chair the meeting, which of course would have been ridiculous. I'd quietly asked David if he would do it for me and also somehow allow Andy to put over his side of things without sending Grimsey off into a temper. My biggest worry was that he might walk out.

I made an introduction and, as best I could, explained how difficult this was for all of us but particularly for Andy as the former Finance Director. I asked that the meeting should be calm and that as soon as it was over we should concentrate on running the business, which had been neglected for months. I also said that much as I wanted to, I had been advised not to resign.

David then took the Chair. The meeting was scheduled to last all day but the morning was reserved for reviewing the figures. David started by asking Andy to pass round his binders. Grimsey looked startled and said, 'What's this? What's this? I don't know anything about this.' David told him in a measured tone that Andy had prepared some information which he would like to present to give his side of things. Grimsey stood up, his eyes were bulging and he looked like he was losing control. 'I've not seen this information. Mr Chairman, you will have to adjourn the meeting.' Andy countered, 'I've not been allowed to see your figures.' I thought a full-scale row was about to erupt but David skilfully calmed things down and somehow managed to get Andy's binders passed round to everybody. Grimsey was steaming.

We went through the list, item by item. Hoskins explained why he had reduced each number and then Andy referred to his papers and explained, not why his number should stay but why he had taken the view he had. It was nothing more than a ritual. Occasionally, Eamonn McGrath would be asked his view on a point and he would support Hoskins. Sometimes Andy would argue but it was only half-hearted. It lasted all morning and nobody else said a word throughout the whole meeting. I didn't know why they were all there except to witness the execution. We broke for sandwiches which had been brought into the end of the room. Everyone stood up and were milling about as Grimsey and Hoskins went round collecting up all Andy's binders. The non-execs disappeared and left me chatting with Tim Steadman. I went to the loo and as I walked past the open door of the adjoining room I saw the non-executives in there and they indicated I should join them. Alan Smith said they were really sorry but neither Andy nor I could possibly stay on after this and we had to resign. I called in Tim and said I didn't know what to do. I didn't want to prejudice my position. Tim suggested I could resign as a director but not as an employee. I was retiring anyway in eight weeks but this would give me time to think about things. I was delighted. I couldn't sensibly stay on anyway after today and endorse what Grimsey was doing.

I spent the rest of the day talking to Stephen Gate and Lucy Hutchinson, Herbert Smith's compliance experts, as the FSA had already requested information on my share sale. Everyone else carried on with the meeting. The banking position of the company was on the agenda during the afternoon and Andy had already pointed out that, with all the exceptional write-offs, they'd have breached the company banking covenants. He said he'd already mentioned this to Hoskins who'd said, 'Don't worry about that, we have a good relationship with the banks.' After all the trouble we'd had with Barclays financing the merger, if Hoskins thought that wouldn't be a problem he'd another think coming!

I saw Grimsey before I left at about 6.30pm. I told him he'd now got everything he wanted and the only thing I would ask from him was that he 'played fair by Andy and gave him a proper pay-off'. His response was as self-righteous as ever and all he said was 'Don't ask me to do anything that will jeopardise the interests of the shareholders.' I told him I'd clear my office by the weekend.

Ranny had come down on the train that afternoon with Andy's wife Debbie. It was Ranny's birthday and we thought we'd celebrate and commiserate at the Four Seasons. Tom Knowlton joined us briefly for a drink but John Berry, who'd been at the meeting, avoided us. As Company Secretary he was trying to be 'professional' and not create a conflict. We read all the papers at breakfast and most of them seemed remarkably well informed. Hudson Sandler were still acting for Iceland but now in Grimsey's interests of course. Grimsey seriously disliked Keith Hann and didn't trust him because of his relationship with me but he knew Michael Sandler very well as he had acted for him at Wickes. I thought we could expect the Sandler PR machine to go into overdrive now in building Grimsey's reputation, probably at the expense of mine.

I went into my office on Saturday and Kathy had packed everything into boxes and arranged a van. Janet was there, tearful, embarrassed and apologising that she'd been asked to oversee my departure. She'd been told to ensure I didn't take any company papers. It was a relief to be out of it but there was still so much uncertainty. Andy was desperately worried about his future and his pay-off. He was convinced he wouldn't get one but I assured him he would. Grimsey would have to pay out his contract and deduct almost nothing for 'mitigation'. The non-execs would ensure fair play.

The press were relentless and I wished some other news would knock me off the pages but nothing much seemed to be happening. Ben Laurance and Teena Lyons did another spectacular three-page spread on Sunday. Photographers had been skulking round my house over the past few days and sure enough a picture appeared of the house with my wife and daughter Caroline superimposed over it. I had never in 30 years involved my wife or children in the publicity I often courted for the business. Until last year when, after a lot of pressure for an 'organic' feature, I allowed the *Mail*'s *You* magazine to photograph my garden (but not my house) and Ranny and Caroline were in the picture. I felt to bring them into this was a disgrace. The *Financial Mail on Sunday* gave a long account of recent events and even described how, when I left Herbert Smith's offices after I resigned, I attended 'a long-standing commitment to the 20-Club, a private forum for retail executives, which met in the board room of

Selfridges. "He sat there with a fixed smile and gave nothing away."'
That was Ranny's birthday evening and I'd never even heard of the
20-Club. I would have to get used to being harassed by Ben Laurance
and the straightforward lies and invention (as opposed to misreport-
ing) in their stories for a long time to come.

23
Animal Farm

On Monday morning, for the first time since I left school, I didn't have to go to work. However, I didn't have the sense of freedom and liberation I had been expecting, with a new carefree period of my life stretching before me. Instead I felt that there was a lot of unfinished business and many loose ends to tie up.

In anticipation of my retirement I'd already converted a garage at home into an office. Desks, filing cabinets, computers and copiers had all been delivered and Andy and I sat there wondering what to do next. We were both still on the Iceland payroll for another eight weeks and then we would be on our own. As a friend pointed out, we were about to discover the price of petrol!

I decided to sort out some 'housekeeping points' first and emailed Grimsey. I was still an employee so could I please use Kathy for typing until I sorted myself out, and what about my company car and expenses? His answer set the tone for our future relationship. No, I couldn't use Kathy. I wouldn't be incurring any expenses on behalf of the company so my credit card was cancelled and I could put in an offer to buy my two company cars. An invoice followed for £300 for my home laptop.

Two company cars are an unusual perk these days but it was a hangover from the past and in my contract. I had an Aston Martin and a Mercedes SLK. I offered £50,000 to buy the Aston and £19,000 for the Merc. His answer astonished me: £19,000 wasn't enough, he wanted £20,850 for the Merc, and the Aston wasn't for sale, I had to hand it back. He was going to use it as a 'staff incentive' car! Imagine a 24-year-old 'manager of the month', who normally drives a Ford Fiesta, winning the Aston for a week and getting a chance to kill himself! I remembered the relationship I had created with John Apthorp by giving him his Bentley after the Bejam takeover. The guy had just picked up £70 million but that gesture was important to him. He was as helpful to me as he possibly could be afterwards. Stuart Rose had even given Napier his Mercedes after the Booker takeover.

I bought the SLK but the Aston sat outside the Iceland office for the next nine months, unused, looking sad and losing value. I'm sure it was meant to be some kind of symbol of my departure.

Grimsey then set about destroying all evidence that I had ever been there. Photographs and memorabilia were removed from the walls, the history of Iceland was rewritten on the website (largely to exclude me) and my office was filled with Price Waterhouse consultants. I'd bought a number of paintings for the offices over the years and these were sold off, though they turned out to be one of the best investments the company had made. I bought two pictures from the company for £90,000 (my cheque had to be cleared before the paintings were released) which was double what I'd paid for them originally, while others were sold at auction. These included a Lowry that cost the company £30,000. I saw this offered later for £530,000 at a gallery in London.

I was in touch with many of the staff for a while on a daily basis and kept up to speed with the gossip. It was only to be expected that Grimsey would make changes but I was sad he chose to rewrite history. The name Malcolm Walker no doubt cropped up everywhere but Grimsey wanted to be the hero now. Staff dared not mention my name for fear of him exploding. I'd never existed. The pride went out of Iceland only days after I'd left. It was almost as if the directors' offices and boardroom were being deliberately trashed. Young consultants were everywhere, working late hours, treading curry takeaways into the carpets and burning the boardroom table with hot pizza. Nobody cared. The FD Bill Hoskins led the gang smoking fags outside the office doors and tab-ends permanently littered the ground.

Grimsey, as he'd promised, did turn out to be a complete control freak. No doubt he had to assert his authority quickly and get to grips with what he saw as a business with serious problems but he made few friends in the company. Senior staff were terrified of him and saw him as unpredictable and irrational. Kathy saw him totally lose control several times for no apparent reason. He'd pick up a stack of papers and bang them on the desk several times and shout, 'This fucking company, I'm sick of this fucking company!' and then he'd storm down the corridor shouting and swearing. Kathy was well used to bad language after nearly twenty years looking after a succession of bosses at Iceland but she claims she'd never experienced behaviour as bad or as nasty as this. She once saw him move from this rage within seconds and into a meeting of junior staff, emerging to turn on a smile in front of them and twinkle 'Any messages for me, girls?' He was Jekyll and Hyde between junior and senior staff but many people thought he was seriously unbalanced.

I should have gone on a long holiday to get away from it all but I felt I needed to be around for a while. I decided to spend some time looking at As Nature Intended. Andy set himself up as a consultant and I became his first client. We both based ourselves in my garage but inevitably spent more time on the post-mortem of recent events than in developing our new businesses. We actually agreed that Grimsey had to do what he did but it was a question of method and degree. It wasn't in Grimsey's interests to help us push the profits to the maximum. It would have given him a difficult number to beat the following year and it was very much in his own interests to 'lower the bar'.

So which profit number was right? The answer is they both

were. Accounting is by no means an exact science and even though the difference seems impossible to reconcile, an over-optimistic or over-pessimistic approach can produce a huge divergence, which the auditors, in each case, would support. Over 30 years we had produced consistent results. Over-pessimism in the accounts, which will destroy shareholder value, is just as bad as over-optimism.

In a hostile takeover you might have expected him to behave as he did, but even then not to that extreme. The difference was that we had invited him in. We agreed that this was like inviting someone into your home for the weekend and having him steal the silver. I tried to discuss the potential problem with Grimsey three times in the first two weeks he was there but he wasn't interested in discussing it. He had his own agenda. Even now, after everything, if he'd quietly apologised and treated everyone fairly and with respect, we wouldn't have forgiven him but it would have taken a lot of the anger out of the situation.

Andy was still desperately worried about his job prospects and his likely pay-off. I reassured him and said he would get at least eighteen months' salary. He said if he did he would be happy, but he refused to believe it would happen. I knew I wouldn't get my promised bonus but I couldn't see that the non-execs would do anything other than the right thing by Andy. David Price had told us that Herbert Smith were dealing with the severance issue and they would make a recommendation in due course. I couldn't see why they had to be involved as this wasn't a contractual issue but one of fairness and conscience. It was up to the directors to make the decision. Andy rang Herbert Smith several times but was eventually told a decision would be made at the March board meeting.

The press were constantly pestering me. They were still fascinated by the story but had run out of news for now and the only way to find a new angle was to interview me or, failing that, speculate about what might happen next. The FSA were now formally involved and in correspondence with Iceland. I knew anything I said to the press would only provoke further coverage and I didn't need that.

The story wasn't over yet. I really did want to get my version of events across but I knew it would be a long time before I could do that.

Ben Laurance thought of a great new angle to prolong the story. He wrote in the *Financial Mail on Sunday* that he felt I had profited unfairly from my share sale and should therefore give the money to charity. He invited his millions of readers to write in with suggestions as to which charity should benefit. This kept the story running for a few weeks until he finally sent me his readers' letters. Just eighteen letters, three of which were supportive of my position! The others included suggested donations to the hedgehog society and Whitby dog rescue! A former analyst himself, his socialist tendencies made it easy for him to criticise the wealth creators in society and those who have actually achieved something in life. He was on a personal crusade against me now but I don't suppose he ever considered for a second the millions of pounds that Iceland had already given to charity over the past few years or the number of hospitals that could have been built with the taxes paid both by me personally and the company I created.

I wasn't quite expecting the volume of supportive phone calls, letters and emails that soon started to arrive. Many were from Iceland staff, some from people that I'd never even met. People wrote the kindest things and it meant so much to Ranny and me. I began to appreciate then the importance of something I'd never been very good at. Often when someone you know has a crisis or even a bereavement, there can be embarrassment about making contact. Sometimes you feel you don't like to intrude. I know now how important and how appreciated that contact can be. I received hundreds of letters of support and only one letter of criticism from a shareholder who blamed me for the collapse of the share price.

I had lunch a couple of times with Keith Hann. Keith was an acquired taste but I liked him. He was outstandingly good at his job and had the drollest sense of humour, which I appreciated. However, he was always on the edge of a personal crisis and this time he'd decided he wanted to leave Hudson Sandler. Grimsey hated him, presumably because he'd had a close association with me, he didn't enjoy his job any more but felt locked in to the company because of his 'earn-out'. (Hudson Sandler had recently been sold and he stood to pick up a chunk of money in the next year or two.) In the mid-1980s Keith had taken a year off work to write a novel. He finished it but never had it published. I suggested he should do this again in the form of a thinly disguised story about a retailer who builds up an empire and is cheated by a rogue at the end! We both thought this was a great idea and Keith promised to do it if I would spend time helping him with the background. Another ten years on and I'm still waiting to see his first draft!

Stories started to emerge from Iceland. Consultants were everywhere, sackings of senior people had started and the influx of new recruits had begun. It seemed the only qualification needed now was to have worked previously for Wickes. The old Iceland style had been easy and freewheeling but command and control was now firmly in place. Structure, process, order, control and accountability were the new creed. I could agree with that up to a point but Iceland had never been a 'stable' business that could be managed by conventional methods. Iceland shouldn't exist. It shouldn't have existed after about 1980. The reality is that Iceland existed and thrived for years because of energy, enthusiasm, innovation and staff that were more than just committed, they felt part of the company. You can't run Iceland by a management textbook. It's much too volatile.

Bill Grimsey threw away years of knowledge and experience by the 'ethnic cleansing' of the old regime. The Buying Director Steve Archdeacon was one of the first to go, fired without compensation. He was convinced his efforts to help me substantiate the buying synergy numbers had sealed his fate.

The new regime attached great importance to the production of monthly management accounts, including a balance sheet. The only problem with this was that our system simply wasn't designed to generate these figures: we had always produced a weekly profit and loss account and consolidated the numbers quarterly. Since the system couldn't be adapted to meet the new requirements, a reliable source informs me that the finance team produced the new monthly accounts by simply making the numbers up: an extreme form of 'creative accounting'.

While all these new rules, restrictions and procedures were being put in place, the one thing many of the remaining 'old school' were surprised about was that nobody ever seemed to discuss sales or were even worried about them. Sales were plummeting but that didn't seem to matter. The year didn't end until March and the worse sales were this year the softer the comparison would be next year when Grimsey was in charge! The trouble is, customers lost are not easily won back.

Grimsey brought in Alan Besbrode on a consultancy basis at £1,500 per day to help with the buying function. Besbrode used to work at the Co-op and Tesco. I've never met him but he is widely regarded by those who have as the most objectionable and uncouth slob imaginable. His nickname was 'soup-stain' which was a reference to his tie! Grimsey also brought in Sonia Tsui, a very attractive Chinese lady who had followed Grimsey around since his time in Hong Kong. She enjoyed a special relationship with Grimsey in that it was noticed by everybody that she was the only person he would ever allow to criticise or contradict him in public.

Everyone lived down south and the jet would do a shuttle every Monday morning bringing up the new team. They would all stay at the Crabwall Manor hotel. No doubt they remembered that travel paid for by the company to your principal place of work is taxable.

Mike Pegg, who was Grimsey's personal guru from 'the mentoring centre' also started to make an appearance. He was now on the company payroll and would drive up to Deeside on a regular basis. In addition to the frequent 'one-to-one' counselling and self development sessions with Grimsey, he spent a lot of time talking to directors and advising them on 'how to relate to Bill'. Jeremy Woodward thought it was weird when Pegg had a session with him to explain specifically what an honest man Grimsey was and exactly how he had to behave in his dealings with him.

One of Grimsey's first decrees, in the interests of a more egalitarian company, was to abolish the reserved car parking spaces for directors, yet he would be chauffeur-driven everywhere. Roger, the company chauffeur, was a retired policeman I had taken on in 1995. At his interview I recognised him as the traffic policeman who had given me a speeding ticket on the M53 the previous year. This gave me twelve points and a six months disqualification but I don't bear grudges! If Grimsey was travelling the 300 yards from the Iceland head office to Woodward's (slightly further than the overflow staff car park) he would call in Roger four miles from his home to drive him there. He was certainly enjoying his new empire but all this seemed at odds with the way he met the warehouse shop stewards and showed them his Labour party membership card: 'I'm one of you lads!' Hoskins by contrast would drive himself everywhere. He used his company car allowance to buy himself a new car, more suited to a pop star than an accountant and Finance Director ... a black AMG Mercedes with blacked-out windows!

Morale was on the floor, fear was everywhere and enterprise was stifled. All communication with either Andy or me suddenly stopped. Senior staff bought their own mobiles and wouldn't talk on home or office phones or company mobiles. They were convinced their calls were being monitored and phone records checked. 'Are they mad or just paranoid?' I asked Andy. Apparently security people 'checking for bugs' were seen in the offices lifting ceiling tiles and tampering with telephones and then Bill announced at a meeting that they had found several 'bugs' on the premises, the implication being that the old regime was somehow involved. Some of the staff speculated that they were placing them themselves!

On 15 March I had a phone call from Andy. I knew Iceland were having a board meeting that day and we were expecting them to make a decision on our severance. They would also be holding an analysts' meeting to present the profit figures up until 30 December and, more importantly, the latest estimate of profits for the March year-end. It was 2pm and Andy was in his car driving down to Devon to see his Mum. David Price had just rung him with his pay-off details. He gave Andy two choices. Either he could resign today and he would be allowed to keep 50 per cent of his share options (which were worth about £180,000 before tax) and his salary would be paid until that night. Or, if he refused, he would be fired immediately with no pay-off and his share options would be withheld. David Price asked Andy to ring back with his decision in two hours.

Andy was distraught. Eighteen years he had worked at Iceland to be treated like this at the end. The share options were given to him five years ago and were an entitlement for past performance. His pay-off was nothing. What on earth were the non-executives doing to allow it? I asked Andy what he was going to do and he said he would see them in court. Soon after I'd finished talking to Andy, David Price rang me. He said they had considered our settlements and since I was retiring anyway at the end of the month there obviously wouldn't be any pay-off for me. He also said he didn't think I'd be surprised to know they weren't going to pay the bonus which they had previously agreed. I said I wasn't surprised about that but I was amazed at the way they had treated Andy. David admitted he felt very bad about that, especially the timescale they had given him. He asked if I would I tell Andy he was sorry and he could have a few extra days to think about their offer. David said the company was short of money; they would have to conserve all their cash and wouldn't be able to afford to pay him anything. I rang Iain Sharp who was on his way to the airport. He was obviously embarrassed and didn't want to talk much. I told him Grimsey would have 'millions tucked away'. Iain just said he really didn't think he had.

The next day Grimsey revealed his latest profit estimate for the year ending March. He had reduced the figure yet again from £62 million to £40 million and increased the exceptional items from £34 million to £66 million. This showed a net loss of £26 million and to me (and I think to everyone else) was absolutely astonishing. To go from an expected profit of £130 million to a loss of £26 million in just a few weeks was beyond belief.

What I didn't find out until later was that, at their meeting on 15 March when they decided Andy would get no pay-off, the board had voted to increase the salaries of both Hoskins and Grimsey and also voted them a special bonus.

The board minutes read: 'The committee resolved after discussion to recommend to the board that Mr Grimsey's annual remuneration be increased to £600,000 [he was previously on £500,000] with effect from 1st April 2001 to reflect the significantly increased workload and responsibility he was having to undertake.'

'In addition the committee agreed to recommend to the board he would be given a one off payment of £225,000 to reflect salary and benefits foregone from his previous employer in joining the Company. This payment was on the basis that this sum would be immediately invested by Mr Grimsey in shares of the Company.'

'It was further agreed to recommend to the board that Mr Grimsey's pension arrangements be amended to provide that 25 per cent of his salary be paid into his personal pension and if this was in excess of the pensions earnings cap, the balance would be paid as additional salary and be subject to deduction of income tax.'

Grimsey was then quoted as recommending that Hoskins should also have a pay increase to £300,000 per annum and a one-off bonus of £180,000 'to reflect the major contribution he was making to the company's recovery'.

In the case of Grimsey's payment being in lieu of salary foregone from his previous employer, this was of course complete rubbish. It may have been useful to put it in the minutes as an excuse to justify the bonus payment but it had no basis in fact. He had agreed to drop all claims relating to Wickes when I took him on.

A share scheme was also introduced giving both Grimsey and Hoskins shares to the value of one-and-a-half times annual salary immediately and one times salary every year thereafter. On top of this, a bonus scheme was introduced to give them the chance of doubling their salary if they met certain performance criteria, which would be agreed after the 2001/02 budgets had been set. David Price also had his salary increased from £30,000 per annum to £100,000 per annum to reflect his increased responsibilities as non-executive Chairman.

To my mind, the hypocrisy of it all was breathtaking. Grimsey and Hoskins had been there only a few weeks but in that time they had taken over the company, trashed the expected profits, the share price had collapsed, and the old management who had created the business over half a lifetime had been ousted with no pay-off. They had increased their own salaries to about double that in their previous employments and also collected a massive bonus for just a few weeks' work. Grimsey was quoted in the minutes as saying he 'could not justify any compensation payment for Andy to shareholders!'

Funnily enough, the share price didn't drop by more than a few pennies after this last profit downgrade and then it started to rise. The newspapers were full of phrases about 'kitchen sinks'. Most of the board had enough confidence to buy shares in the business and Grimsey and his wife bought several lots of shares, spending nearly £0.5 million. Grimsey was not a very wealthy man and that amount of money represented a considerable investment for him. This seemed much more than a new Chief Executive demonstrating his commitment to the business. He was showing an unusual level of confidence in the company's 'recovery'.

The expression 'kitchen sink' is one used by financial commentators to describe the act of 'throwing everything in' (including the proverbial kitchen sink!) Almost any new Chief Executive will take a one-off opportunity to have a clean sweep of the books and tidy up the business. Things will be written off that could conceivably cause a problem to profits in the future but it is generally accepted that some of the items written off will later be found to have been too prudent and will find their way back into the profit figures at a later date. Technically this is stealing profit from one year and showing it the next. In my book that isn't a problem if continuing management are 'smoothing out' the figures over the long term but a new Chief Executive could destroy his predecessor's reputation and shareholder value by trashing the profits and using what is 'tucked away' to enhance his own performance in the following years. Everyone expects it will happen but it's all a question of degree!

Alistair Osborne in the *Daily Telegraph* on Saturday, 17 March reported that 'analysts had called Mr Grimsey's more conservative accounting "the last bit of kitchen sinking".' In February, Patience Wheatcroft in *The Times* had commented that Grimsey's time in DIY had taught him a lot about kitchens and sinks! 'The worse things look before a new boy begins to perform, the more impressive his act can appear.'

However, excessive provisions or 'profits tucked away' can be a two-edged sword. If sales in a business are declining, how can those extra profits be released without the numbers looking funny? Achieving sales growth can then become more important than trading profitably just to enable those reserves to be released. Signs to watch out for are when companies with poor sales somehow manage to show the expected profits but talk about 'improved margins' and 'cost savings' helping the bottom line.

Grimsey was now approaching a new trading period for which only he was responsible. He had new sales initiatives planned and was no doubt expecting that the 'turnaround' would begin immediately. He cut 200 prices and launched a 'glassware promotion'.

He was confident enough to tell the *Daily Mail* on 16 March that he would get the group 'back on track within eighteen months'. 'As of tomorrow, I am responsible for this group,' he said.

Fiona Walsh in the *Evening Standard* quoted Grimsey as saying he was confident the worst was over and he predicted the recovery process would take between fifteen and eighteen months.

The same day he told the *Daily Telegraph* that 'People should be realistic, it's eighteen months to two years before we get the recovery. Only then will you see where Grimsey has been.'

Hoskins was also quoted in the *Financial Times* as saying 'This is the last time we can be the messengers, as of tomorrow we must take full responsibility.'

Of course, it's easier saying it than actually doing it and, for all the millions he spent on consultants in the first year and the army of Wickes people he brought in, it was obvious he didn't understand the business. It was quite amusing to read what he was saying exactly one year later.

'This is a mess, a big mess and it was not what I was expecting. But I am going to build a quality business over three years.' *Daily Telegraph*, 3 March 2002.

Three days later he'd added on a year, 'The key message is that [we are] in this recovery process, which we've always said would take three to four years.' *BBC News* (website).

He was also quoted in the company annual report saying that 'recovery' would take four years, while avoiding any blame for the poor sales during his first year.

'It is from now that we want to be judged.' *The Guardian*, 7 March 2002.

'We are signalling today that we have the plan, we have the people. The management team we have needs to be judged from now.' *Evening Standard*, 6 March 2002.

Meanwhile, Andy was in shock. He could keep his share options if he conceded defeat, which would pay off his mortgage, but he had no job, no salary and no company car as from today. At first he was full of bravado about fighting his battle in court but soon the realisation of the cost of this began to outweigh what he would lose in the value of his options and he really had no alternative but to accept the offer. As if getting a job wasn't difficult enough, they even made him sign a competition agreement that prevented him working for another food retailer for the next six months.

I tried to cheer him up and suggested that he should take this crossroads in life as an opportunity and set himself up in business. We discussed this for a while and I said I would come in with him and why didn't we start again in the frozen food business! It was a joke but the more we talked about it the more serious we became. Wasn't the safest option to go into a business we knew? We felt the frozen food business was far from exhausted and it would be fun. What's more, we knew it would drive Grimsey bonkers when he found out!

24
Starting Again

I had a few days out with Andy looking for new store sites and researching the property market. We considered several parts of the UK for our new venture but, in spite of the high level of competition in the North West, we decided the advantages of operating the 'start-up' on our own doorstep outweighed the competitive disadvantages. We found our first store in Wrexham, which is only a few miles from where we both live. Since Andy wasn't allowed to work for another food retailer for the next few months he kept on the sidelines. It was great fun setting everything up again and planning the new venture. I had to talk to several people in the industry about our plans and knew it would only be a matter of time before Grimsey found out. Because of that we decided on a code name for our new venture: 'Frozen Out' seemed appropriate!

The biggest obstacle to starting any new retail business is the sheer cost of setting up a storage and distribution network. In our case a cold storage network would be even more expensive! So I went to see Nigel Woodward. Since we had bought his wholesale business five years earlier he had concentrated on Cold Move, his storage and transport company. Nigel was delighted to help us start up again and agreed to handle all our storage and distribution requirements. He gave us a dedicated 1,000-pallet cold store which was a tremendous start for a new venture with a single shop! That was a major part of the jigsaw solved and made everything else possible. I made contact with all the other people we would need to help us such as shopfitters, refrigeration suppliers, solicitors and property agents. Geoff Mason still did a lot of work for Iceland but he decided to give it up and go with us. Geoff's son Andrew was running the practice now but he was also keen to work with us.

I'd kept in touch with my PA Kathy Wight since I left Iceland but she has always been the ultimate professional and I knew better than to ask her too much about what was going on. However, I knew she wasn't happy there and decided to offer her a job looking after my personal affairs, which seemed to be growing ever more complicated as I was starting to get involved in various new ventures. Kathy resigned from Iceland on Monday, 26 March 2001. Grimsey's reaction was not what she expected. He told her how much he valued loyalty (she had been there twenty years) and even said he would invite Kathy and her husband Alan to Chester races with the directors as a 'thank you' for her long service. He then gave her a lot of work by way of 'catching up' which involved her working very late for the next two nights. On Wednesday, when Grimsey was in Wellingborough, Iceland's Personnel Director Janet Marsden called Kathy into her office. Janet was very aggressive towards Kathy and accused her of going to work for me. It was a fair guess that she might have been and hardly surprising. Why that should have been a problem I can't imagine. No one knew anything about our new venture at this stage so the reaction could hardly have been about potential competition. Janet then asked Kathy to leave the premises immediately but first watched her pack her personal belongings to ensure that she didn't steal anything. She asked a driver to follow her home to collect her laptop.

The next day Alan, who has his own company organising conferences and making video training films, and who counted Iceland as his biggest client, got a phone call from Janet, telling him he would never be allowed to work for Iceland again. The reason she gave was 'a personal issue between Malcolm and Bill'. Kathy was obviously very upset by all this. I was less surprised but still stunned at Janet's behaviour. She seemed to have 'gone native' and carried out her task with too much enthusiasm. Kathy now joined Andy and me in our garage headquarters. I suggested that the three of us had now all been fired by Iceland but Kathy insisted that she'd only resigned, but then been frog-marched out of the building!

The deal with Andy was that I would help finance the new business but only work on a part-time basis after the company had become established. I was supposed to have retired and I didn't want another full-time job so soon after leaving Iceland. We also needed another person as part of our team to look after the buying function. I decided to approach Andy Errington. Andy had previously worked for Iceland as our very first buyer. He was a very strong individual and quite aggressive. I thought he'd fit in well! After Iceland, Andy got a job with the frozen food company Eismann, which is based in Germany. First he learned to speak German, then commuted to Germany every week for the next six years. He was now working as Buying Director for Dunnes Stores in Ireland and commuting there on a fortnightly basis. I'd heard he was fed up with all the travelling and thought he might come back to Iceland, which was why I'd suggested his name to Grimsey in early January.

I spoke to Andy on the telephone and he told me that he'd had an interview with Grimsey, Janet Marsden and Alan Besbrode over a dinner. He said he knew he'd blown it with his usual outspoken opinions! Grimsey, he concluded, only wanted 'yes men' and conformists.

Andy then told me something very strange. It wasn't his first dinner with Besbrode. Apparently they used to work together at the Co-op and hadn't got on at all well then, which made it even more unusual for Besbrode to ring Andy in Dublin and invite himself over for dinner in late 2000. As he was leaving, Besbrode had said to Andy, 'See you in Iceland, then.' This was the strangest thing to say, but it made it clear that Besbrode had already been recruited by Grimsey, before Grimsey himself had even started at Iceland.

Andy said he was interested in joining us and he came over for a meeting. We had a lot of catching up to do and I noticed he'd mellowed only slightly since his days at Iceland, but I knew he would be great to have on board. He was very excited at our plans and agreed to join us immediately. He also bought a share in the business.

On his first day in the garage office, Andy Errington asked if anyone had a current year's diary that he could have. Kathy said she had one at home and brought it in the next day. She happened to mention it was Grimsey's old diary and of course everyone wanted to see it and we were all intrigued to know how she'd got it. She explained that at the end of January Grimsey had gone 'electronic'. He had eventually got the hang of it and then given his old diary to Kathy and told her to 'get rid of it'. She flicked through it, thought it was a nice diary and since it was virtually unused she took it home. I had a look through. There was nothing in it except appointment times for most days in January with Iceland senior managers but on 29 December 2000 there was an entry in Grimsey's own handwriting that stunned me.

'Price Waterhouse, meeting, Hilton Watford, TAKEOVER PROJECT.'

So the whole thing was planned. Grimsey had seen an opportunity and gone for it. It all started to fall into place. Hoskins had obviously been recruited as Finance Director before Grimsey started work for Iceland, hence Andy Pritchard was moved sideways on day one. Besbrode was recruited to run buying, probably at the same time. Norman Bell, an old pal of Grimsey's from Wickes, was brought in as 'Strategy Director' in early January followed by a whole team of former Wickes people including Price Waterhouse as consultants.

Over the next few months the 'takeover' was completed. Rothschilds, ABN Amro and Charterhouse were all fired and replaced by Warburgs. Herbert Smith were replaced by Linklaters. Both companies had previously worked with Grimsey at Wickes.

Ernst & Young were replaced as auditors by Price Waterhouse and finally the Finance Directors of Iceland and Booker, Tarsem Dhaliwal and Mike Camp, were fired just before the first year-end figures were put together. Andy Pritchard had of course already gone so, by the time Hoskins was putting together his first set of accounts, nobody was left in the finance department who had been involved with making all the provisions and conservative assumptions the previous year.

During the first few months lots of the Iceland 'old guard' were fired and a raft of ex-Wickes people brought in. Carl Hamill (the maverick grey market expert) was fired, putting at risk a very profitable part of the business. John Berry was replaced as Company Secretary by Suzanne Chase, who was much less experienced but ... from Wickes! Grimsey's usual pattern was to either fire people without compensation for alleged misconduct, or pay them the absolute minimum and insist they work their notice. This behaviour contrasted with his own demands for a full pay-off if he had to go.

Grimsey was starting again but so was I. The only problem was Andy Pritchard. A few years previously he'd been diagnosed at a routine medical examination as having a faulty heart valve. This was no real cause for concern as he had always been a keen sportsman and had never been affected by it. Stuart Rose had even mentioned that he had the same issue and it wasn't really a problem. Since leaving Iceland, Andy had been increasingly unwell and in August he went for a check-up, was detained as an emergency and had a heart operation a couple of days later. This problem affected him throughout 2001 but by the end of the year he was back to his old self.

Our first store was due to open in July 2001. Grimsey was eventually told about it through a supplier currying favour and soon the news and the name Frozen Out had found its way into the press. Grimsey's reaction was, of course, out of all proportion to what we were doing. By all accounts he went completely ballistic and then went to see his lawyers to see if he could stop us. Alan Smith was the only one of the non-executives who had kept in touch and he'd even invited me to his 60th birthday party. (I'd bought him a book for a present called *The Biggest Business Blunders*, after all he'd had a few!) As soon as news of our new venture got out I never heard from him again.

We hoped that we could keep the location of our first store secret and put out misinformation that it was in Prestatyn, but Grimsey soon found out it was in Wrexham.

My garage at home became a hive of activity. We were planning our new frozen food chain which we'd really decided to call Cooltrader. I'd also moved the accounts function for As Nature Intended up from London. Whatever happened to retirement?

We opened in Wrexham on 26 July 2001 to a blaze of publicity. It made a good story for the press. The opening day was packed with customers and we knew it was going to be a huge success. One of our biggest customers that day turned out to be Iceland who'd sent in a number of staff to buy every single product we sold. They analysed everything and reported us to trading standards for two imported products which didn't quite comply with UK labelling standards. Funnily enough Iceland sold exactly the same products! The local trading standards brushed it off as a minor infringment but I decided to go on the attack. The next day I visited two local Iceland stores and had no trouble in finding a number of out-of-date products on sale, which I bought and took to trading standards. I then emailed Grimsey and reminded him that he had 760 shops to manage while I had only one, so he wasn't going to win on this one.

Apparently he'd set up a task force called 'Project Snowdrop' which was supposed to put us out of business. He cut prices in the Iceland Wrexham store, put in extra staff, installed a storage container in the yard and spent a great deal of money and effort but to no avail. We opened our second store in Bootle a few months later and he slashed prices and invested heavily in Iceland there. We moved the office out of my garage and into new offices above our third store in Moreton and from there we relocated a second time to a Regis-serviced office on the Chester Business Park. We had a serious and growing business and managed to open 25 stores in the first three years. In the same time, Iceland opened one.

My problems with Iceland were still not over and, as anticipated, an inquiry was started first by the Financial Services Authority (FSA) into whether Iceland had made any misleading statements and whether or not I'd followed the correct procedure for my share sale, and then another inquiry by The Department of Trade & Industry (DTI) into any possible insider dealing offence. I had no contact from the FSA and no contact from the DTI until I was asked to go for an interview.

I attended two interviews with the DTI which were conducted by a retired lawyer called Ronald Lindsay, who lived in Portugal (he flew to the UK on a regular basis to conduct the inquiry) and an accountant called Peter Thornton who didn't seem to have any sense of humour or to understand accounts too well. I believe the inquiry went on for three years with dozens of people interviewed, no doubt at huge expense, but I had no knowledge of any of this apart from what I read from time to time in *The Guardian* or the *Mail on Sunday* – particularly the latter. Eventually I read that the file had been passed to the Serious Fraud Office (SFO) but again no one thought to inform me. My only contact throughout all this was the two letters inviting me to the DTI interviews. However, the press wouldn't let it go and I had a cloud hanging over me for all this time. 'There's no smoke without fire' was the widely held belief.

I quite liked Lindsay and found him generally agreeable but I left the meetings without any clear idea of how it had gone. He wasn't hostile in any way, which was more than could be said for Thornton. At the end of the second meeting, I suggested that when they had finished their deliberations, they were bound to conclude I had done nothing wrong. And in that case, it was clearly unjust that they wouldn't be able to put out a statement to that effect. How was I going to clear my name and restore my reputation? Lindsay said he had some sympathy with my predicament and, even though they were prevented by statute from disclosing their findings, the

Department was starting to 'soften' its stance and there was a partial way around the problem. He gave by way of example Jeffrey Archer and the insider dealing allegations relating to his Anglia Television share sale. When the DTI dropped the case, this was dealt with by way of a press release put out by Archer. Lindsay said that if my lawyer were to contact them after a respectable period of time – say, a year – and if they had then decided to drop the matter, then they would 'tip my lawyer the wink'. I could then put out a press statement saying the case had been dropped and they wouldn't contradict it. So much for the transparency of the system.

While the enquiry allegedly dragged on, Ben Laurance of the *Mail on Sunday* became the bane of my life. He seemed to take a personal interest in my supposed wrongdoing and never missed an opportunity to try to rehash and rekindle the story. Every few weeks he seemed to find a new twist or turn and give it more column inches. It was destroying my reputation with the constant drip, drip of coverage and I was in no position to respond. To make it worse, Laurance and his colleague Jenny Little won the 2002 'Business Journalist of the Year' award, handed out at some prestigious black tie dinner, for their coverage of the DTI enquiry story. Somehow that seemed to give it even more credibility.

I was in London at a meeting with my pension adviser about a year after leaving Iceland and glanced at a copy of the *Daily Mail* in reception while I was waiting. There it was again. I decided to take action. I had Ben Laurance's mobile number so I called him up. He was almost startled to hear from me.

'Ben, this is Malcolm Walker speaking.'

'Oh, OK.'

'You remember that story about the English and German soldiers in the trenches during the First World War? It was Christmas Day and they held a truce and played a game of football, swapped mementoes and cigarettes. Do you fancy lunch?'

'Err, OK, when?'

'Now, today.'

We met for lunch at The Oriel Café in Sloane Square and after asking for our meeting to be off the record I told him the whole story. He was sceptical but said he'd think about things and get back to me. He called me back the next day, said he'd done some checking and now believed I was telling the truth.

That seemed to change everything and I wished I'd made the call earlier. We met several times after that and became quite good friends. There were no more stories in the press and he became very sympathetic to my predicament. I'd started writing the early chapters of this book by then and I gave them to him to read. He suggested he might be able to help with the editing so I invited him to come and stay at my house and go through the manuscript.

Rhianydd was quite nervous about meeting the dreaded Ben Laurance and I was quite nervous she might try to kill him. But he came bearing gifts, she forgave him and we all got on really well. He stayed two nights and suggested changes to this book which in the event I didn't use. I have always preferred my own words and style.

Eventually in October 2004, after three-and-a-half years, I received a letter by second class post informing me I'd been cleared of any wrongdoing.

Meanwhile Grimsey's tenure at Iceland wasn't proving as easy as he had presumably hoped. The shares had already halved in value between December 2000 and January 2001. This was probably not bad news for Grimsey, who would be issued with his share options in March at the lower price, but the shares continued to fall steadily.

In spite of his promises to the City about 'recovery' and 80 new store openings, sales steadily collapsed. An army of consultants was brought in and five different formats were trialled for the Iceland stores. Freezer centres were considered old hat and a programme to turn the estate into convenience stores was launched. This was expensive to fund so a large number of Iceland freeholds were sold off at what turned out to be well below market value. Grimsey was Group CEO and two successive Managing Directors for Iceland itself were recruited beneath him, but failed to reverse the company's fortunes. These were Mike Coupe, who is now at Sainsbury's, and Andy Clarke now the CEO of Asda.

By now I'd become very friendly with Steven Walker (no relation), a young guy who had just sold his Yorkshire pudding business and made a serious amount of cash. He spent a lot of time in my garage office and we did quite a few property deals together. At one point Cooltrader was struggling for cash and without any persuasion he took a stake and put £300,000 into the business. To my surprise we had never been able to get any serious bank funding for this new venture and had to invest mostly our own money. Steven's help was much appreciated.

As things at Iceland deteriorated Steven had this idea that we should go back into Iceland and take it private. As their share price collapsed this looked more and more possible but I really wasn't interested. Sometime in 2003 I was contacted by Aidan Barclay. His Dad was one of the famous Barclay brothers. I went to see him and he wanted to know if I'd be interested in working with them to buy The Big Food Group (BFG) as Grimsey had renamed the Iceland-Booker holding company. I said I wasn't interested in getting involved but I would be happy to advise them all I could. I never heard any more.

However, Steven wouldn't give up and kept going on and on about buying the business. Eventually, when the share price bottomed out at 25p valuing the £5 billion-turnover company at only £75 million, I decided it was worth a look. I went to see Jon Moulton of Alchemy, the private equity firm. He was lukewarm about the idea but promised to put me in touch with his local man in Manchester. I'd no sooner left his office than I got a call from Ossie to say that shares in BFG had just doubled in value as a result of some Icelandic investment house called Baugur buying a stake.

I rang Jon Moulton but he assured me that it was a temporary blip and we should ignore it and carry on with our proposal. We met his man from Manchester several times in my garage office but didn't seem to make much headway. We gave up on him but by now

I was getting more enthusiastic about the project and I decided on another approach.

I contacted Jon Asgeir Johannesson of Baugur and arranged to see him in his office in London. Both Charles Wilson (formerly of Booker) and John Richards (a former retail analyst) knew Jon Asgeir and they paved the way for the meeting. I was surprised when I met him. Tall, long greasy hair, leather jacket – he looked more like a rock star than a businessman. I told him my story and suggested he had a problem. By now they had a 25 per cent stake in BFG and it was only going one way. He had no confidence in Grimsey but he didn't know me. Only what Grimsey might have told him, which wouldn't be good.

I suggested that he might be considering making a full bid for BFG, but Iceland was his problem. Booker and Woodward's were considered valuable assets but Iceland was seen as a real dog by the City and had negative value. I offered to take it off his hands for nothing, leaving him free to make the best deal he could out of the rest of the business. He agreed that it made sense and we should instruct our advisers to progress the deal. I contacted Simon Eccles-Williams of Hawkpoint and Baugur instructed Deutsche Bank.

/

25
The Vikings

It seemed like a good deal. We'd get Iceland for free. Iceland was perceived as such a basket case by the City that the The Big Food Group would have been worth more without Iceland, which was considered a liability. So much so that we called our approach Project Aspirin, because Baugur had a headache in Iceland, and we were the solution. But then Jon Asgeir came back to me with second thoughts. He would now give us only half the company for free and keep half himself. He intended to make a bid for BFG, which he was confident would succeed, and he would split out Iceland into a separate company. BFG shares were then trading at around 70p and he seemed very confident that an offer of around £1 would be accepted.

I didn't really want to go back to run the company at this stage and we didn't even know if it could be saved, but I was keen to get my hands on the books and find out what had been going on. I agreed with Steven Walker that I would 'front' the deal and he would take over from me as CEO after a period of time, with Andy Pritchard working alongside him. We would also reverse Cooltrader into the new Iceland company. We considered who else we might want to involve and I was quite clear that we should bring Tarsem into the fold.

We had an interesting few months dealing with the Vikings.

Jon Asgeir was impossible to get hold of, never answered his phone and was usually an hour or so late for meetings – or, more likely, didn't turn up at all. Often we'd be sitting in a meeting room with Hawkpoint and Deutsche Bank, killing time while waiting for Jon Asgeir, only to find out that he was still in Iceland (the country). Unsurprisingly the deal progressed slowly but for some reason the BFG share price started to rise. When it got close to £1 there seemed to be no point in progressing the matter and the takeover just fizzled out.

Steven by now was getting impatient to get back into business and decided to buy three restaurants in the Manchester area, which he hoped to grow into a chain. I had already invested in my local radio station in Chester, Dee 106.3, and now put money into a fresh fish distribution company with Tarsem, which we renamed The Big Fish Group to wind up Grimsey. Meanwhile Andy concentrated on running Cooltrader, which by now was growing into a serious business.

Another year went by but the fortunes of BFG (Food not Fish) did not improve. We kept a close eye on what was happening and by the summer of 2004 the share price was down to around 60p again. Every six months they had to report their numbers to the City and it was very funny to read all the press cuttings and see how Grimsey's time scale for 'recovery' extended with each set of results. In March 2001 he was quoted as saying 'as from now we are responsible for this company' and stated that recovery was going to take one year, which then became eighteen months, then two years, then three, then 'We've always said this is a three- to four-year project'.

I could never understand why he couldn't grow profits. He had at least £60 million tucked away from the provisions he'd made, and the bar had been lowered from £130 million to £40 million, so it should have been easy for him to show growth. Something must have seriously gone wrong not just with Iceland but also with Booker. By now the City had given up on him and he was rumoured to be looking for a face-saving exit.

I decided to make contact again with Jon Asgeir but it was only just in time. He was already well advanced with preparing another bid. This time he'd changed his mind and would not consider giving us Iceland. He wanted to keep it but would consider taking us on as managers. This wasn't attractive to me but finally he offered to sell us Iceland for £160 million.

There was only one outstanding issue now. Where were we going to find that kind of money? I rang Philip Green. 'Would you be interested in helping us buy Iceland?' 'Not unless you know something I fucking don't,' was his answer. So that door was firmly closed, but I did persuade him to give me Peter Cummings's mobile phone number.

Peter was a banker at HBOS and was famous for making big bold bets on companies. He had recently financed Philip Green to pay a £1 billion dividend out of Arcadia. My worry was that Cummings would already be involved with Baugur and that proved to be the case. He did say that while he couldn't be involved another division of HBOS might help and he passed me on to a colleague in their London office.

Jon Asgeir was anxious to progress things and he had given us just one week to come up with the money or he would go ahead alone. KPMG had helped us prepare a business plan so we went to see HBOS and made our presentation. Normally you would expect these things to take weeks to come to fruition, several meetings would be involved and finally the credit committee would make a decision. On this occasion we needed an answer immediately. Our presentation went down well, our man from HBOS made positive noises and I got the impression we might be in luck. I decided to push it and asked for a decision. I needed to go back that day to Jon Asgeir with an answer. They said they would back us.

This was not a lot of money in the scheme of things. Iceland's sales had dropped from £2 billion when we left to £1.5 billion, but it was still a big business. If we couldn't recover the profits our fallback plan was to sell maybe 200 stores to Sainsbury's or Tesco, so we felt the bank's money was safe. It was one thing HBOS agreeing verbally to back us but if I was to have any credibility at all with Jon Asgeir I needed it in writing. I asked if they would give me a letter. The HBOS contingent left the room and KPMG then told me I was mad to ask for a letter as they would never give it. To everyone's surprise HBOS came back into the room and said they would prepare the letter. We should go to lunch, they would call me when the letter was ready and then we could send a driver to collect it. We would then go straight round to Baugur's office to deliver it. We were jubilant.

We had a good lunch but by 3pm I still hadn't received the call. I tried to contact the bank but no one was available. Eventually I did get through only to be told they'd changed their mind. Someone had quashed the deal. Maybe Cummings decided they didn't want to be involved at both ends. We were devastated but decided to try to negotiate another deal with Baugur. In reality we were the only option they had to run the Iceland business but they were obviously mistrustful of us and had no doubt been told all kinds of bad things about us by Grimsey. But they were no great fans of his either. For the past year as shareholders in the business they'd employed a photographer to go round the Iceland shops every week taking photos of empty shelves. These they'd show to Grimsey but nothing ever improved. If he couldn't keep stock on the shelves how could he hope to sell it?

Eventually they offered us a deal. We could have 10 per cent of the new company in return for selling Cooltrader to Iceland, plus another 10 per cent if we met certain targets. We didn't think it was enough and walked away. We expected they'd come back with a better offer but they didn't. After ten days we panicked and went back to them and said we'd accept. Andy and Tarsem had been to see Palmi Haraldsson at a hotel in London and tried to negotiate a better deal, but he just kept repeating, like a mantra, 'Either you're in the box or you're not in the box.' The reality was that we wanted a different and bigger box, but he made it clear that this simply wasn't on offer.

Even though we were wound up to do a deal, we were still not

100 per cent convinced it was the right thing to do. We had no real idea of the state of Iceland or what we would find when we got there. Could we make it work? Could we reverse the apparently unstoppable decline in sales? How much money if any could we personally make out of this deal? We had many meetings in my garage office to discuss this. Eventually Tarsem summed up the situation perfectly in one sentence. 'How the fuck can we not make money out of £1.5 billion of sales?' That was it in a nutshell. Without doing any more analysis and just looking at the big picture Iceland still had massive sales. They may have declined by 25 per cent during Grimsey's tenure, and the company would certainly require radical change and a lot of surgery, but there was a big opportunity in front of us.

Only six months previously we'd run out of money to expand Cooltrader. Steven's money helped but we desperately needed a cash injection to keep growing. Steven's restaurant business was flying by now and he was up to about twenty. He'd recently brought in a private equity group called Gresham to help him fund the growth and he recommended them to us as a source of finance. We were also talking to Lloyds private equity, but they turned us down. We finally did a deal with Gresham but it proved to be a very unhappy relationship and I realised I would never be able to adapt to their way of working. I resolved then never to do a deal with private equity again. The problem we had now was persuading them to sell their share in Cooltrader only a few months after they'd bought in to the business. They were greedy and nearly scuppered the deal. They'd doubled their money in just a few months but weren't happy about it.

Somehow we got dragged along with the Baugur deal and even acquired an Icelandic adviser of our own, called Arev. The next few months proved entertaining to say the least. The most complicated deal imaginable was put together. It involved breaking up BFG into three companies: Iceland, Booker and Woodward's. All the freehold properties were to be sold off to help finance the deal and leased back on what turned out to be onerous terms. That sale and lease-back would mean paying additional rents of £12 million for Iceland, which would be a huge challenge for a company that was already losing money.

Each company had a different mix of shareholders, mostly Icelandic pals of Jon Asgeir. Everyone wanted to be involved with Booker and Woodward's but no one wanted to invest in the Iceland part of the deal and it seemed impossible to get any bank to finance it. We had meeting after meeting with an army of bankers, lawyers and accountants which went on for weeks. At one point we had to make a big presentation to a load of mainly Icelandic bankers in a hotel in Liverpool, before which we took them for a tour of the Iceland store in Bootle. Seeing a load of men in suits approaching the store manager challenged us but we explained 'We're from Iceland' (which was true in one sense) and he was then happy to let us wander around pointing out everything that was wrong with his store. At other times we used an accomplice in London to take potential investors around the stores there.

Grimsey had by now found out we were in the consortium but I think he was anxious to get his exit before the company finally went bust. We were never allowed to meet, however, and were always kept in separate rooms during meetings.

Tarsem and I finally signed a deal with Palmi on 24 November 2004 in the London flat of Arev's John Scheving (like all the Icelanders we met, he had a swish flat in Chelsea overlooking Stamford Bridge). We would buy the Iceland business for a fixed £160 million. Best of all we negotiated to leave the pension deficit behind with Booker. We agreed to pay a further £20 million, phased over our first year in the business, to take us out of the BFG pension scheme altogether and make a fresh start. This was without doubt the best £20 million we have ever spent.

We also managed to negotiate a shareholders' agreement whereby no dividend could be paid or any refinancing take place without the consent of the management. We were frightened that Baugur might want to strip cash out of the business. Why they agreed to it I don't know but they were pretty broad-brush in their approach and once the deal was agreed in principle they weren't too interested in the detail, particularly where Iceland was concerned: they were focused on the big opportunities in the property portfolio and Booker. We also negotiated that if they ever wanted to sell the company we had the right to buy provided we could match the price. These conditions later proved to be worth their weight in gold.

The price for The Big Food Group as a whole was agreed at 95p per share, which valued the company at £326 million. This was less than a quarter of its value before Grimsey arrived. I tried to persuade Jon Asgeir that this was still too much to pay and that he could have got it for less, but this was his first big deal in the UK and he was anxious not to lose it. It didn't matter to us as in any case we were buying the Iceland division for a fixed price.

The final meeting when the deal was due to be signed took place on 16 December 2004 and proved to be a complete circus. Fifty or 60 people in the offices of the lawyers Allen & Overy, all signing documents and still negotiating details. No one was wearing a name badge and it was hard to work out who they were: we spent some time trying to negotiate details of our deal with someone who finally asked: 'Why are you telling me all this? I'm here to buy Booker!' Our principal lawyer had a stammer, which got worse when he was nervous, so by the time he managed to make a point on our behalf the conversation had usually moved on to something completely different. At one crucial point all the bankers from HBOS scurried off together, which is never a good sign. The best thing that could be said of the occasion was that the trolleys of food and drink that were wheeled in at regular intervals were of a very high standard.

Everything had to be signed before midnight otherwise due to some technicality the finance would fall away. As the deadline approached we remembered that one crucial thing we had to do was to email all the details of the deal through to the pensions regulator. Someone said, as a joke, 'I hope you've got the right email address!' Which was, of course, when we discovered that we hadn't, but at least it gave us time to track it down!

Larus Welding was the 29-year-old CEO of Landsbanki and he had finally agreed to loan the £160 million for our part of the deal. Andy was at home following an eye operation so I was there with Tarsem and our discussions with Landsbanki went on until nearly midnight. There were so many people involved in the group deal and so much still to agree, contracts to type up and sign, and it was obvious that it was never going to happen. Finally at five minutes to midnight Alan Paul of Allen & Overy called everyone into the stairwell and said 'This deal can never happen in time so I am going to invoke a verbal contract. Everyone raise your hands if you agree to agree that this contract is binding.' And the deal was done.

I was driving home with Tarsem at 2am when we called Andy. He said he wasn't happy with the deal we had agreed which rather put a dampener on things. He felt we would never see any money out of it. I think he would have been happier to take a couple of million for his share of Cooltrader and walk away. But Tarsem and I were happy and convinced we had done the best deal it was possible to do.

Completion was set for 11 February 2005. In any other situation we would now have been allowed into Iceland to start planning the handover but Grimsey was having none of it. I certainly wasn't going to be allowed in until completion day, although Tarsem was permitted to go into Iceland's offices before this to sort out some of the shared service issues that had to be unravelled to allow BFG to be split up into its component parts. He did glean a certain amount of useful information, though the principal benefit was the knowledge that his presence was thoroughly pissing off Grimsey.

My motives for doing the deal were mixed. I wasn't sure the company could be turned around, but it was worth a try. I felt I had something to prove, I thought there was a possibility we could make some money, but the real reason was to get my hands on the books. Palmi Haraldsson was a friend of Jon Asgeir's, a shareholder in our new company, and also our Chairman. He asked me if I thought it possible the company could ever make £100 million at some time in the future. I said it was impossible but hoped one day we could maybe reach £50 million. He was happy with that. Within seven years we would be making over £230 million.

I went on holiday to the Maldives with Ranny the week before we were due to take over. I thought it might be a good omen and it also felt like we had some unfinished business there, where our holiday had been so rudely interrupted four years earlier. The media were having a field day and I was dubbed 'the comeback kid'. It was tempting to talk to the press but I decided not to. There seemed no point crowing about events as there was every possibility we might fail.

One strange thing troubled me. In spite of everything that had gone on it was reported in the press that Grimsey and Hoskins would stay on and run Booker. I was amazed and tried to talk Jon Asgeir out of it. Was he mad? They'd wrecked the business over a four-year period and now he was going to let them continue to run half of it. The week before they were due to start Grimsey changed his mind and decided he didn't want to do it. Hoskins went in as Finance Director but after ten days was unceremoniously ejected from the company. A black hole had been discovered in the forecasts. Apparently Jon Asgeir had previously asked Charles Wilson to come back to run Booker, but he had only just started working at Marks & Spencer with Stuart Rose. He wouldn't be available for a year and the banks insisted that a management team be put in place. Grimsey and Hoskins had been his only option as a stopgap.

Booker limped along after the deal and haemorrhaged cash but eventually Charles Wilson did come on board and he has transformed Booker into a hugely successful and valuable company. Seven years after the deal was done Iceland and Booker combined were valued at over £3.5 billion compared with the just over £300 million that Grimsey got for his shareholders.

26
Full Circle

The deal was completed on Friday, 11 February 2005. It was my 59th birthday. I'd also got flu and felt awful. Andy, Tarsem, Kathy and I met for breakfast at the Grosvenor Hotel in Chester. We were excited but apprehensive. I'd arranged to meet Andy Clarke, the MD of Iceland, in the hotel, and briefly interrupted my breakfast to meet him in the lobby and fire him. It was a good-natured conversation, but we didn't need him and he was glad to be out of it.

We drove to Iceland, my usual car parking space was left vacant and we walked in through the front door for the first time in four years. It was a strange experience. I had to switch my phone off as the press were calling constantly. No one looked up from their desks as we walked through the building and into my old office. It felt deathly quiet and a sad and sombre place. I'd heard that my office had been used as a meeting room and that all my furniture had been disposed of, but it was all back in place just like I'd never been away. Idris, our office services manager, had kept it safe. He said he knew I'd be back. We went into the boardroom and Anne our tea lady presented me with a cake with 'many happy returns' iced on it – a double meaning if ever there was one.

We asked for all the directors or heads of departments to come into the boardroom, where most of them had been enjoying a champagne celebration just before we arrived, because their share options all crystallised on completion of the deal. They all sat around the table, probably more apprehensive than we were. For the last six months it had been rumoured I was coming back. Everyone recognised that the company was beyond hope and good people had been leaving in droves. Morale was on the floor and those who knew me thought I could maybe save the company. Those that didn't know me hoped for a miracle but no doubt also hoped they wouldn't be a casualty themselves.

We went round the table and everyone introduced themselves. I gave a speech about the state of the business and showed some slides to illustrate the financial state of the company. They were shocked; even the senior people in the room weren't fully up to speed on how bad things really were. I explained we'd take a few days to familiarise ourselves with the situation and then we'd act quickly.

Towards the end of the meeting Tarsem put his hand under the boardroom table and found something stuck to it: chewing gum! For him, that summarised everything about how far the business had sunk while we were away.

As ever products and prices were the first key to everything and Iceland was a complete mess. Karl Martin was the incumbent Buying Director but we didn't intend to keep him. Nigel Broadhurst, our former Buying Director, had left Iceland a few years before I did and I'd invited him back to join us. He jumped at the challenge but couldn't start for a couple of weeks. He was the only man I'd trust to sort out our products and prices, and would play a vital role in our recovery. We invited John Berry back as Company Secretary and Tim Yates as our Property Director. Kathy was back, of course, as my PA. We soon made up our minds as to who we were going to keep and who would go. Nick Canning was the Marketing Director and a Grimsey recruit so I assumed we would get rid of him but we chatted, he seemed confident and more than capable, and he has ended up with Nigel and Tarsem as one of the three key people in the business.

For the first few days I thought we'd made a terrible mistake in coming back. I was ill and lacking energy and it all seemed beyond hope. But very soon I realised it was going to be dead easy to get Iceland back on track. Because, quite simply, there wasn't one single part of the business that hadn't been comprehensively screwed up. The scale of mismanagement was unbelievable.

Sales were running at minus 10 per cent. The company was actually losing money. The bank overdraft limit was £300 million but there was little or no headroom left. We discovered a fictitious 'SAP accounting failure' that had been reported over Christmas, which meant that the company hadn't been able to pay any bills for a fortnight. As a result, suppliers hadn't been paid for weeks and credit insurance had been withdrawn.

Our selling prices were 10 per cent more than Tesco's across the board and there was an internal expression for many of the prices that were even more out of line: 'insult prices'. Our frozen chips were £1.69 when everyone else in the market was at £1.20. Yet to line up on just that one price would cost us £4 million off our profits.

Range extension was out of control. There were five types of feta cheese, eleven types of frozen lasagne, nine types of mayonnaise. How could anyone with any retail knowledge allow a metre of Earl Grey tea to be displayed in Kirkby, Liverpool, one of the most deprived parts of the city? We sold fresh fish in some stores, flowers, sandwiches, newspapers, toys and every store had a cigarette kiosk. Opening hours had extended to ridiculous times. No one seemed to know what business we were in. We weren't a supermarket, we weren't a discounter, we weren't a convenience store and we definitely weren't a freezer centre. We were in no man's land.

We had 60 stores without a manager. Many light fittings were dead in every store, with chewing gum trodden into the entrance mats. Store staff levels had been cut to the bone but had exploded at head office. When I left there were 600 people in head office and annual sales were £2 billion. When I returned there were 1,400 in head office but sales had declined by 25 per cent to £1.5 billion. The company was out of control and standards were a disgrace.

The first thing we did was set about raising standards – getting pride back into the company. At head office we cleaned the carpets, painted the walls and replaced the window blinds. In stores we replaced the lighting and deep cleaned every store. We cut the paperwork by 80 per cent. We increased the number of area managers to one for every fourteen stores instead of the twenty they were previously trying to manage.

We had to make 400 people redundant at head office, not just to save money but to free up the log jam of bureaucracy. It was like the civil service, with masses of process, procedure, steering groups and committees, but nothing ever actually got done. Most importantly we started investing again. Years ago I'd opened 'The Roxy American Diner' as the staff canteen at head office. It was complete with a Harley Davidson motorbike and a Wurlitzer juke box. Now it had become a greasy spoon so we spent £400,000 on fitting out an amazing new staff restaurant. Gradually morale recovered.

We stopped all advertising, fired the agency and immediately stopped all Buy One Get One Free promotions, which by now accounted for 30 per cent of sales. The company had got into the cycle of promotional activity that was like a drug, and they couldn't wean themselves off it. We cut out all non-core products, which accounted for 40 per cent of the range, and had a massive sale at half price to get rid of £30 million worth of old stock. We called it 'silt', because it was gumming up the system. We worked through the product range item by item cutting out duplications, improving quality and reducing our prices. Funnily enough sales started to improve very quickly. At the same time, we very quickly achieved £40 million of annual cost savings by hacking back the bureaucracy at head office, simplifying our product range and talking to all our suppliers. In short, by focusing on the things that actually mattered.

Our grand plan for saving the business consisted of just four words or phrases: Focus, Simplicity, Accept Reality and hopefully have some fun. The first two are obvious and necessary in any business. Accepting reality means not deluding yourself about a situation, as we all can do: hoping against hope something will work or get better when it won't. Having fun is an integral part of our philosophy, which became our main focus over the next few years.

I was curious to find out what Grimsey had been up to but there was no evidence of him ever having been there. Computers had been wiped, no paperwork existed. He'd done a good job at cleaning up after himself. I then decided to look into the accounts. We seconded an accountant to start piecing together the financial history over the last four years and at the same time I employed KPMG Forensic and also Kroll to carry out an investigation and produce two independent reports. Their reports were so damning I thought there was enough to warrant an investigation by the DTI so they were duly sent a copy but we heard nothing. They weren't interested. I imagine that after the long and costly investigation that started four years previously they hadn't the appetite to start again.

Our main findings were:

- Of the £65.6 million of provisions recorded in the 2001 annual report and accounts which resulted in the 2001 profit collapse **OVER £53 million** was simply released back into profit over the next three years and not against any costs incurred. None of these provision releases was documented in the annual report and accounts. In the first year alone provision releases accounted for 68 per cent of declared profit before tax and amortisation.

- Decisions not to issue profit warnings in 2004/05, although based on professional advice, were apparently based on forecasts, prepared by management, which were not realistic.

- If the large (£14.9 million) prior year tax adjustment that was made in 2003/04 had been classified as an exceptional item (as it should have been), it would have been excluded from the calculation of adjusted earnings per share. This would have had the consequence that targets for the LTIP (Long-Term Incentive Plan) would not have been met so management would not have received the shares (920,425 for Bill Grimsey and 460,722 for Bill Hoskins) that were issued to them under the scheme.

- Spending appeared to be profligate and out of control. £16 million was spent on consultants in the four-year period with £11 million paid to PricewaterhouseCoopers alone during one eighteen-month period. A consultancy called System 21 charged £1.5 million for a supposedly cost-saving head office review, covering all processes, which saved nothing at all; a year later we saved £40 million. Another £8 million was spent on legal and professional fees. £200,000 was spent on 'mentoring'. £8 million was spent on hotel accommodation and £4 million on air travel, subsistence and entertaining, while £8 million was posted as sundry personal expenditure.

During the four years we were away from the business reference was often made to our lack of financial controls. This could not be further from the truth. We had tight controls and weekly management accounts. By contrast on our return we discovered one lady in the accounts department had bought a horse on the company and another had paid for her wedding. Bank account reconciliations of store takings were running six to eight weeks in arrears, and in the resulting confusion one store manager was able to walk off with a cool £250,000, which we never got back.

By September we were ready for a relaunch. One of our key strategies and points of difference was to re-engineer all our products and pack sizes so the price could be adjusted to 'round pound'. This was something we'd developed at Cooltrader. The original idea came from a tiny frozen food store we'd seen in Birmingham that called itself 'The Pound Frozen Shop'. The shop itself was pretty grotty and their products were thoroughly obscure. At first we laughed when we saw the shop but the seed had been sown and we began to wonder whether this wasn't something we could try at Cooltrader. Slowly we changed our prices and rounded them to the nearest pound and while the results weren't exactly spectacular we did see an increase in sales.

While we were away Iceland had become a very complicated business not only in terms of systems and process, but also as far as the customer was concerned. From the customer's point of view, Buy One Get One Free (BOGOF) promotions were a con. A product would be displayed at an artificially high price, with minimal sales expected, and then promoted as a BOGOF, which is effectively half price. Sales would rocket for the period of the promotion and then drop back again when the promotion finished. This created all kinds of problems for the supply chain and also educated the customer just to look for promotions. Why not sell it at 'half price' all the time and be honest about it?

We decided to abolish all promotions and rely on selling products that offered honest, everyday good value. We reduced our prices so as to undercut the supermarkets and designed a price flash to go on the front of every product very clearly and prominently stating 'Only £1' (or £2 or £3). This was in bold red and yellow colours and in a typeface called 'Impact'. It took three months to work the packaging changes through the manufacturers and have everything ready for our relaunch.

We'd already reduced the number of products in store, getting rid of the crowded jumble sale effect so that everything could now be displayed clearly with enough space to display each product properly. We simplified the ticketing with big bold tickets in red and yellow advertising the new round pound prices. The stores were cleaner, brighter and less cluttered. New staff uniforms were also introduced. We set up a trial store in Mold, North Wales to evaluate the new look and grew in confidence that the relaunch would work.

It was all planned for September and to launch it we had a new advertising campaign featuring Kerry Katona. In February, during our first week back in the company, we had realised that the relaunch would take time to plan: we'd only get one shot at it and it had to work. Key to its success would be a new advertising campaign and I told Nick Canning we should bring back Tom Reddy, a long-suffering advertising man who had helped us on numerous occasions in the past. He had coined the phrase 'Mum's gone to Iceland' and also produced our best-ever Christmas TV ad with Chris Rea singing 'Driving home for Christmas'. Nick wanted to invite a few agencies to 'pitch' for the business, which would be the normal way of doing things. I agreed to this to keep him happy, although I always knew that Tom would get the job. Nick put the brief out and the day came when three agencies including Tom would each make a presentation to Nick, Nigel, Tarsem and me in our boardroom. The result was entirely predictable ...

Two of the agencies were from London and were very slick and professional. Each London team consisted of two guys in smart suits, one being a director we'd probably never see again but who was there to add 'weight'. The second guy was the account director who would be our main point of contact. There was a guy with a ponytail and denim jacket who was the 'creative director' and finally a very attractive girl in a business suit with a tight skirt.

Each made a similar presentation. Lots of Powerpoint slides about their agency and the big clients they worked for. Lots of photographs of Iceland shops to prove they'd been round a few. Market data and demographic information profiling our customers to prove they understood our business and then finally, the big idea. This is where they seemed to run out of inspiration, or maybe they thought no one had ever proposed we use an Eskimo, penguin or polar bear in our adverts before. Their big ideas were predictable and uninspiring.

And then in came Tom. Tom is seriously overweight, his shirt is usually hanging out of his trousers and he always looks very dishevelled. He is well past retirement age and came puffing into the boardroom accompanied by his wife and daughter. It's a family business. Nick looked horrified. Tom got straight to the point. He dropped magazines on the table all featuring 'Mum of the Year' Kerry Katona. I'd never heard of her. Apparently she was really well known, a former member of the girl group Atomic Kitten, and was getting a serious amount of press coverage. She was well liked, but brash and 'in your face'. Tom explained that we needed a celebrity in our adverts, a strong personality our customers could recognise, someone who would stand out and grab attention, but it was also high-risk. He explained that the trouble with celebrities is that you sign them up and then they go and do something stupid like being caught taking cocaine.

Anyway, we liked the idea. Tom got the job, Kerry was in our adverts shouting loudly about everything being only a pound and sales went off like a rocket. We were immediately recording increases of 15 to 20 per cent against minus 10 per cent when we took over. We were on a roll. We reintroduced our annual conference in October, and it turned out to be a fun-filled celebration of success. We gave away prizes and unveiled a BMW sports car as the prize for a Christmas sales incentive. Our managers were on fire. Morale was higher than it had ever been and we knew we were on the road to success.

Our relationship with Baugur was excellent. They completely left us alone to get on with the job and were fully supportive of everything we did. By the end of the first year we were able to show an operating profit of £52 million and we had generated enough cash to pay back our shareholders all their original investment. We were all in for free.

Our original safety net plan was that if profits didn't recover we could sell maybe 100 stores to one of the supermarkets to raise cash. We started the process as soon as we arrived back and both Tesco and Sainsbury's each said they would be interested in up to 100 stores. We sent them information and gradually their interest reduced to 50 stores, then twenty, then ten, and then none. We ended up giving just one store to Sainsbury's that Grimsey had taken, but which we thought unsuitable and didn't want to fit out and open as an Iceland. Meanwhile Marks & Spencer expressed interest in 29 stores, which eventually we sold them for £28 million. By this time it was clear we didn't need the money but it was a good price and I was outvoted.

The irony is that M&S sold several of them back to us a couple of years later for just £1 each and closed most of the rest. They couldn't make them work.

Over the next few years sales and profits grew strongly. We were soon able to claim we were the fastest growing food retailer in the UK. We were able to start increasing managers' salaries and soon they went from being the worst paid in the high street to the best. In the second year we were able to refinance and pay another dividend out to shareholders of £290 million. Our standing with banks and landlords went from zero to hero.

Baugur were obviously delighted with our progress and it came as a pleasant surprise when they suggested we buy a new aeroplane. To my surprise Grimsey had kept our old plane and used it a lot. They flew 2,070 times in four years, mainly to and from the office. We inherited the plane on our return but mothballed it as we intended to sell it. But as sales and profits improved we started to use it cautiously. Then, to our astonishment, at the end of the first year, Palmi suggested we needed a new one. We changed the old Citation Bravo for a bigger and brand new Hawker 850.

The Icelanders largely left us to get on with it and, even when we did see them, it was hard to engage their attention. They would typically be juggling three different phones and a laptop each, and their first question on walking into a room was always 'What's your wireless?' They were deeply shocked on their first visit to Iceland head office when they found we didn't have one! We held one memorable dinner in Prague where Jon Asgeir flew in literally for one course, then flew out again. He seemed to be constantly on the move. We never thought to ask who he was trying to keep one step ahead of.

We tried to introduce them to the finer things in English life and took them pheasant shooting. To be fair, Gunnar Sigurdsson took the trouble to look into the etiquette and spent £4,000 at Holland & Holland kitting himself out like an English gent. Palmi turned up in a ski suit and the only birds he shot all day were two protected blackbirds. He also nearly shot a beater, who failed to see the funny side, and it was no surprise that Palmi was subsequently banned from the shoot.

Baugur were taking over the British high street and buying everything in sight. People wondered where the money was coming from and suggested it was somehow 'dodgy Russian money'. The truth was that the three main Icelandic banks were on a roll, paying high interest rates to lenders and borrowing money themselves on the wholesale money market. With hindsight it was of course unsustainable, but at the time it didn't seem like that. The press, the City and the investment community all lauded the Viking Raiders – they appeared unstoppable. As always, though, when it went wrong the same people were quick to criticise them.

Baugur had a 10 per cent stake in Woolworth's, which was another company going nowhere. They'd already made a tentative offer to buy the company, been rebuffed and then suggested we might like to get involved. We did some basic research and reached an obvious but not widely shared conclusion. Generally Woolworth's was seen as an old-fashioned concept, past its sell-by date and with no future, much like Iceland had been until recently. That couldn't be further from the truth. Woolworth's was simply incredibly badly run. Home Bargains, B&M Bargains, Wilkinson's and the pound shops had stolen their place in the market and were making good profits. Woolworth's had the name, the number of stores, the store locations and it should have been flying, but the board led by Richard North was frozen in the past. What convinced me was seeing the management 'family tree' – 100 pages of utter bureaucracy.

Working with Rothschilds I sent a letter to Richard North with an indicative offer but got no reply. After a while we decided to send another reduced offer of £50 million, but leak it to the press. This forced him to respond but only with a letter claiming there was £500 million of value in the retail business and rejecting our approach. I found Richard North arrogant and intransigent throughout the whole process. Soon after the company went bankrupt, all the stores were closed and everyone lost their jobs.

We were at least able to salvage something from the wreckage, and give a powerful boost to our expansion plans for Iceland, by acquiring 51 redundant Woolworth's stores from the receiver. This massively increased the pace of our store openings to a record 74 in our financial year to March 2010: our biggest increase in store numbers in a single year since we bought Bejam in 1989. Having started my retail life at Woolworth's, it gave me some satisfaction to be able to put new life back into at least 51 high streets, and to create around 2,500 new jobs in the process.

Meanwhile, in February 2009, Baugur had gone bust. It was inevitable. Their shares in Iceland were taken over by the Icelandic banks Landsbanki and Glitnir to which Baugur owed money, but only a few months later the banks themselves went bust. For a while nobody really knew who owned the shares in Iceland the company.

27
Long-Term Greedy

There was a huge amount of accusations, recriminations and blame seeking in Iceland (the country) about who had caused the financial crisis and Jon Asgeir took the brunt of the blame. For a long time the banking industry was in complete disarray but eventually each bank was split into two – a 'good bank' and a 'bad bank' – and a 'Resolution Committee' was set up to manage their assets and eventually sell them off to pay their creditors. Landsbanki appointed three directors to Iceland but for some reason they appointed Jon Asgeir as Chairman. The politics and relationships involved were unfathomable.

We flew out to Iceland to see the Resolution Committee and it was like walking into a meeting of a particularly disorganised parish council. There were papers literally everywhere and it was hard to believe that anyone had a clue what they were doing, or the capacity to make a decision about anything. The idea that they had the financial destiny of a whole nation in their hands was mind-boggling. To add to the joy of the occasion, when we stepped outside Reykjavik's fashionable Hotel 101, which was owned by Jon Asgeir's wife, a group of protestors spotted Jon Asgeir with us and began enthusiastically pelting him with snowballs.

Day-to-day we weren't affected by the Icelandic meltdown, as the banks were happy to leave us alone and let us get on with the job. After all we were producing spectacular results. But our long-term horizon had changed. We'd gone from being a private company where the shareholders were happy to stay in forever and take a dividend every few years to a company that would eventually have to be sold. This didn't worry us. We saw it as a great opportunity as we had the pre-emption clause in our shareholders' agreement, which gave us the right to match any other offer they might otherwise accept. We also had a complete block on any refinancing or dividend payments.

Jon Asgeir told us that the Icelandic nation was so short of foreign currency they were desperate to raise cash and he thought the banks would accept an immediate and low offer from us to buy the business. We made an offer, which valued the company at £600 million. That turned out to be a mistake, as they were not happy with us and saw us as being opportunistic – which of course we were. Relations from then on were prickly with each side suspicious of the other.

When we got back into the business and put our original budget together in 2005 we were understandably conservative. After years of chasing analysts' forecasts as a public company we wanted no such pressure. We could now run the business with a different mindset. Instead of squeezing the maximum amount of profit each year, and often making short-term decisions at the expense of the future, we could run the business for the long term. It didn't matter if we made an investment that might adversely affect this year's profit number if we thought it would benefit us in the future. The phrase we adopted to summarise our approach was that we were 'long-term greedy'. Baugur were happy with this. As it turned out we beat our first profit forecast by a much bigger margin than expected. Of course we wanted to under-promise and over-deliver but we surprised ourselves with the result. This pattern continued every year to the point where Baugur and later Landsbanki thought we were playing games and deliberately under-forecasting. Baugur were relaxed about it but Landsbanki saw it as a big problem and started to disbelieve any forecast we put forward.

We couldn't get any sense out of Landsbanki as to when they might want to sell the business or how they might manage the process. To be fair, although we wanted to do a nice cosy deal with them (and we were the logical buyers) they had to be seen to get the best price and the Resolution Committee all seemed to be terrified of making a mistake and getting sued by their creditors. We thought they would want to sell quickly and get in the cash but they reckoned they could wait for years. This sort of left us in limbo. One of their main reasons for hanging on was our profit performance. The profit graph had gone up in a straight line and somehow they seemed to think that would go on forever. It was bound to level off. We'd had spectacular growth, but it wasn't possible for it to go on at that rate much longer. Landsbanki just refused to believe this and decided that, based on future growth, the company was worth £2 billion. We ourselves couldn't get the number past £1 billion. We were never sure who had the real authority on the Resolution Committee as names kept changing but our contact and board member was Baldvin Valtýsson (known as Baddie). Our relationship was cordial but mistrustful. He wanted to sell Iceland for the highest price he could get, while we obviously wanted to buy it for the lowest.

With that as a background we carried on building Iceland into a more and more successful business, thereby putting up the price we might one day be forced to pay. Most other supermarkets had now copied our round pound pricing strategy and even the typeface and colour of our tickets. It didn't seem to matter. We were innovating new products all the time and sales kept on growing. Our main concern was building staff morale. This we saw as a key weapon in building the business. We'd increased wages ahead of most other retailers and now paid a better hourly rate than even Sainsbury's, John Lewis or Marks & Spencer. Even so our front line staff still only got £6.75 an hour but in a *Sunday Times* survey of the Best Companies to Work For Iceland came out number one in employee satisfaction with their rate of pay. Number two was Goldman Sachs! The point here is that it's not just the actual rate of pay that matters, but how people feel about the company they work for.

We really were building fun back into the business. Area meetings, regional meetings and Christmas parties were all designed to include an element of fun. Our managers' conferences got bigger and better each year culminating first in a conference at Disney World in Paris in 2007, and then two years later we took 1,000 of our managers and senior people to Walt Disney World in Florida. We charted three jumbo jets to do this and spent £4 million on the event. Every penny was an investment in staff morale. Happy staff make happy customers. Happy customers put cash in the till.

One of our main morale-boosting events every year is charity week. Every August store staff go mad running marathons, washing cars, dressing up and doing other crazy things to raise money. For years I made a token contribution, usually cooking lunch for head office staff in the Roxy restaurant. Then in 2011 I decided to lead by example and do something indisputably crazier than absolutely anyone else.

28
On Top of The World

It was all Lord Kirkham's fault. He'd rung me out of the blue at the start of 2010 to announce that he'd organised a birthday treat for me: 'I'm taking you to the North Pole!' I'd known Graham for over 30 years and he'd always had the capacity for the unexpected, but this did seem a bit extreme even for him. I suppose he thought it might be an appropriate destination for me. 'Yeah right,' I said, but then realised he wasn't joking when he explained we were going with the famous Arctic explorer David Hempleman-Adams. He'd also invited his pal the Kwik Fit founder Sir Tom Farmer on the trip.

Any more information was in short supply until the kit list finally arrived. Scott of the Antarctic managed with leather boots and Harris Tweed but clothing technology had moved on. Four hours in four different specialist shops saw me with base layers, mid layers and outer shells made from fibres I never knew existed. I always get cold feet (in the literal sense) when it gets below freezing but inner socks, vapour barriers and outer socks would do the trick. It's not often the advice and guidance from a young sales assistant could be a matter of life and death.

The trip was to take five days and I envisaged pulling sleds across frozen wasteland and possibly losing a few fingers to frostbite. More people have climbed Mount Everest than have ever been to the North

Pole and this wasn't something to be undertaken lightly. Only two days before departure the itinerary finally arrived. It didn't exactly make it look cushy but I was rather reluctant to dilute the admiration of my friends and family by showing it to them. A four-and-a-half-hour flight by private jet to Spitzbergen, just on the Arctic Circle, followed by a two-and-a-half-hour flight in a Russian jet to within 30 miles of the pole and finally a half-hour flight by Russian helicopter to land at the pole itself.

Spitzbergen is the size of Switzerland with a population of 2,000 humans and 5,000 polar bears. It's minus 25°C and the cold was a shock as we got off the plane. We overnighted at the Polar Hotel and were warned not to leave the hotel without a guide with a rifle – polar bears were everywhere!

The Arctic ice cap is only a few inches thick but the Russians clear a runway for just four weeks every year and manage to land an Antonov S.T.O.L. to service their scientific research station. We spent the night at 'base camp' in an unheated tent we erected ourselves. The temperature was minus 35°C. Surprisingly no one was ever cold; the specialist gear did the trick.

The old Russian helicopter probably presented more of a risk than actually walking to the Pole but we finally made it to the top of the world. We had a couple of hours taking photos and drinking hot punch before we finally retreated in the face of near frostbite and went back to base camp.

Our journey back via Spitzbergen involved a stay several days longer than we had intended thanks to the Icelandic volcanic ash cloud that blocked air traffic across Europe, but we filled the time making long journeys into the wilderness each day either by snowmobile or driving dog sleds. And naturally we talked, which is where I took my next serious wrong turn. David Hempleman-Adams mentioned that he was leading an expedition to Everest the next year and like an idiot I said, 'Can I come?'

I don't know why I did it. I'd never been much of an adventurer outside business and, while I enjoyed scout camps as a boy, I recognised long ago that my natural habitat is a five star hotel. I suppose it was an attempt to prove to myself that I was still young. At any rate, now that I had committed myself, the adventure seemed to provide a perfect opportunity to raise at least £1 million for a charity that had become very close to my heart, Alzheimer's Research UK. For once I could say, hand on heart, to all our staff who were doing triathlons, climbing mountains and pulling trucks to raise money for our 'Charity of the Year' that I really was leading by example!

Raising money for good causes had been woven into the culture of Iceland from an early stage. We were a founder member of the Per Cent Club in 1986, pledged to give half a per cent of our profits to charity each year, and we particularly liked to support less fashionable charities where our support could make a real difference. During the mid-1990s we raised more than £1 million to help build a National Institute of Conductive Education for Petö UK, a charity for children and adults with neurological motor disorders.

Good causes took something of a back seat during the Dark Ages between 2001 and 2005 while I was away from the business, but between 2006 and 2009 we raised over £3 million for the Alder Hey Children's Hospital in Liverpool. We also became a long-term partner of the prostate cancer charity Prostate Cancer UK, for which we had raised more than £500,000 by 2013.

Our biggest charity year so far had been 2010, when our adoption of Help For Heroes really captured the imagination of our people, customers and suppliers, helping us to raise a record £1.5 million. I was delighted to present Help For Heroes co-founders Bryn and Emma Parry with a cheque at a spectacular charity ball held at my house in Cheshire on 18 November 2010, 40 years to the day after we had opened the doors of the first Iceland store in Oswestry. We invited more than 350 people including suppliers, advisers, senior staff and many of those who had been with us at the start and through the early years, including Peter Hinchcliffe, Bernard Leigh and Richard Kirk (as Dick Kirk now likes to be known). They enjoyed an evening of fine food and great entertainment, including performances by Dame

Edna Everage and Tom Jones. It was certainly a night to remember, though I am not sure how many of us actually could when we woke up the next morning.

After the party it was time to face up to the grim reality of tackling the world's most famous mountain, probably the toughest challenge on the planet. I was personally responsible for a huge leap in like-for-like sales at Snow+Rock, as I stocked up with more specialist clothing and equipment, including a down-filled 'summit suit'. I climbed Kilimanjaro by way of preparation, and also spent a couple of days climbing in the Alps. The fact that I did any training at all was largely at the insistence of my son Richard, who had asked to come with me as soon as I told him I was heading for Everest, and kept accusing me of not taking it seriously enough. He probably had a point.

However, I did take a serious look into the reasons why so many past Everest expeditions failed. The weather was top of the list and clearly out of our control, but we could guard against altitude sickness by taking time to acclimatise properly, so we arranged to spend two weeks trekking in Nepal before we even headed for Base Camp. The other big issue was sickness and stomach upsets, which can be life threatening at 25,000 feet, so I decided to take a 60-day supply of hygienically prepared, high calorie Iceland food! This was specially devised and produced for us at the Loxton's factory in Manchester, which we later took over and renamed Iceland Manufacturing.

I also took along a selection of delicacies from my favourite restaurant, Piccolino (the fact that I am Chairman of its holding company having no bearing at all on this), including Parma ham, Parmigianino cheese, olives, fine wines and vintage brandy. To ensure that this would be consumed under appropriately civilised conditions, I also insisted that we were equipped with a proper mess tent, with a table and chairs. And, most importantly, fully functioning portable toilets!

My role models were Mallory and Irvine on their expedition of 1924, when they headed up the mountain laden with Fortnum &

Mason's tinned quail in foie gras, vintage champagne, truffles and crystallised ginger. In an attempt to avoid joining them among the 200-odd dead bodies littering the aptly named Death Zone, we recruited a hugely experienced climber called Alan Hinkes as our guide, with an unambiguously simple brief to bring us back alive. Although I secretly hoped to make it to the summit, I also set a public goal of reaching the North Col at 23,000 feet, which is 3,000 feet below where the Death Zone starts.

We flew out to Kathmandu on Sunday, 28 March 2011, our confidence perhaps slightly dented by the fact that the expedition leader David Hempleman-Adams nearly missed the flight after getting lost at Heathrow Airport!

On the following Thursday we set out on a twelve-day 'acclimatisation trek' that would take us up to 16,000 feet and was meant to get us used to the thin air we would encounter on Everest itself. The party comprised nine experienced climbers, including two super fit ex-paratroopers and a Red Arrows pilot, plus two novices, Richard and me. It certainly brought out my competitive spirit and got us used to extreme cold and served its purpose in that none of us got altitude sickness on Everest itself.

Then, on the night before we were due to cross the border into Tibet to head for Everest Base Camp, one of our three lorries laden with specialist climbing equipment and supplies drove off a cliff and was completely destroyed. The driver, his assistant and an accompanying Sherpa jumped clear in the nick of time, but were lucky to escape with their lives. This was a real threat to the whole expedition not just because of the stuff we had to try to recover from the crash site, but because our group permit to enter Tibet was only valid for one day. If we didn't make it, we'd be stuck for weeks while the wheels of Chinese bureaucracy ground out a new permit, which would almost certainly mean that we'd miss the 'weather window' for an Everest summit attempt.

Luckily we did make it in time over the oxymoronically named Friendship Bridge and past the unsmiling Chinese border guards into

Tibet: first the border town of Zhangmu and then Nyalam, the true armpit of the universe. I'd thought Kathmandu was a bit of a dump, mainly because of the locals' penchant for slinging litter everywhere, but this place made it look like Chelsea. Even worse, the only hotel in town where you might be prepared to let your dog stay claimed to be full and to have no record of the booking we'd made (and paid for in full) three months earlier. We finally managed to persuade them to give us a couple of rooms while the rest of the team went to another place where, on a previous visit, our deputy expedition leader Graham Hoyland had found himself sharing his bed with a rat. None of the hotels in Tibet ran to heating and I was colder than I had been in my tent on the trek.

Then we drove onwards and upwards to spend two nights in a place called Tingri that was, unbelievably, even more of a dump than Nyalam. At least, I reflected, Everest couldn't be any worse than this!

We reached Base Camp by road on Friday, 15 April and set up our comparatively civilised tents. One minor disappointment was discovering that the state-of-the-art satellite communication equipment we had lugged all the way from England, and which had luckily survived the lorry crash, would not work because no one had taken account of the rather large mountain that would be blocking the signal. Which was a bit worrying when you reflected that our lives depended on the organisational genius of these same individuals in the coming weeks.

We made offerings to the gods at a three hour Puja ceremony to bring us luck on our climb, and it obviously worked because I have survived to write this!

Even the acclimatisation trek had not prepared us for the reality of how incredibly difficult it is to do anything at all at very high altitudes. Above 6,000 metres (Base Camp is at 5,182 metres, Advanced Base Camp at 6,492 metres) the human body starts to deteriorate really seriously. You lose your appetite and your body literally starts to consume itself. The average weight loss of an Everest climber is

10 to 15 kilos. Unfortunately I only found out after I got there that it's muscle you lose and not fat!

The real challenge, though, was coping with the extreme boredom of simply hanging around in squalid conditions waiting for the weather to allow us to move on. We climbed up to the ghastly interim camp, on the way to Advanced Base Camp (ABC), then the weather closed in and Richard and I took Alan Hinkes's advice to return with him to Base Camp, while the rest of the team hung on in the hope of continuing to ABC.

Richard and I finally made it to ABC on 29 April, just in time to miss the rest of the team's Royal Wedding celebrations. I recorded in my blog at the time: 'I've had a bad sore throat for three weeks now. I've lost weight and my appetite has gone. I just can't face dinner. I have a cut on my thumb which won't heal and the recognised cure at this altitude is superglue which does seem to work quite well. My nose is always blocked and every time I blow it there's a tissue full of blood. Again all quite normal. My lips are chapped and bleeding – oh, and I have one false tooth, an implant, which for no apparent reason dropped out. Other than that I'm quite well.'

Richard and I made it to our target of the North Col (7,000 metres or 23,000 feet) on Tuesday, 3 May 2011. To put that in perspective, the North Col is higher than any mountain on Earth outside the Himalayas. To get there, you have to make your way up a terrifying ice cliff on a series of fixed ropes, anchored by screws into the ice. Often five or six climbers will be on one rope putting all their weight on it. The cliff seems vertical in places but is 60 degrees most of the way.

It took about three-and-a-half hours of the most physically exhausting work it's possible to imagine to get up it, then we had to cross 'the ladder' over an apparently bottomless crevasse maybe 15 metres wide. It's called 'the ladder' because the Tibetan rope fixers had acquired three aluminium ladders that looked for all the world like they had come from B&Q. These were lashed together with rope to make one long, wobbly, saggy ladder that was propped across the chasm. Not for the faint hearted but actually not that difficult! The worst bit was manoeuvring up the ice wall on the other side, clipping and unclipping safety devices. A few more metres and the prayer flags and tents on the North Col came into view. There has never been such a welcome sight!

Richard had made it an hour-and-a-half ahead of me and was undoubtedly the fittest member of the whole expedition team. No one was in any doubt that he could make it to the summit if he wanted to. We could clearly see the route to the top and it looked deceptively easy. The problem was that all climbers who make it to the North Col then have to go all the way back down to Base Camp (or lower) for maybe ten days to recover before climbing all the way back up for the summit attempt. The thought of this was more than I could bear. I was ready to go home and Richard kindly decided to accompany me.

Everyone knows how the news of Hillary and Tenzing's summit triumph in 1953 reached London on the morning of the Queen's Coronation. Another pleasing coincidence was that on the very same day that we reached the North Col, Bill Grimsey's latest company, Focus, went bankrupt. Another pinnacle in our respective careers!

While I was recuperating back in the UK, the rest of the team returned to Base Camp and four of them – Rodney Hogg, Graham Duff, Justin Packshaw and David Hempleman-Adams, with their wonderful supporting Sherpas – finally made it to the summit and unfurled the Iceland flag there on Saturday, 21 May. And, with the great support of our staff and customers during charity week in August, we raised over £1.2 million during the year for Alzheimer's Research UK, to fund a research project into early-onset Alzheimer's disease.

I should have learned my lesson on Everest but the bug to do daft things for charity bit me twice more in 2012. In September I abseiled from the top of The Shard in London along with my fellow director Lord Kirkham. Although I genuinely have no head for heights, this proved a piece of piss compared with what followed in December.

Again, I don't really know how it happened but somehow I found myself agreeing to take part in another expedition organised by David Hempleman-Adams, this time trekking unsupported across the Antarctic ice sheet to the South Pole. I suppose because I'd been to the North Pole it seemed right to try to complete the set. The expedition was timed to mark the centenary of Captain Scott's ill-fated adventure, which with hindsight did not seem like a good omen, and included three wounded soldiers from the legendary Captain Oates's old regiment, the Royal Dragoon Guards. We called it 'In the Footsteps of Legends: The Iceland Antarctic Expedition' and dedicated it to raising money for Alzheimer's Research UK and Walking With The Wounded.

Given that it was the sheer squalor of life on Everest that made me quit after reaching the North Col, the brief for the Polar quest did not look too enticing. There would be no Sherpas to do the heavy lifting, no Iceland meals, no wine and no mess tent. I took about 70 changes of underwear up Everest, among the supplies that we carried up to Advanced Base Camp on no fewer than 120 yaks. For this trip 'Hempie' told me that I was allowed a maximum of two pairs of underpants, and suggested that I saw the handle off my toothbrush to save weight. Everything we did take we had to haul ourselves on sleds. The soldiers prepared for it by yomping through the hills above Catterick every day for weeks, hauling tanks behind them. I did nothing.

We flew out from Punta Arenas in Chile on 23 November, on a Russian Ilyushin jet that transported us to the Union Glacier base in Antarctica. Four days later a Twin Otter plane took us on to our starting point at 88 degrees south, 140 miles from the geographic South Pole. The Antarctic plateau isn't just incredibly cold, getting down to minus 45°C, it's also at high altitude – over 3,000 metres – so the physical challenge was at least as great as climbing Everest. And we had one critical handicap. We were burning 8,000 calories a day, which we needed to replace, but all we had to do it with was near inedible 'expedition food', rather than the Iceland ready meals we had taken to the Himalayas.

It did not take me long to work out why Captain Scott came up with his famous quote: 'Great God! This is an awful place ...' Even so, I got through the first few days surprisingly well, despite gale force headwinds and sastrugi in the snow that forced us to walk rather than ski. I also managed to avoid suffering any ill effects from altitude or frost burn. I was conscious of reaching my physical limit by the end of each day, but recovered in a few minutes once our five-man tent went up. Then on Sunday, 2 December, it all went seriously wrong and I started being so sick that I ended up retching blood. I thought I was going to die. More worryingly, I later found out that David Hempleman-Adams thought so, too.

I was airlifted out to Union Glacier, attached to a saline drip, and felt fine by the time I got there. But there was that same Ilyushin plane just about to head back to Punta Arenas so I thought I might as well take the opportunity to enjoy a night in a comfortable hotel and a decent steak dinner. Unfortunately the rich food made me so ill that I ended up back on the drip, which rather made the decision for me as to whether I should head back to the UK or look to rejoin the rest of the team for the final trek to the Pole. They arrived there on 11 December. Sadly we didn't make anything like as much as we had hoped for Walking With The Wounded, but Iceland raised another £1 million for Alzheimer's Research UK over the year, which made a significant contribution to their total research funding.

I think maybe the South Pole experience has cured me of the desire to do extreme adventures for charity, and this year I'll go back to griddling steaks in the Roxy. On the other hand I always said 'never again' after every unsuccessful diversification away from Iceland over the years, until I thought of the next one!

29
The Auction

Knowing that an auction for the business would start one day we began to talk to bankers and possible backers to get our finance in place. All the private equity houses were interested and we spoke to almost every one of them. They were all in 'sell mode' so were charming and agreeable. I would explain that I didn't like private equity and didn't trust them. They would typically buy a business, ramp up the profits and want to sell again in three or four years. They always wanted control and, while from our point of view as management it would be a safe option because the money was assured and our returns could be great, it wasn't what we wanted. We wanted to control the business ourselves and run it for the very long term. Of course each one of them assured me they weren't like all the others. They claimed they were all nice people to work with and would be happy to hold for a longer term than usual.

Tarsem took over negotiations with the banks and all were eager for part of the action. We retained Rothschilds as usual to act on our behalf but also took on a young former Goldman Sachs banker called Dan Yealland to work alongside them. We employed George Knighton of Allen & Overy as our lawyer and Grant Thornton as our tax advisers. Eventually in May 2011 Baddie informed us Landsbanki were starting the process of selling their 67 per cent shareholding and

Glitnir's 10 per cent stake in the business. He seemed to be under the impression they were selling the company (which in reality would be the case) but technically they were only selling their own share-holdings. The management owned the remaining 23 per cent of the company and we resented the way they were going about things. This should have been a joint venture but they decided they were in control.

They retained two banks, Bank of America Merrill Lynch and UBS, to advise them and carry out the sale process. They needed to put together a sales document which would require extensive due diligence on the company to be carried out. They retained OC&C to carry out the commercial due diligence (that is, to report on our place in the market) and Ernst & Young to carry out financial due diligence (checking our numbers and forecasts). I rang Baddie and asked why, of all the top accountancy firms, they had to choose Ernst & Young. They had been involved in approving Grimsey's provisions in 2001 and I didn't want to have any involvement with them ever again. Baddie told me it was his choice and I would have to accept it. He wanted me to meet them the following week. I refused and said I would not allow them into the building. This stand-off continued for over a week. I had phone calls from various people trying to persuade me but I refused to budge. Eventually the situation was in danger of getting seriously out of control so I agreed to meet Harry Nicholson, a partner of Ernst & Young, on neutral ground at Rothschild's offices. I explained what I felt about them but obviously he was not going to admit they'd made any mistakes or done anything wrong, although he did apologise for how things turned out. He also tried his best to persuade me to cooperate and let them in. In the end I agreed, but only on condition that they would make a donation of £10,000 to our Alzheimer's charity. They did.

We had our first meeting in Deeside with their banks and Philip Noblet of Bank of America took charge. He was a caricature of your typical investment banker. Fat, loud, with red braces and a bullying manner. He explained how it was all going to work and insisted we should drop our pre-emption rights and dividend veto as of course this would adversely affect the price. I explained to him the facts of life as we saw it. We would not give up anything and their best plan would be to work with us. We intended to invoke pre-emption and we would buy the business. The interests of all shareholders were to be considered here and not just the Vikings.

Their plan was to have three rounds of bids. The first would be to send out the sales document to more or less anyone who requested it and those that were interested would put in an indicative bid. Then a short list of bidders would be invited into the second round. This would involve them having access to more detailed information and being allowed into the company to carry out their own due diligence. Finally a third round would see maybe two bidders putting in their final and binding bids. We were not happy with this. It would be disruptive to staff and any of our competitors, whether they were really interested or not, could gain access to the company and see all our secrets. It was even requested we should make our cost price file available. We argued over the coming weeks and eventually reached a compromise that gave us some kind of security. Limited information would be made available to other retailers but more information to other bidders. The usual data room containing sensitive documents was requested to be made available electronically. We didn't trust anyone with this, as we would have no control over what happened to electronic files or who might see them, so we insisted they only see hard copies of documents that they wouldn't be allowed to copy.

Morrisons and Asda were interested and I had several meetings with Dalton Philips of Morrisons and one with Andy Clarke of Asda. Dalton was desperate for the deal and basically promised us a free hand if we would do a deal with him. In the event both Morrisons and Asda dropped out, leaving only private equity bidders.

These private equity bidders were then whittled down to two we thought we might be able to work with, BC Partners and Bain Capital. All the private equity firms would only want to be involved with the incumbent management so gradually they all dropped out as we made clear we weren't interested. Of course Landsbanki weren't happy about this. Finally we fell out with Andrew Newington of BC Partners who we accused of trying to do a deal behind our back and then we fell out with Felipe Merry del Val of Bain. At one meeting he made it clear that he would only bid on the basis that we would work with him. On the basis of this promise we gave him much more sensitive information but in the event he went and bid in round two without our involvement as did Andrew Newington. It was interesting to note that despite his promises to work with us for the long term, Andrew Newington left BC Partners around six months later.

Both had decided to go ahead without us in the final round of bidding, but I still failed to understand why they were going to all this time and trouble and spending maybe £500,000 on due diligence when they knew we could come in at the last minute and match their bid. As it turned out we later found out Landsbanki was paying for their due diligence. It was the only way they could get people interested and risk their bid being matched by us.

I had no desire to work with private equity. The problem was if they came in at a high price we couldn't match we would have to either sell out or work with them. This is what they were both gambling on. Baddie told us the bids were around £1.4 billion, which was far more than we could afford, but neither of them were ready to make their offers unconditional. Underwriting costs would be involved and no one wanted to risk that until they knew where we were.

My good friend Lord Kirkham, who had recently sold his company DFS, told me he was interested in investing with us. Rothschilds introduced me to Landmark, a company based in Dubai and run and owned by Renuka and Micky Jagtiani. They were fabulously wealthy and keen to invest money in the UK. Dan Yealland introduced me to Christo Wiese, a very wealthy guy from South Africa. All were retailers, all owned their own companies and all would invest their own money. Christo planned to make his investment through an investment vehicle called Brait which was run by John Gnodde. More importantly they all were looking for a very long-term investment and weren't interested in a short-term exit.

They were ideal backers for us. Like-minded people who understood retail. We met several times and got on well. They were all enthusiastic about Iceland. One problem was that never had we had such a good run for profit as we were doing in 2012. We ended up making £230 million EBITDA (Earnings Before Interest, Taxes, Depreciation and Amortisation). We also came first in the *Sunday Times* Best Companies to Work For. Everything was going our way but we were putting the price up to ourselves. We were nervous our prospective investors would buy into us as a growth story. We made it clear to everyone that as far as we were concerned there would be very little profit growth in future years and we would only be able to expand at about fifteen new stores each year but we were a phenomenal cash generator. Our investors accepted this.

An agreement was reached and each investor agreed to take an equal stake in the company. It was important that we as management had control even if we ended up with a minority stake. It all depended on the price we paid and the total bank borrowings we took on. If we increased our borrowings we could end up owning over 50 per cent of the company between Tarsem, Nigel, Nick and myself. Andy had decided to cash in his shares and leave so we had to find even more money to buy him out. If we wanted to sleep at night and take less borrowings we would end up with just over 40 per cent but, while having a minority was emotionally difficult to accept, it didn't matter if we had control written into our shareholders' agreement.

The problem now was to do the deal with the Resolution Committee. We did not want to pay £1.4 billion but it looked like that was the offer from both BC and Bain. Of course we could wait until they went unconditional and then pre-empt but it would be better all round if we could do a deal now and better for Landsbanki and Glitnir if they had certainty. The problem was we'd done such a good job convincing them we couldn't raise the money, as we tried to keep the price down, that they were reluctant to deal with us. If they thought we had the money they might try to engineer a higher price. Finally, on the advice of Larus Welding who was now out of a job with the bank but happy to help and advise, we went direct for a face-to-face meeting with the Resolution Committee, without any advisers present.

We suggested we could pay their price of £1.4 billion but only if they helped us by lending us the money and lending it at a very low rate of interest. We asked for a loan of £250 million at 5 per cent. They agreed with such alacrity that Tarsem said afterwards that he wished we'd asked for £350 million at 4 per cent! It was like going to see a car for sale, putting in an offer, then asking the vendor to lend you the money to buy it. It was a spectacular result for us. I don't suppose they would have been quite so keen to lend us the money if we had told them about our three new investors or the fact that we were buying out Andy Pritchard as part of the deal!

From the moment that we announced that we were in exclusive talks to buy the business, on 15 February 2012, we had 42 days to get the deal done or all our shareholders' rights would fall away. Everyone thought that this was an incredibly tight deadline but in fact we managed to complete it in little more than half that time on 9 March 2012. Almost 42 years after I started the company it was now back in private hands. Our new shareholders have proved to be outstanding. They leave us alone, offer advice when needed, are fully supportive but most of all enjoy life and have fun with us in the business. They've even agreed to us buying a new aeroplane!

I've decided I never want to retire. I'm in this for life and completely focused on Iceland, apart from owning or having stakes in a hairdressing salon, a vodka distillery in Iceland (the country), property businesses in Poland and the UK, a film production company, an ice-making business, a media monitoring agency, an African biofuels company, a chain of restaurants and an upmarket fish and chip shop. That diversification bug that plagued us through our early years has certainly proved hard to shake off!

I'm proud of the fact that my son Richard has now decided to come into the business. My children have always been successful doing their own thing with no pressure from me. They are well brought up, know the value of money, have a strong work ethic and to top it all they are really nice people. That is an even greater achievement for my wife and me than building Iceland.

Index

ABN Amro (Hoare Govett) 83, 108, 111, 118, 152, 186, 197, 201, 236, 255

Alpine Frozen Foods 48–9, 66

Alzheimer's Research UK 318, 323, 327

Apthorp, John 89, 93, 94, 96, 97, 99, 100, 104, 106, 107, 112, 116, 133, 267

Archdeacon, Steve 204, 230, 271

Arthur Hapgoods 46, 60

As Nature Intended 207, 248, 268, 285

Astaire, Mark 167, 186, 195, 199, 233, 261

automated box picking 101–2, 103

Bain 132, 133–4, 137, 156

Barclays Bank 25, 41, 46, 64, 68–9, 70, 86, 152, 190, 191–3, 195, 196, 263

Basham, Brian 107

Baugur 289, 291, 293, 295, 308, 309, 310, 311, 313

Beck, Charlie 12–14

Bejam 84, 89, 90, 93, 95, 112, 116, 127, 133
    board 98, 99
    hostile bid 102, 106, 107, 108, 110, 111, 112, 117
    merger 97–8, 100, 112, 115, 118
    sales 113, 117

share price 95, 100, 104, 106, 109
    shareholders 106, 108, 109

Berry, John 1, 5, 89, 111, 232, 234, 237, 284, 301

Bhs 173

Big Food Group (BFG), The 289, 292, 295, 297

Birchall, Alan 48, 49, 66–8, 72, 75, 80, 167

Blank, Sir Victor 138–9, 140

Booker 177–9, 180, 182, 184, 186, 188, 189, 190–2, 194, 196, 198, 200, 202, 209, 221, 227, 234, 244, 290, 296, 299

Booker Prize 218–9

Brent, Andy 143, 157

British Rail Pension Fund (BRPF) 70, 72, 74, 78, 105

Broadhurst, Nigel xi, 65, 301

Brown, David 143, 148, 172, 173

Buchanan, Robin 132, 136

Budgens 165–6, 178

Bullivant, Peter xi, 58, 71, 83, 89, 123, 217, 219

Business Enterprise Award 109

Buy One Get One Free (BOGOF) 210–11, 234, 236, 240, 303, 306

buying synergies 204, 209, 212, 213, 216, 230, 234, 247–8, 252, 271

Camp, Mike 184, 246, 284
Canning, Nick xi, 301, 307, 330
Cazenove 83, 201
CBE 135
central distribution 41, 42, 43
charity fundraising 6, 119, 168, 270,
    315, 318, 323, 327
Charterhouse 117, 201
cold store 39, 40, 63, 64, 70, 74, 77, 101,
    103
Cooltrader 285, 289, 291, 294, 295, 305
Corah 43–4
Cordon Bleu 72–3
Coyle, Tony 17–18

Dale, Barry 128, 131, 138
Davies, Gary 41
Davis, Sir Peter 140
Deakin, Paul 151, 152
Department of Trade and Industry
    (DTI) 259, 286–7, 288, 304
Deutsche Bank 290, 292
Dhaliwal, Tarsem xi, 167, 184–5, 230–1,
    246, 252, 253, 254, 256, 284, 291,
    292, 294, 295, 296, 298, 300, 301,
    307, 326, 330, 331
Directors' Report 42, 52
diversification 50, 60, 72, 90, 94, 116,
    122, 130, 155, 176, 331
Don, Laurence 96, 98, 99, 104
Dunnes Stores 128, 129

Edey, Russell xi, 95, 104, 107, 114, 117,
    129, 136, 138–9, 143, 152
Ernst & Young 59, 88, 185, 186, 229,
    260, 327
Errington, Andy 65, 245, 282
European Coal and Steel Community
    Fund 64
Everest 319–22

Financial Services Authority (FSA)
    investigation 258–9, 263, 269,
    286–7, 288
flotation, Iceland 82–4, 85, 87, 88, 91, 120

Ford, Russell 157–8, 161–3, 169–70,
    171–2, 176, 187, 188, 205, 209,
    211, 216, 230–1, 240, 241
France 120–1
freezer centre 50, 72, 84, 94, 120
frozen foods, loose 25, 48, 50, 94

Gate, Stephen 3–4, 263
genetically modified (GM) food 160–1,
    163, 168, 171
Glitnir 311, 327, 330
Grange Moor 8, 79
Green, A. V. 7, 125
Greenpeace 168, 169, 202
Greenway, Robin 55
Grimsey, Bill xi, 1, 3, 4, 218, 223–5, 226,
    227, 230, 232, 235, 238, 240, 242–
    5, 247, 248, 250–2, 254, 261, 263,
    264, 267, 268, 272–3, 275, 278,
    283, 288, 292, 296, 299, 304–5
Gubay, Albert 55, 74–5, 76
Gulliver, Jimmy 72–3

Hallas, George 67–8
Hamill, Carl 244, 284
Hann, Keith xi, 85, 198, 206, 217, 219,
    233, 235, 236, 257–8, 264, 270
Haraldsson, Palmi 294, 296, 298, 309
Harris, Derek 65
Hawkpoint 151, 290, 292
HBOS 293, 294, 297
head office, Bejam 113
head office, Deeside 63, 64, 69, 73, 74,
    77, 82, 101, 114, 132, 167, 205,
    227
head office, Flint 33
head office, Rhyl 41, 43, 63
Heath, Edward 47
Hempleman-Adams, David 316–17,
    320, 324, 325
Herbert Smith 3, 83, 152, 255, 261
Hinchcliffe, Peter xi, 7, 21, 22, 27, 30,
    45, 53, 66, 71, 73, 75, 81, 87, 88,
    95, 98, 104, 105, 107, 110, 113, 118,
    120, 122, 123, 131, 132, 134, 145

Hoare Govett (ABN Amro) 83, 108, 111, 118, 152, 186, 197, 201, 236, 255
home delivery 146–7, 149, 151, 152, 153, 154, 165, 167, 173–4, 213
home shopping 174, 212, 236
Hoskins, Bill 1, 241, 242, 246, 250, 255, 256, 261, 262, 268, 273, 275, 299
How, Tim 104, 112, 116–17
Hudson, Mark 136, 137, 142, 143, 145, 155, 166
Hudson Sandler 154, 198, 201, 218, 264, 270, 271
Hungary 122–5

Iceland 2, 26, 30–1, 38, 39, 41, 47, 49, 53, 58, 62, 64, 66, 69, 70, 71, 73, 77, 79, 82, 84, 91, 101, 115, 122, 126, 129, 135, 137, 143, 148, 155, 164, 170, 180, 183, 186, 192, 194, 200, 203, 207, 215, 221, 224, 233, 240, 243, 264, 284, 290, 291, 293–4, 298, 300–3, 312, 330, 331
  AGM 102, 145, 167
  at Littlewoods 127–8
  auction 326–330
  capital reconstruction 151–3, 154, 165
  first store 8, 24, 34
  flotation 82–4, 85, 87, 88, 91, 120
  number of employees 6, 65, 81, 118
  number of stores 70, 81, 91, 137
  profit 35, 65, 70, 81, 91, 118, 125, 135, 142, 147, 211, 218, 234, 239, 243, 260, 273–4, 276–8, 302, 308
  sales 43, 65, 81, 91, 113, 125, 135, 142, 148, 159, 169, 174, 187, 234, 239, 288, 293, 295, 302, 314
  share price 85, 127, 132, 147, 150, 167, 170, 199, 218, 220, 249, 255, 276, 289
  shares 53, 70, 84, 86, 106, 112, 118, 151, 153–4, 206, 228, 233, 235, 237–8, 249, 255, 256, 258, 270, 288
  stock market valuation 101
  takeover 249, 250–2, 253, 283
Iceland (the country) 289, 312, 313
ICFC (3i) 64, 69, 70, 151
inflation 45, 47
internet shopping 169, 173
Ireland, Republic of 120
Ishaq, Majid xi

Johannesson, Jon Asgeir xi, 290, 291, 293, 296, 297, 299, 309, 312, 313
Jones, Alan 47, 57, 58, 62

Katona, Korey 306, 307, 308
Kirk, Richard (Dick) 57, 62, 72, 81, 88, 95, 98, 104, 105, 107, 113, 120, 125, 132, 134, 136, 142
Kirkham, Lord (Graham) 85, 158, 316, 332, 329
Knowlton, Tom 159, 196, 210, 246, 261
Kroll 172, 304
Kwik Save 55, 72, 74, 78

Laing, Stephen ('Stainless') 59–60, 88
Landsbanki 298, 311, 312, 313–14, 326, 330
Laurance, Ben 165, 257–8, 264–5, 270, 287–8
Leigh, Bernard (Bernie) 52, 53, 54, 59, 71, 75, 77, 82, 89, 95, 98, 105, 107, 110, 126, 132, 150, 154, 157, 167, 170
Littlewoods 126, 127, 128, 130–1, 137, 139, 140, 173
Lyons, Teena 256, 257, 264

management conference 71, 165, 315
management consultants 132, 136, 267, 271
Marks & Spencer 29, 43, 126, 140, 181, 216

Marsden, Janet (formerly Weinstein) 5, 65, 120, 226, 241, 242, 264, 281–2

Mason Owen and Partners 55, 58, 129

Mason, Geoff xi, 55, 56, 58–9, 63, 74, 75, 281

McLachlan, John xi, 70, 78, 158, 196

McWilliam, Jill 115, 119, 135, 163

Melchett, Peter 168, 169, 202

Mills, Nigel 109, 110, 117

mobile shop 212–13

Monk, Alec 76

Moores, John 128, 140

Murphy, John 48, 49, 66–8

Napier, John 190, 191, 196

non-executive directors 158, 186, 261, 264, 275

North Pole 316, 324

Northern Ireland 120

Orchard Foods 88, 91

organic food 170–1, 187, 203, 209, 211, 230–1, 234, 250

Orsborn, Mike ('Ossie') 83, 117, 186, 195, 199, 201, 227, 229, 233, 237, 261, 289

Oswestry 24, 29

overage 15–16

Owen, Barry xi, 55, 110

Palmer, Tony 73, 77

Perry, Bill 93, 94, 96–7

Prestt, John 58, 74, 167

price earnings multiple (PE) 84, 182

Price, David 3–4, 233, 255, 259, 261, 269

Prince Charles 135

Princess Diana 119

Pritchard, Andy xi, 1, 157, 167, 170, 176, 183, 184, 189, 194, 200, 205, 219, 225, 230, 234, 237, 240, 246, 249, 255, 256, 260, 262, 264, 266, 269, 274, 278, 284, 291, 294, 300, 330, 331

product range 26, 32, 33, 48, 78, 244, 303

profit warning 147, 246, 250

profit, Iceland 35, 65, 70, 81, 91, 118, 125, 135, 142, 147, 211, 218, 234, 239, 243, 260, 273–4, 276–8, 302, 308

Prudential 110

Rankine, Kate 201, 214, 216, 220, 238

Rathgay, Charles 114, 115

recession 118

recycling freezers 119, 168

Reddy, Tom 307–8

Resolution Committee 312–4, 330, 331

retail analysts 148, 150, 153, 167, 200, 202, 223, 227, 233, 235–7

retirement 194, 200, 207, 214, 217, 227, 233, 248, 266, 331

Rhyl 30, 40

Richardson, Sir Michael 83, 85, 117

Rose, Stuart 181–3, 185, 187, 189, 193, 196, 200, 203, 204, 206–7, 209, 213–16, 219, 240

Ross, William 46

Rothschilds 83, 86, 87, 95, 98, 99, 100, 104, 105, 108, 117, 128, 129, 136, 143, 152, 201, 255, 310, 326

Royal Bank of Scotland (RBS) 150, 190, 192–3, 195

sales, Iceland 43, 65, 81, 91, 113, 125, 135, 142, 148, 159, 169, 174, 187, 234, 239, 288, 293, 295, 302, 314

Salisbury, Bob 52

Sandler, Michael 85, 198, 264

shares, Iceland 53, 70, 84, 86, 106, 112, 118, 151, 153–4, 206, 228, 233, 235, 237–8, 249, 255, 256, 258, 270, 288

shares, selling 4, 167, 206, 228, 233, 235, 237–8, 249, 255, 256, 258, 270

Sharp, Iain 159, 196, 229, 246, 261, 274

Sheldon, Roy 51

shrinkage 15, 18, 43

Sigurdsson, Gunnar xi, 309

site finding 45, 58

Smith, Alan 139, 173, 178, 181, 223, 227, 261, 263, 284

South Pole 324–5

St Catherine's Freezer Centres 73, 77, 78, 90

Steadman, Tim 3, 195, 258, 262, 263

Stock Exchange 87, 100

Stringfellow, Peter 10

supplier partnering 136, 156, 166

Takeaway, The 34, 35, 37–8

takeover, Iceland 249, 250–2, 253, 283

Tesco 144

Tilney 83, 118, 138

Tutt, Trevor 177–8, 181, 213

United Kingdom Listing Authority (UKLA) 3

Valtysson, Baldvin ('Baddie') 314, 326, 327, 329

Walker, Alexia 82, 166–7, 175, 259

Walker, Caroline 82, 175, 207, 264

Walker, Rhianydd 1, 9, 19, 38, 82, 91, 111, 124, 135, 175, 207, 219, 248, 254, 257, 263, 299

Walker, Richard 2, 82, 166–7, 175, 319, 320, 322, 323, 331

Walker, Steven xi, 289, 291, 292

Walker-Arnott, Edward 3, 83, 258

Weeks, Michael 55, 78

Welding, Larus xi, 298, 331

Whitam, Stephen 89

Whitehead Mann 137, 218, 222, 241

Wickes 218, 271

Wight, Kathy xi, 5, 251, 258, 266, 281, 300

Wilson, Charles 183–4, 185, 198, 200, 205, 209, 213, 216, 222, 242, 299

Wizard Wine 116–17

Wogan, Terry 79–80

Woodward, Bill xi, 26, 40, 42, 46, 53, 68–70, 79

Woodward, Nigel xi, 26, 280

Woodward, Norman xi, 26, 40, 42, 48, 53, 68–70, 79

Woodward's 26, 27, 30, 33, 40, 64, 155, 157, 194, 212, 234, 290, 296

Woolworth's 7, 10, 12–15, 20, 27, 29, 50, 58, 310

Yates, Tim 120, 301

Yealland, Dan xi, 326, 329